LANGUAGE AND LITERACY SERIES

(cont

CRITICAL ENCOUNTERS
in Secondary English
Teaching Literary Theory
to Adolescents

THIRD EDITION

Deborah Appleman

TEACHERS COLLEGE PRESS

TEACHERS COLLEGE | COLUMBIA UNIVERSITY
NEW YORK AND LONDON

Published by Teachers College Press, 1234 Amsterdam Avenue, New York, NY 10027

Copyright © 2015 by Teachers College, Columbia University

Library of Congress Cataloging-in-Publication Data

Appleman, Deborah.
    Critical encounters in secondary English : teaching literary theory to adolescents / Deborah Appleman. — Third edition.
        pages cm. — (Language and literacy series)
    Includes bibliographical references and index.
    ISBN 978-0-8077-5623-2 (pbk. : alk. paper)
    ISBN 978-0-8077-7355-0 (e-book)
        1. English literature—Study and teaching (Secondary) 2. Literature—History and criticism—Theory, etc.—Study and teaching (Secondary) 3. American literature—Study and teaching (Secondary) 4. Literature—Study and teaching (Secondary) 5. Criticism—English-speaking countries. I. Title.
    PR33.A66 2015
    820.71'273—dc23   2014032415

ISBN 978-0-8077-5623-2 (paper)
ISBN 978-0-8077-6430-5 (hardcover)
ISBN 978-0-8077-7355-0 (ebook)

Printed on acid-free paper
Manufactured in the United States of America

For John Schmit.
With boundless love and gratitude,
I dedicate this book to you.

Contents

Preface to the Third Edition

What we have loved, others we love, and we will teach them how.

—William Wordsworth

Nonfiction is never going to die.

—Tom Wolfe

I read the same amount of nonfiction and fiction.

—Anne Lamott

Let's be honest. Most of us got into this English teaching business because we love fiction. Following Emily Dickinson's words, "there is no frigate like a book," we have traveled to many places using literature as our transport. And we have taken our students, willing or reluctant passengers, with us. As teachers of literacy, we have generally privileged the reading and teaching of fiction over nonfiction, eschewing the pragmatic contours of informational texts and other nonfiction in favor of the literary arts, such as fiction, drama, or poetry. We have subscribed to the opinion of Ellen Hopkins who writes: "Nonfiction speaks to the head. Fiction speaks to the heart. Poetry speaks to the soul" (Hopkins, 2014).

Yet, for many complex and interrelated reasons, our literary landscape in K–12 literacy is shifting, as more and more teachers turn to nonfiction to teach skills of both reading and interpretation. It is this shift that this Third Edition of *Critical Encounters* addresses. In this edition, I hope to demonstrate how nonfiction can be fruitfully integrated into the secondary literature curriculum. I also hope to illustrate how the lenses of literary theory, which are still the core focus of this text, can enrich the reading of nonfiction. Additionally, I will argue that nonfiction itself can powerfully illustrate the importance and relevance of reading with theory. First, though, it's important to make the case for using nonfiction to the literature lovers that are English teachers. Here are a few reasons why you should consider using nonfiction in the secondary literature classroom, along with literary theory.

REASONS TO USE NONFICTION

Engaging Readers

Although much in the world has changed, the texts we teach to young people have remained remarkably constant (Applebee, 1993). As enamored as we may be of the classic chestnuts that we think should comprise the core curriculum of the literature classroom, many teachers, in their most candid moments, would admit that texts such as *Adventures of Huck Finn, The Scarlet Letter,* or even more recent additions to the canon such as *Beloved, Their Eyes Were Watching God, Peace Like a River,* and *The House on Mango Street* don't always engage readers. While we can argue for more diverse and engaging kinds of fiction, which many teachers have done, for purposes of student engagement, nonfiction deserves our serious consideration. As Smith and Wilhelm argue in their aptly named book, *Reading Don't Fix No Chevys,* many adolescent readers, especially males, become impatient with the purely aesthetic and ethereal qualities of literature and want to experience the sense that what they are reading has something of pragmatic value (Smith & Wilhelm, 2002). This brings us to the next reason for incorporating more nonfiction into the classroom: the increasing demands of literacy outside of the classroom, or, as some have called it, "real-world literacy" (Cooper, 2014).

Real-World Literacy

There is much talk about the increasing demands on young people for information literacy—a situation created by a variety of factors, including the proliferation of technology in all facets of students' lives, both in and out of school. Since it has become increasingly important for adolescents to learn to use these tools and multiple platforms, we teachers, who, after all, are responsible for encouraging students' developing literacy, need to rethink what we teach. That means that the kinds of informational and nonliterary texts that students will encounter in everyday life need to be incorporated into our curriculum.

There is also a push on many fronts to make all educational endeavors, from kindergarten through college, more pragmatic, more vocationally oriented, and more focused on helping students prepare for meaningful postsecondary opportunities in addition to job-ready skills (Carnegie Corporation of New York, 2013). As a professor in a liberal arts college and a teacher of the liberal arts (literature and writing) to incarcerated students, I could (and have) argued against this pragmatic stream in education (Appleman, Caligiuri, & Vang, 2014). But this vocational expectation, fueled in no small part by the rising costs of postsecondary education, is here to stay. Combined with the expectations of stakeholders, such as parents, administrators, and state boards of education, there are many forces which, for better or worse, have redirected our collective pedagogical energies to the consideration of texts that might better prepare our students for navigating a world beyond school.

Improving Reading Skills

In addition to engagement with texts and consideration of real-world literacy, the use of nonfiction and informational texts has additional value in the secondary literature classroom, and that is the teaching of reading. Many reading experts have come to believe that informational texts can help bolster students' reading skills. Several recent studies have indicated that the inclusion of informational texts helps increase students' reading skills on a variety of measures, including fluency and vocabulary. Some of these studies have caused educators to link nonfiction reading with student success. For example, a recent educational leadership article cites the following findings:

A comparison of an enrichment reading program and basal reading programs (Reis, Eckert, McCoach, Jacobs, & Coyne, 2008) found that the enrichment reading group scored significantly higher in oral reading fluency than did the basal reading group. Students in the enrichment reading group received instruction on thinking skills during teacher read-alouds; independently read self-selected books; participated in individualized reading conferences; and engaged in a variety of enrichment activities of their choice, including book discussion groups, creative writing, and other interest-based projects. The researchers concluded that providing "structured silent reading of self-selected challenging books, accompanied by supported, individualized reading instruction . . . may be a promising way to increase reading fluency" (p. 312).

Common Core State Standards

Finally we come to the reason that some might have thought is the primary reason for including nonfiction: the adoption of the Common Core State Standards (CCSS) and its effect on practice and curriculum. The resulting push to include more nonfiction and informational texts into secondary literature classrooms has been keenly felt in the corners of our classroom, from textbook publishing, Common Core institutes, and scores of resources on including nonfiction texts (of which, a cynic might say, this is one). In some ways the push to include nonfiction texts into the literature classroom rested on a misinterpretation of the anchor standards. Initially, the charge to have 70% of texts in the curriculum be informational texts was read to mean in the *literature* curriculum. That created a nationwide panic among literature teachers that reverberated everywhere. It was a counter-intuitive call, one that seemed to ask us to invert the proportions of everything we were teaching, to throw the baby as it were, out with the bathwater. As it turned out, our initial reading was inaccurate; it's 70% of reading across all classes. But you already knew that.

While I and many of my colleagues share some serious concerns about the CCSS, or at least the way instruction has been envisioned by proponents of the Common Core (Appleman, Smith, & Wilhelm, 2014), there are still many good reasons to heed the CCSS and include more nonfiction on our classes, including building vocabulary, becoming familiar with increasingly complex texts, and learning to distill information from and write about the texts that students will encounter both in college and in the marketplace.

The CCSS document itself cites several valid reasons for the importance of including more nonfiction and informational texts into the curriculum:

> In grades 6–12, ELA programs shift the balance of texts and instructional time towards reading substantially more literary nonfiction . . . including essays, speeches, opinion pieces, biographies, journalism, and historical, scientific, or other documents written for a broad audience. . . . The standards emphasize arguments (such as those in the U.S. foundational documents) and other literary nonfiction that is built on informational text structures rather than literary nonfiction that is structured as stories (such as memoirs or biographies).
>
> To become career and college ready, students must grapple with a range of works that span many genres, cultures, and eras and model the kinds of thinking and writing students should aspire to in their own work.
>
> Materials aligned with the . . . standards should help students acquire knowledge of general academic vocabulary because these are the words that will help them access a wide range of complex texts. (Coleman & Pimentel, 2013)

In other words, secondary English teachers should incorporate both fiction and nonfiction into their curriculum to better prepare students for the range of reading experiences they will have after high school. If it is a "both/and," rather than an "either/or," as we had originally feared, perhaps the additions of nonfiction will not only enhance our students reading experiences, but will enrich their experiences with fiction as well. This makes good sense for those who care about adolescents and their reading habits and skills, both in and out of school.

LITERARY THEORY AND NONFICTION

The central question, of course, is this: Can the lenses of literary theory be fruitfully applied to nonfiction as well as fiction? Of course they can. Indeed, I assert in this book that the incorporation of nonfiction into a literature curriculum that is focused on lenses can serve to enrich and strengthen students understanding not only of the fiction used but also of the lenses themselves.

Although our practice of reading with theory is grounded in literature, the origins of the theories themselves often come from scholars and philosophers who have tried to make sense of the world—the real world, not a fictional world.

FORMAT OF THE BOOK

While many texts have rushed to add the imprimatur of the Common Core State Standards on their products, we have taken a different approach. This Third Edition attempts to maintain the bulk of the material that teachers have come to depend on. The literary lenses are all there, including a new chapter on new historicism. Rather than including an atheoretical chapter that illustrated the use of nonfiction, I selected new historicism, and used primarily nonfiction texts, because it lends itself to that kind of treatment.

At the end of each chapter, you will find a list of suggested nonfiction pieces that work well for the particular lenses in question. For example, we suggest pieces such as Stephen Jay Gould's "Women's Brains" for the gender lens and Lars Eighner's "On Dumpster Diving" for the class lens. We have in our selections attempted to heed the advice of Sarah Mosle:

> I love fiction and poetry as much as the next former English major and often despair over the quality of what passes for "informational texts," few of which amount to narrative much less literary narrative. What schools really need isn't more nonfiction but better nonfiction, especially that which provides good models for student writing. Most students could use greater familiarity with what newspaper, magazine and book editors call "narrative nonfiction": writing that tells a factual story, sometimes even a personal one, but also makes an argument and conveys information in vivid, effective ways. (Mosle, 2012)

For many teachers, one of the most valuable elements has been the actual classroom-tested activities that animate each of the lenses. With the guidance and generosity of several classroom teachers across the country, I have created and tested several new classroom-ready activities that can be found in the Appendix. They are designed to be easily integrated into well-established literature curricula, as well as to stand alone as separate, self-contained activities that promote the close reading and interpretation of both informational and literary nonfiction texts. They are designed to serve the demands of the Common Core State Standards as they deliver complex and challenging nonfiction texts. They also reinforce the contours of the philosophy of each lens to reinforce students' understanding of the emphasis of individual lenses. Additionally, the nonfiction lessons can be used to illustrate the central concept of this text, the importance of multiple perspectives.

In the first chapter of this book, entitled "What We Teach and Why," I make the argument that combining the teaching of literature with the teaching of literary theory helps encourage young people to have the critical consciousness required for them to become enlightened witnesses: The charge for those of us who engage with adolescents through literacy, as Paulo Freire (Freire & Macedo, 1987) has pointed out, is to help students read both the world and the word. Our job is not simply to help students read and write; our job is to help them use the skills of writing and reading to understand the world around them. We want them to become, in the words of bell hooks (1994), "enlightened witnesses," critically vigilant about the world we live in. To become enlightened witnesses, young people must understand the workings of ideology.

In this increasingly complex, information-rich world, this goal has never been more important. Combining literary theory with the informational and nonfiction texts, not only helps teachers help students meet the Common Core State Standards, but it also encourages them to read everything they encounter critically and vigilantly, as bell hooks would have them do.

Integrating nonfiction into the literature curriculum will undoubtedly help teachers and their students meet the current demands of the Common Core State Standards. But whether those standards will endure, the simple fact remains: The world is filled with many kinds of texts, both fiction and nonfiction. As literature teachers, we are charged with helping young people make their way meaningfully through the world. Therefore, we must help them make sense of a myriad of texts, to read and if necessary, resist the ideologies embedded in those texts.

Yes, as secondary English teachers, we want young people to be able to have critical encounters wherever they turn, whatever they read—whether it's a canonical literary text, an informational text such as a newspaper or magazine article, an essay, or an online post. It is my hope that the additions to this Third Edition of *Critical Encounters* will help teachers guide their students to have those critical encounters.

I am grateful to Teachers College Press and most particularly to Emily Spangler, whose kindness and patience makes her an author's dream of an editor. Thanks, too, to Annie Larson for her terrific assistance with the manuscript production and permissions. Thanks to the English teachers across the country, who let me know that the lenses work for their students and sometimes even let me into their classrooms! Thanks to my English Language Arts colleagues at the Singapore American School who gave new life to the lenses and the theory cards. Special thanks are reserved for John Schmit, whose invaluable support and contributions made this book, and all of my efforts, possible.

Introduction

Often literary theories change our views of a work of literature by proposing new distinctions or new categories for looking at the work. This is a bit like putting on a new set of glasses: Suddenly you see things more clearly.

—Stephen Bonnycastle, *In Search of Authority*

On a promising spring day after a brutal winter, I'm guest teaching in a high school in Minnesota. St. Paul is no longer Lake Wobegon, if it ever was, and Jamie's third hour American literature class reflects a changing school district that is rich in every kind of diversity. There are 32 10th-graders in this class: African American, Latino, Hmong, Vietnamese, and White. Jamie notes that all of his students have postsecondary aspirations, and many will be the first in their families to attend college.

Jamie's focus this year has included contemporary literary theory. The students are preparing to read Ralph Ellison's *Invisible Man*. Jamie thinks his students are always underestimated; he believes that high expectations are the key to their success, and he wants his class to be challenging in both content and approach. He also knows that as a teacher of literature he needs and wants to deal directly with issues of gender, class, and race. He thought he might incorporate the lenses of feminist/gender literary theory, postcolonial theory, class or Marxist theory, and reader response to help engage these topics.

It hasn't been easy. The students haven't been exactly captivated by the hand-me-down theory articles that Jamie pulled from his college notebooks. The students have never even heard the term *literary theory* before, despite the fact that since middle school their previous English teachers had clearly employed both New Critical and reader-response techniques. The students had even studied a variety of archetypes. But this—this term *theory*—seemed new and strange. Worse, to some of the students it seemed artificial and contrived, a "teacher game" not unlike the transparent symbol hunts or the fishing for themes, designed to make reading literature even more complicated than it already was. It seemed a fancy tool that came without instructions. Jamie remembered my frequently repeated entreaty to all secondary teachers I know, "invite me into your classroom, make me walk my talk." So he did.

Introduced as a special visitor, I come armed with 35 copies of Sharon Olds' "On the Subway," a powerful poem about an encounter between a White woman and an African American male on a New York subway. I also bring four different sets of handouts, each with a focus on a different literary theory or "critical lens," 35 sets of theory cards, and a battered pair of Ray-Ban sunglasses, especially ground for driving. I pass the sunglasses around, asking students to look through them. When all have tried them on, I ask them to comment on what they noticed. It's an exercise I've done many times over the past 20 years, and it never fails.

As hundreds of students before them have done, the students get it immediately. "I see red," says Tamika. "Check out Josh's sweater, and hey (looking at me), your hair!" Annie joins in, "I really see yellow when I have these things on; it's crazy. I never even noticed how much yellow there is on the posters on the wall." "The greens are super-green," says Luis, "which is awesome since our school colors are green and white. Go Shamrocks." The class erupts in a spontaneous cheer, and Jamie casts me a nervous sideways glance.

"I've got this," I assure him, not at all sure that I do. "Do the glasses turn colors that aren't green or red or yellow into green or red?" I ask. "No," someone replies, "they just seem to bring out what's already there. Bring it out, so you can't miss it." After I tell them that the sunglasses are intended for driving, Pa volunteers, "I get it—red, yellow, green—stop, wait, and go. The glasses bring out what's there 'cause you can't afford *not* to see it."

I shuffle my handouts, pull out the theory cards, and tell the students that what the sunglasses did for the green and yellow and red, literary theory does for the texts we read. They provide lenses designed to bring out what is already there but what we often miss with unaided vision. Like the sunglasses, contemporary theories highlight particular features of what lies in our line of vision. If used properly, they do not create colors that weren't there in the first place. They only bring them into sharper relief. And, like the sunglasses, they have purpose outside the classroom. There are things we can't afford *not* to see, especially around issues of race and class and gender. These issues are not beyond the concerns of literature teaching; they are the stuff of which great literature is made.

I put away the Ray-Bans and ask the students to get ready to read the poem. "There are a couple of critical lenses I'd like you to peer through," I say. "Let's see what we encounter."

CHAPTER ONE

What We Teach and Why

Contemporary Literary Theory and Adolescents

The paradox of education is precisely this—that as one begins to become conscious one begins to examine the society in which he is being educated. The purpose of education, finally, is to create in a person the ability to look at the world for himself, to make his own decisions. . . . But no society is really anxious to have that kind of person around. What societies really, ideally, want is a citizenry which will simply obey the rules of society. If a society succeeds in this, that society is about to perish. The obligation of anyone who thinks of himself as responsible is to examine society and try to change it and to fight it—at no matter what risk. This is the only hope society has. This is the only way societies change.

—James Baldwin

Everything we do in life is rooted in theory.

—bell hooks

Over 14 years ago, in my introduction to the First Edition of *Critical Encounters in High School English: Teaching Literary Theory to Adolescents,* I made the following statement: "We live in dangerous and complicated times and no one is more aware of it than our teenagers" (Appleman, 2000, p. 1). It's ironic to note that when I wrote those words, the 9/11 attack hadn't happened, the war in Iraq hadn't begun, and Columbine had just heralded the era of mass shootings in schools. Now, more than a decade later, the times we live in have become considerably more dangerous and even more complicated. We are all, in the 21st century, poised precariously within ecological, economic, and political crises. It has become more and more difficult to navigate our way in an increasingly ideological world.

In addition to the crises wrought by war and both natural- and human-made disaster, we are also bombarded with messages, slogans, and pleas from the political left and right. The radio airwaves, the Internet, print and television ads, and films and documentaries all compete for our attention as they attempt to sell us their version of the truth. While this cacophony of ideologies can be deafening even to adults, it can be absolutely over-whelming to young people. The charge for those of us who engage with adolescents through literacy, as Paulo Freire (Freirie & Macedo, 1987) has pointed out, is to help students read both the world and the word. Our job is not simply to help students read and write; our job is to help them use the skills of writing and reading to understand the world around them. We want them to become, in the words of bell hooks, "enlightened witnesses" (1997, p. 8), critically vigilant about the world we live in. In order to become enlightened witnesses, young people must understand the workings of ideology.

IDEOLOGY

What *is* ideology? Bonnycastle (1996) offers an adolescent-friendly definition:

> In essence an ideology is a system of thought or "world view" which an individual acquires (usually unconsciously) from the world around him. An ideology determines what you think is important in life, what categories you put people into, how you see male and female roles in life, and a host of other things. You can visualize your ideology as a grid, or a set of glasses, through which you can see the world. (p. 32)

Bonnycastle rightly emphasizes the unconscious quality of ideology. One is reminded of Leo Lionni's classic *Fish is Fish* (1974), where a tadpole's lively description of what he observed on land is translated by his fish listener into mental pictures that all look like fish-cows, fish-birds, even fish-humans. The fish is unaware that everything he hears is translated unconsciously into his own limited, fishy paradigm.

While Lionni's depiction is playful and points to the foibles of limited experience and imagination, Mark Ryan (1998) offers a somewhat more sinister definition of ideology:

> The term ideology describes the beliefs, attitudes, and habits of feeling, which a society inculcates in order to generate an automatic reproduction of its structuring premises. Ideology is what preserves social power in the absence of direct coercion. (p. 37)

In other words, when we teach the concept of ideology to young people, we are helping them to discern the system of values and beliefs that help create expectations for individual behavior and for social norms. Although ideology can be individual, it is generally a social and political construct, one that subtly shapes society and culture. As history has taught us, ideologies are not always benign or harmless, and they need to be questioned and sometimes resisted. Although ideological constructs help each of us learn how we fit into the world, like Lionni's fish, for us ideology is often invisible and transmitted unconsciously. It is what Norman Fairclough (1989) has dubbed "ideological common sense." He writes, "Ideological common sense is common sense in the service of sustaining unequal relations of power" (p. 84).

I was recently on an airplane when a woman in a pilot's uniform boarded the plane. The gentleman sitting next to me whispered, "That's the copilot." As a frequent flyer on the airline, I recognized the pilot's uniform and knew my fellow passenger was mistaken. His ideological common sense kept him from seeing that a woman was the pilot. While this example may seem trivial, ideological common sense also influences who we think are trustworthy renters, likely friends, college-bound students, or plausible presidential candidates.

IDEOLOGY AND THE STUDY OF LITERATURE

A literature or language arts class at the secondary level is an ideal place to help students learn to read and, if necessary, resist the ideology that surrounds them. In our literature classes, we teach texts that are full of ideology. As Fairclough (1989) explains:

> Ideology is most effective when its workings are least visible. . . . Invisibility is achieved when ideologies are brought to discourse not as explicit elements of the text but as the background assumptions, which, on the one hand, lead the text producer to textualize the world in a particular way, and on the other hand, lead the interpreter to interpret the text in a particular way. Texts do not spout ideology. They so position the interpreter through their cues that she brings ideologies to the interpretation of texts—and reproduces them in the process! (p. 85)

When we read Robert Frost's "The Road Not Taken," we attend to the assertion that "taking the road less traveled by" makes all the difference. From Fairclough's perspective, the text "positions" us to embrace the American ideologies of individualism and nonconformity. In Mark Twain's *Adventures of Huckleberry Finn* the racialized portraits of Huck and Jim normalize a particular kind of America, whose ideology of inequality was unquestioned for too long. Our responsibility as literature teachers is to help make the ideologies inherent in those texts visible to our students.

LITERARY THEORY AND IDEOLOGY

The best way to uncover and explore these ideologies as they are found in literature is through the explicit teaching of contemporary literary theory.

Literary theory provides readers with the tools to uncover the often-invisible workings of the text. Many people consider literary theory (if they consider it at all) as arcane and esoteric. It's dismissed as a sort of intellectual parlor game played by MLA types whose conference paper topics are the annual object of ridicule by the *New York Times*. As Terry Eagleton (1983) put it, "There are some who complain that literary theory is impossibly esoteric— who suspect it as an arcane elitist enclave somewhat akin to nuclear physics" (p. vii). What could poststructuralism, new historicism, deconstruction, social class/Marxist, and gender/feminist literary theory possibly have to do with the average adolescent, just struggling to grow up, stay alive, get through school, and make the most of things? It sounds as if I'm promoting a sort of theoretical fiddling while the Rome of our sacred vision of successful public education burns.

Teachers, too, may not be convinced of the relevance of contemporary literary theory. High school literature teachers often feel distant and detached from recent developments in literary theory. Literature teachers find it difficult to see, at least initially, how contemporary literary theory can inform their daily practice. They are already overwhelmed as they juggle curricular concerns as well as the varied literacy skills and needs of their increasingly diverse student body. Students and teachers alike find it hard to believe that something as abstract and "impractical" as literary theory could be relevant to their lives, both in and out of the classroom. Nothing, however, could be further from the truth.

Literary theories provide lenses that can sharpen one's vision and provide alternative ways of seeing. They augment our sometimes failing sight and bring into relief things we fail to notice. Literary theories recontextualize the familiar and comfortable, making us reappraise them. They make the strange seem oddly familiar. As we view the dynamic world around us, literary theories can become critical lenses to guide, inform, and instruct us.

Critical lenses provide students with a way of reading their world; the lenses provide a way of "seeing" differently and analytically that can help them read the culture of school as well as popular culture. Learning to inhabit multiple ways of knowing can also help them learn to adapt to the intellectual perspectives and learning styles required by other disciplines. When taught explicitly, literary theory can provide a repertoire of critical lenses through which to view literary texts as well as the multiple contexts at play when students read texts—contexts of culture, curriculum, classroom, personal experience, prior knowledge, and politics. Students can see what factors—whether it's a character from a text, an author or literary movement, an MTV video, a shampoo commercial, peer pressure, or the school system in which they find themselves—have shaped their own world view and what assumptions they make as they evaluate the perspectives of others. As Stephen Bonnycastle (1996) points out, studying theory:

means you can take your own part in the struggles for power between differ-ent ideologies. It helps you to discover elements of your own ideology, and understand why you hold certain values unconsciously. It means no authority can impose a truth on you in a dogmatic way—and if some authority does try, you can challenge that truth in a powerful way, by asking what ideology it is based on. . . . Theory is subversive because it puts authority in question. (p. 34)

In the last decade or so, critical theory has played an increasingly im-portant role in professional conversations among college literature profes-sors and has become more visible in college literature classrooms as part of what it means to study literature. James Slevin and A. Young (1995) regard theory as the site of some of our most profound professional reexaminations as we reconceptualize what it means to teach literature, "the new directions in literary theory and criticism that mark the last two decades can be seen as responses to these very concerns, reexamining the assumptions that underlie literary study" (pp. ix–x).

Similarly, Bonnycastle (1996) writes:

Literary theory raises those issues which are often left submerged beneath the mass of information contained in the course, and it also asks questions about how the institution of great literature works. . . . What makes a "great work" great? Who makes the decisions about what will be taught? Why are authors grouped into certain historical periods? The answers to fundamental questions like these are often unarticulated assumptions on the part of both the professor and the students. . . . Literary theory is at its best when it helps us realize what we are really doing when we study literature. (p. 20)

In the early 1980s, Terry Eagleton (1983) wrote, "Not much of this theoretical revolution has yet spread beyond a circle of specialists and en-thusiasts; it still has to make its full impact on the student of literature and the general reader" (p. vii). More than 3 decades later, the presence of liter-ary theory is more clearly (some might argue, oppressively) present in the college literature classroom, yet these new developments in theory and the reconsiderations of curriculum that have been generated have not, for the most part, been introduced into the high school literature classroom. As Arthur Applebee (1993) points out:

The certainty of New Critical analysis has given way to formulations that force a more complex examination of the assumptions and expectations about authors, readers, and texts as they are situated within specific personal and cultural contexts. The challenges to New Criticism, however, have taken place largely within the realm of literary theory. Only a few scholars have begun to give serious attention to the implications of these new approaches for classroom pedagogy . . . and most of that attention has been focused at the college level. It would be fair to say that, despite the recent ferment in literary theory, the majority of college undergraduates still receive an introduction to literature that has been little influenced by recent theory. (pp. 116–117)

In fact, Applebee (1993) found that 72% of the high school literature teachers he surveyed in schools that had a reputation for excellence "reported little or no familiarity with contemporary literary theory" (p. 122). As one high school teacher put it, "These [theories] are far removed from those of us who work on the front lines!" In one of the few texts about theory written explicitly for secondary teachers, Sharon Crowley (1989) agrees, "The practice of teaching people to read difficult and culturally influential texts is carried on, for the most part, as though it were innocent of theory, as though it were a knack that anybody could pick up by practicing it" (p. 26).

While it is not widely reflected in the practice of secondary teachers, the notion that literary theory can be useful has gained greater voice in the field of English education. In *Literary Theory and English Teaching*, Peter Griffith (1987) describes the tension between presenting literature as cultural artifacts or literature as a vehicle for transmitting ideology. Additionally, the aim of many progressive educators is to use literature as a vehicle for self-exploration and expression. Griffith points out that the teaching of literary theory to secondary students is a useful way to bridge this gap:

> Certain applications of literary theory can lay bare what the text does not say and cannot say as well as what it does and, as part of the same process, to make certain aspects of the context in which the reading takes place visible as well. . . . To be able to offer pupils this sense of power over their environment seems a desirable goal, especially if the sense of power is more than a delusion and can lead in some way to an effect on the pupil's environment. (p. 86)

Dennie Palmer Wolf in *Reading Reconsidered* (1988) urges us to reexamine our notions of what literacy is, of what students should read, and of what it means to read well. She encourages us to teach students ways of thinking about texts. She writes, "Not to teach students these habits of mind would be to cheat them just as surely as if we kept them away from books written before 1900 and burned all poetry" (p. 4). Wolf reminds us that reading is "a profoundly social and cultural process" and urges us to provide all students with deeper and richer ways of thinking about literature, using terminology such as "holding a conversation with a work," "becoming mindful," and "reading resonantly" (p. 9).

In *Textual Power: Literary Theory and the Teaching of English*, Robert Scholes (1985) argues that there are three basic textual skills: reading, interpretation, and criticism. Although there are many secondary English teachers skilled in all three, all too often they relegate only the reading to their students. It is they, rather than their students, who determine the appropriate critical approach for each literary text. After their critical stance has been articulated, the teachers either allow students to create interpretations within the context of that critical approach or they provide a single privileged interpretation for the students. While the teacher may be well-schooled in theory, the students are not and are therefore limited in the interpretive choices they can make.

THE CALL TO THEORY

The call to theory has just begun to be heard by secondary school practitioners. As he contemplates the shape high school literature should take in the coming years, Bruce Pirie also invokes Scholes as he calls for a repositioning of the study of literature that "clarifies its relationship with the rest of the world" (1985, p. 24). Critics such as Scholes have pointed out that contemporary literary theory opens the barriers between the literary text and "the social text in which we live" (Scholes as quoted by Pirie, 1997, p. 31). It is at his intersection of text and social context, that the explicit study of contemporary literary theory can help adolescent readers make meaning of literary texts.

Kathleen McCormick (1995), a scholar notable for her unique ability to gracefully straddle the theoretical world of the university and the seemingly more pragmatic world of reading instruction in elementary and secondary schools, argues for the relevance of contemporary literary theories, especially those she calls "culturally informed theories," to the development of pedagogies in the schools. She writes:

> While so often the schools and universities seem quite separate, it is primarily the research carried on in the colleges and universities that drives the reading lessons students are given in the schools. If feminists, theorists of race and gender and cultural studies, teachers, and researchers in the universities were to begin to engage in more active dialogue with the developers of reading programs and the teachers who have to teach students—young and older—"how" to read, it might be possible to begin to change the dominant significations of reading in the schools—so that more students could begin to learn to read the world simultaneously with learning to read the word—so that readers can begin to see themselves as interdiscursive subjects, to see texts as always "in use," and to recognize that different ways of reading texts have consequence. (p. 308)

McCormick's suggestion that theoried ways of reading have significant consequences for our students of literature echoes an eloquent plea Janet Emig made almost 25 years ago for the teaching of literary theory. In a conference paper as president-elect of the National Council of Teachers of English, Emig (1990) wrote, "Theory then becomes a vivid matter of setting out the beliefs that we hold against the beliefs of others, an occasion for making more coherent to others, and quite as important to ourselves, just what it is we believe, and why" (p. 93).

Emig underscores the power of the approach to teaching literature that I present in this book. The purpose of teaching literary theory at the secondary level is not to turn adolescents into critical theorists; rather, it is to encourage adolescents to inhabit theories comfortably enough to construct their own readings and to learn to appreciate the power of multiple perspectives. Literary theory can help secondary literature classrooms become sites of constructive and transactive activity, where students approach texts with curiosity, authority, and initiative.

BUT ISN'T IT TOO POLITICAL?

There are those who may say that they signed on to teach English, not social studies, and that this approach is too political. I have two rejoinders to that objection. First, teaching is essentially a political act, a political stance— a stance that advocates for the literacy rights of everyone, a stance that acknowledges that when you give someone literacy, you give them power. Second, even our seemingly neutral reading of texts is political. In our literature classes, then, we should focus on helping students read texts with an eye toward the ideology that is inscribed in those texts. An African proverb puts it this way: "Until lions tell their stories, tales of hunting will glorify the hunter."

Our canon has been filled with tales of the hunter. In the last 2 decades, tales of the lion, works by authors such as Toni Morrison, Alice Walker, Louise Erdrich, Sherman Alexie, Amy Tan, and many others have begun to fill our schools' bookrooms and our students' sensibilities. In addition to hearing from the lion, we can continue to teach tales of the hunter but with the remediating lens of literary theory—a postcolonial lens for *Heart of Darkness,* a gender lens for *The Great Gatsby,* a social class lens for *Hamlet,* just to name a few possible examples.

For those who say, we should simply teach the literature "neutrally," I offer the perspective of literary scholar Shirley Staton (1987):

Contemporary theory holds that there is no such thing as an innocent, value-free reading. Instead, each of us has a viewpoint invested with presuppositions about "reality" and about ourselves, whether we are conscious of it or not. People who deny having a critical stance, who claim they are responding "naturally" or being "completely objective" do not know themselves. (p. 43)

We could continue to uncritically teach *Adventures of Huckleberry Finn* or *To Kill a Mockingbird* because they are classic pieces of literature, without regard for the problems engendered by the use of culturally offensive customs and terms. That decision privileges the arbitrary literary value of a canonical text over the significance and relevance of a changing student demographic. It ignores the deeply politicized history of the word *nigger*, for instance, and how it differently affects different populations. Teachers often make these kinds of decisions, teaching the same texts in the same way without taking changing classroom demographics into account. That, too, is a political decision, as much as offering a postcolonial analysis or reading the texts through the lens of critical race theory.

THE IMPORTANCE OF MULTIPLICITY

On the other hand, it is very important that we don't offer only a single theory to our students, for that truly is dogmatic or propagandistic teaching. It is the monotheoretical approaches of most secondary English classrooms that drew me to the notion of multiple perspectives as an antidote. Even a reader-response lens is limiting if it is the only possible theoretical frame in which one can produce a reading.

Offering students several ways to look at texts does more than help them learn to interpret literature from multiple perspectives; it also helps them develop a more complex way of thinking as they move from the dualism of early adolescence to the relativism of adult thinkers (Perry, 1970). F. Scott Fitzgerald (1964) perhaps most notably stated the virtue of this kind of thinking:

> The test of a first-rate intelligence is the ability to hold two opposed ideas in mind at the same time and still retain the ability to function. One should, for example, be able to see that things are hopeless and yet be determined to make them otherwise. (p. 69)

These multiple ways of seeing have become vital skills in our increasingly diverse classrooms as we explore the differences between and among us, what separates us and what binds us together. As Maxine Greene (1993) has eloquently argued, "Learning to look through multiple perspectives, young people may be helped to build bridges among themselves; attending to a range of human stories, they may be provoked to heal and to transform" (p. 194).

Attending to multiplicity, to the diversity that has come to characterize our interpretive communities, has caused some scholars to reconsider the role that literary theory may play as we acknowledge our need to learn to read across and between cultures (Rogers & Soter, 1997). As Laura

Desai (1997) points out, "Literary theory reminds us that we do not live in isolation nor do we read and interpret in isolation. We understand what we read through some combination of ourselves as readers and the text with which we interact, but this is never free of the multiple contexts that frame us" (pp. 169–170). Desai further argues that literary theory can provide for young people the tools necessary for interpreting culture as well. "Literary theory allows us to recognize our own reactions by providing the contexts we need to understand them. In this complex world, cultural forces are clearly at play in the lives of young people" (1997, p. 170). But young people will remain powerless over these forces unless they can recognize them: "How can we judge culture's impact if we cannot define what it is that is influencing our reactions?" Literary theory provides the interpretive tools young people need to recognize and "read" those cultural forces.

THE CHANGING TIMES

As we begin a second century of teaching literature, it is time we examine these enduring characteristics of literature instruction, asking which are appropriate and essential and which have continued because they have remained unexamined.

—Arthur Applebee, *Literature in the Secondary School* (1993)

In the past few decades, the relatively stable (some might even say, staid) and predictable practice of teaching literature has undergone changes from many directions. At the prompting of scholars, practitioners, and, perhaps most importantly, the changing nature of our students, we have considered and reconsidered the texts, contexts, and pedagogical approaches that comprise the teaching of literature. Our canons are loose, our pedagogy is shifting, and our profession seems to be challenging every assumption we have made about the teaching of literature since 1920. For example, we have reconsidered the relationship of texts to readers, of readers and teachers to authors, of texts to theories, and, of course, of teachers to their students. Multicultural literature has largely been embraced by many teachers, but the complexity of teaching diverse works to diverse and nondiverse classes is just beginning to be confronted. Our profession is challenging its assumptions about our literary heritage, our students, and even who is included in the pronoun "our." This reflection demands that as we challenge the hegemony of the sort of "cultural literacy" proposed by Alan Bloom or E. D. Hirsch, we also challenge the notion of a single theory, perspective, or "truth" about what literature we read together and how we teach it. As Slevin and Young (1995) put it:

If texts no longer organize the curriculum, then what does? If the professor is no longer the privileged agent of education then who is? . . . These pressing questions . . . contemplate the end of coverage as a model, the end of the canon as an agreed-upon certainty, the end of the professor as the agent of learning, and the end of the classroom as a place where education is delivered. These "ends" have been much contemplated, indeed. But what arises in their place? (p. ix–x)

CONCLUSION

In the end, by teaching literature with theory, we help students learn to decipher the world inscribed within the texts we study as well as learn to read the world around them. They can become the enlightened witnesses that bell hooks (1994) calls for, noting how power and privilege are inscribed all around us, and learning to read both texts and worlds with a nuanced and critical eye. Our students can become, with our help, truly educated in the way James Baldwin (1985) envisions, able to critique their own society intelligently and without fear. This kind of teaching is difficult. It requires a willingness to give up one's ultimate authority in the classroom. It reminds us, as Peter Rabinowitz and Michael Smith (1998) suggest, that we are not teaching readings but teaching ways of reading.

Critical Encounters in Secondary English: Teaching Literary Theory to Adolescents, Third Edition challenges current theoretical and pedagogical paradigms of the teaching of literature by incorporating the teaching of literary theory into high school literature classes. The guiding assumption of this book is that the direct teaching of literary theory in secondary English classes will better prepare adolescent readers to respond reflectively and analytically to literary texts, both "canonical" and multicultural. I argue that contemporary literary theory provides a useful way for all students to read and interpret not only literary texts but their lives—both in and out of school. In its own way, reading with theory is a radical educational reform!

Teaching literary theory is also, as Lisa Shade Eckert (2006) points out, a way of teaching reading. She writes: "Teaching students to use literary theory as a strategy to construct meaning is teaching reading. Learning theory gives them a purpose in approaching a reading task, helps them make and test predictions as they read, and provides a framework for student response and awareness of their stance in approaching a text" (p. 8). Similarly, Robert Scholes (2001) offers the notion of the "crafty reader." He explains, "As with any craft, reading depends on the use of certain tools, handled with skill. But the tools of reading are not simply there, like a hammer or chisel. They must be acquired, through practice" (p. xiv).

This kind of teaching changes our conception of what we teach and why. We are no longer transmitting knowledge, offering literature as content, as an aesthetic experience or as neutral artifacts of our collective cultural heritage. Instead, we are offering our students the tools to view the world from a variety of lenses, each offering a unique perspective sure to transform how adolescents read both words and worlds. As Lois Tyson (2006) writes:

> For knowledge isn't just something we acquire; it's something we are or hope to become. Knowledge is what constitutes our relationship to ourselves and to our world, for it is the lens through which we view ourselves and our world. Change the lens and you change both the view and the viewer. This principle is what makes knowledge at once so frightening and so liberating, so painful and so utterly, utterly joyful. (p. 11)

Critical Encounters in Secondary English offers instructional approaches that begin to meet the important challenge that Emig (1990) offered to her fellow teachers, "We must not merely permit, we must actively sponsor those textual and classroom encounters that will allow our students to begin their own odysseys toward their own theoretical maturity" (p. 94).

QUESTIONS ADDRESSED

The Third Edition of *Critical Encounters in Secondary English* addresses some of the following questions:

- Which contemporary theories seem best-suited or most age-appropriate to high school students? Are some more "teachable" than others?

- What are some specific strategies that teachers can use to encourage multiple perspectives as students read literary texts?

- What does a teacher need to know about theory in order to be able to teach it?

- Is theory really relevant to marginalized students or reluctant learners, or is it only appropriate for college-track classrooms?

- Can the study of literary theory help students understand, question, and bridge cultural differences?

- How does the teaching of theory change classroom practice?

- What sorts of texts can be used in teaching contemporary literary theory?

ORGANIZATION OF BOOK

This book combines theory with actual classroom practice. It combines argument with narrative. Classroom examples illustrate the practice of teaching literary theory. Portraits of urban, suburban, and rural classrooms help make the case for particular theories. Throughout the book, actual lessons and materials provide ways of integrating critical lenses into the study of literature. A variety of texts—"classics" such as *Hamlet, The Awakening, Of Mice and Men, Heart of Darkness, Frankenstein*, and *The Great Gatsby*, as well as titles that have been included in our secondary literature curriculum such as *Beloved*, "The Yellow Wallpaper," *The Things They Carried*, and *Native Son*—are used to illustrate a variety of critical lenses.

Chapter 1 sets forth the reasons for teaching critical theory. Chapter 2 argues for the importance of multiple theoretical perspectives as we read and interpret literary texts. Four very different classroom vignettes illustrate the power of multiple perspectives. Through the vignettes I offer specific strategies for introducing the notion of multiple perspectives to students (and to teachers) using several short stories and poems. These introductory activities, designed for Grades 9 through 12, can be used at the beginning of a semester, trimester, or yearlong course, or at the beginning of a specific unit on critical analysis. The focus of the activities will be on the power of viewing literary texts from a variety of perspectives, not on specific literary theories—yet. The emphasis on multiple perspectives and multiple ways of viewing texts helps set the stage for the introduction of theories that comprise the rest of the book.

Is reader response an appropriate interpretive strategy for all students? Is it useful or appropriate for all texts? Chapter 3 explores what happens when students are taught how to apply the basic tenets of reader response to their own reading. By describing what happens when students are given interpretive tools that are explicitly named, this chapter demonstrates that when we make our teaching strategies explicit to students, we strengthen their interpretive possibilities. This chapter also challenges some of the common assumptions and practices of response-centered teaching, especially as they relate to diverse classrooms.

Chapter 4 explores the political prisms of literary theories grounded in issues of ideology, class, and power. This chapter makes the case for the importance of political theory to help students learn to understand and read, and perhaps even resist, prevailing ideology. Using texts such as *Of Mice and Men, Black Boy, Native Son, Hamlet, The Great Gatsby*, and *Beloved*, I explore how these theoretical lenses help us understand the political, social, and economic dimensions of the world in which we live.

Gender theory is the focus of Chapter 5. Here I present classroom situations in which students learn to interpret texts such as *A Doll's House*,

The Great Gatsby, A Room of One's Own, The Awakening, "The Yellow Wallpaper," *Frankenstein,* and a variety of poetry using the gender lens. We also explore the resistances that both male and female students have to reading literary texts through a gender lens. In addition to exploring those resistances, we illustrate how students can also learn to read both texts and the world through the refractive light of gender theory.

Chapter 6 focuses on the postcolonial lens. Postcolonial criticism gives students the tools necessary to interpret a literary text within the context of European colonialism and imperialism. It allows them to see how commercial and military power have advanced Western ideologies among colonized peoples by examining literatures from both sides of the colonial divide. An analysis of these differences allows new interpretive possibilities for both canonical and postcolonial texts.

Chapter 7 offers a lens new to this edition: new historicism. This lens introduces a useful approach to fiction, especially historical fiction. Additionally, new historicism provides teachers with a fruitful opportunity to integrate nonfiction and informational texts into their literature classes within the framework of critical lenses. This chapter is also designed to answer the call for the inclusion of such texts into the secondary literature curriculum.

In Chapter 8 I tackle the more difficult and even more rarely used contemporary theory of deconstruction. Students will contrast the purposes of critical theories that are structural and linguistic to more political, extrinsic critical lenses. In using these theories, students are encouraged to focus on the specific language used in literary texts (mostly poetry) and apply recent postmodern theories to those texts. Again, several specific lessons are provided for teachers along with a discussion of the potential value of these approaches to high school students.

Chapter 9 focuses on three very different readers, describing theoretical predispositions that these readers began to develop when given a choice of interpretive perspectives. This chapter provides especially useful information for teachers who are interested in accommodating their instructional approach to different kinds of students in heterogeneous classes. The three readers are presented as case studies, and I chronicle their prior attitudes toward reading, the resistances and predispositions they brought to their literature class, their backgrounds, abilities, and interests, their written and oral responses to several literary texts, and the degree to which a multiple-perspective approach enhanced their responses to literature. We also consider issues of cultural diversity as we focus on relatively homogeneous suburban classrooms, as well as heterogeneous urban classrooms.

In addition to concluding remarks, Chapter 10 gives specific suggestions on how teachers might implement the teaching of literary theory in their literature classes, whether they be year-long required courses or electives. The chapter includes a discussion of the importance of reading cultural texts, using examples from contemporary media.

Chapter 10 also summarizes the central thesis of the book: Literary theory can and should be taught to secondary students. Using literary theory as they read texts, students become theoried and skilled readers with a variety of interpretive strategies and theoretical approaches. They become constructors of meaning, with multiple literary visions of their own. They become adept at reading the world around them.

CHAPTER TWO

Prisms of Possibilities

Introducing Multiple Perspectives

A man with one theory is lost. He needs several of them, or lots! He should stuff them in his pockets like newspapers.

—Bertolt Brecht, as quoted in Bonnycastle, 1996, p. 8

PRISMS OF POSSIBILITIES

As a former high school English teacher who knows something about literary theory, I've been pressed into service by a colleague who teaches at an urban school in Minneapolis. Stephanie is keen on the idea of introducing literary theory to her 10th-grade, mixed-ability American Literature class, but she doesn't exactly know how to begin. I volunteer to get things started for her, figuring that I'd better be able to walk my talk. I bring each student a set of literary theory cards (see Appendix, Activity 6) (adapted from Lynn, 2007, also in Beach, Appleman, Hynds, & Wilhelm, 2006). The cards are fastened together by a metal ring, which the students immediately being to pry apart. I also bring the poem "Mushrooms" by Sylvia Plath, but the title has been removed from their copies:

Mushrooms
Overnight, very
Whitely, discreetly,
Very quietly

Our toes, our noses
Take hold on the loam,
Acquire the air.

Nobody sees us,
Stops us, betrays us;
The small grains make room.

Soft fists insist on
Heaving the needles,
The leafy bedding,

Even the paving.
Our hammers, our rams,
Earless and eyeless,

Perfectly voiceless,
Widen the crannies,
Shoulder through holes. We

Diet on water,
On crumbs of shadow,
Bland-mannered, asking

Little or nothing.
So many of us!
So many of us!

We are shelves, we are
Tables, we are meek,
We are edible,

Nudgers and shovers
In spite of ourselves.
Our kind multiplies:

We shall by morning
Inherit the earth.
Our foot's in the door.

—Sylvia Plath

This poem has been used extensively with reader-response approaches (see Beach, 1993; Appleman, 2000; and this volume, Chapter 3), but now I enlist it for a different cause. I ask the class if anyone has ever heard of Sylvia Plath. Thanks largely to the 2003 film *Sylvia*, starring Gwyneth Paltrow, five students raise their hands. "Great," I say, "you are our biographical group." I clump the remaining 24 students into groups of four and assign each group the labels of reader-response, gender, and social power. I then pass out the Prisms of Possibilities handout (see Appendix, Activity 8) and ask the students to create a reading of the poem based on their assigned perspective, using just the theory card, their own background knowledge, and each other.

I circulate around the room, answering questions and repeating my admonishments about the metal rings that hold the theory cards. We reconvene, in ragged circles, each group reporting its findings.

"You can tell she was really depressed," the biographical group reports. "Her husband made her feel invisible."

"All women feel invisible," a gender group explains. "Look at the language in the poem about serving and about being subservient."

"It's not just women," the social power group retorts. "It's about any group that feels at the margins: workers, poor people. Immigrants, maybe? People without full rights. But look at the last two lines: 'We shall by morning inherit the earth.' There's gonna be a revolution!"

"Man, our group didn't get so . . . political," says the reader-response group. "We tried to guess what the poem was about, and then we, like, focused on the woods and stuff like that. Jonah's done a lot of hiking in the Boundary Waters Canoe Area wilderness and it reminded him of that."

"Well, who's right?" some students ask. "Which group got it?" "Can there be more than one right answer?"

"Oh, yes," I respond with a smile. "There certainly can!"

WHAT KIND OF WALTZ?

My Papa's Waltz

The whisky on your breath
could make a small boy dizzy
But I hung on like death
Such waltzing was not easy.

We romped until the pans
Slid from the kitchen shelf
My mother's countenance
Could not unfrown itself.

The hand that held one wrist
Was battered on one knuckle
At every step you missed
My right ear scraped a buckle.

You beat time on my head
With a palm caked hard by dirt
Then waltzed me off to bed
Still clinging to your shirt.

—Theodore Roethke

Joe, a 10th-grade language arts teacher in an urban school, distributes this frequently anthologized poem to his mixed-ability class of high school juniors. He asks them to read the poem to themselves several times and waits for the silence to be broken by the stirring of students ready to talk. In a series of gently prodding questions, he asks the class to construct an oral reading of the poem that conveys its meaning. One student, Mark, offers that it is a wistful remembrance of a young boy's affectionate kitchen romps with his deceased father. The teacher asks the student to read the poem aloud with this interpretation in mind and he does so. His changing voice does not betray him as he reads gently and affectionately, stressing words like *papa*, *waltz*, *cling*, and so forth.

Complimenting the student on his reading, Joe turns to the rest of the class and peppers them with questions. "Is this the definitive reading?" he asks. "Is this what Roethke meant to communicate? Would all of you have read the poem the way Mark did, or are there any other ways this poem could be read?"

Slowly, hesitantly, a hand rises from the corner of the room. Marnie, a serious and quiet student, says firmly, "I don't think this poem is about a happy childhood recollection at all." Then under her breath, almost inaudibly, she asserts, "I think his dad was a drunk who beat him." Some members of the class murmur in assent. Mark silently shakes his head in vigorous disagreement. Joe pushes. "How would the poem sound if that were the case? How would it be read? Does anyone care to try?" There are more than a few students who seem willing to take on this reading. Marnie is not one of them.

Josh begins to read forcefully, emphasizing words like *beat*, *death*, *battered*, *missed*, *dirt*, *whisky*, and so forth. After the reading, some students in the room seem to shudder visibly from the effect of Josh's reading. They also seem a bit unsettled. Hadn't they already heard a convincing and sensible reading?

"Which one is right?" one student asks. "How do we know which way to read it?"

"Could they both be right?" Joe asks.

"Not at the same time," one student replies.

"Not to the same person," another one offers.

"But do they both seem to make sense? Do they offer two plausible perspectives?" Amid general murmurs of assent, Joe continues, "There clearly seems to be more than one way to read this poem, more than one way to read the situation. This may turn out to be true for many of the texts we read together, as well as for many of the things that happen to us in everyday life." Joe smiles and hands out another poem, "Thirteen Ways of Looking at a Blackbird" by Wallace Stevens.

INTRODUCING MULTIPLE PERSPECTIVES

Bob, a veteran of 20 years of teaching, surveys his class of restless 10th-graders, a varied assortment of adolescents very different from the Advanced Placement students he is generally used to teaching. In the class are hardworking students who hope to go to college, a few students who are struggling to pass their classes, and a few underachieving students who long ago decided to get off the train on the college-prep track.

The students have read a short piece by essayist Russell Baker entitled "Little Miss Muffet" (see Appendix, Activity 1). Baker recasts the familiar fairy tale of the unfortunate Ms. Muffet and the intruding spider by retelling it through a variety of perspectives, for example, from the eyes of a psychiatrist, a teacher, a militarist, a child. The students respond ambivalently to the essay. They are surprised that anything as childish as nursery rhymes is being introduced by a teacher who has a schoolwide reputation of "making you think without making you sweat." Bob arranges the students into groups. Once in their groups, he asks them to select a nursery rhyme and recast it from several occupations or roles. The students do so and come back to class the next day with fanciful results. Here are three examples:

"Humpty Dumpty": Prosecuting Attorney's Point of View

This whole incident is obviously a conspiracy. There is no way Mr. Dumpty would just fall off the wall. Being in the fragile state that he was, he would have been extremely cautious while up on that wall. He was obviously distracted by a diversion so he wouldn't notice the suspect creeping up behind him, ready to push him off at just the right moment. It was just an "innocent fall" or so the members of the palace would have you believe. The fact of the matter is, all the king's horses and all the king's men are suspects. They all had a motive. They were sick and tired of the egg getting all the attention. And the fact that they couldn't put Mr. Dumpty back together is very suspicious, since they were all trained in egg lifesaving. So far, they've come up with an alibi, but it won't hold. There are almost as many holes in their stories as there are in Mr. Dumpty's poor broken body. (Maggie)

"There Was An Old Woman Who Lived in a Shoe": Democrat's Point of View

This is, no doubt, a serious concern of ours in the United States of America. We are no longer living in a middle-class suburban home with a father, mother, two-and-a-half children, and a family pet. This poor woman needs the federal government's help. With a welfare check every so often, maybe she could feed her children something more nutritious than broth. And she's living in a shoe! What is happening to low-income housing these days? The government should raise some taxes so that she doesn't have to live in a shoe! Something that is so truly heartbreaking is that this poor mother is single and stuck with the burden of the children with no support from the father. We need to catch these absentee fathers and make them pay child support. Welfare, not workfare is the answer to all of the Old Woman Who Lived in a Shoe's problems. (Mandi)

"Jack Be Nimble": Fire Chief's Point of View

This is a textbook example of what happens when fire is in the hands of careless children. Children should never play with fire. It's a cardinal rule. Everybody knows that. This isn't play. No, it's much worse than that; fire is not a toy. What we see developing is a blatant disrespect for the animal which is fire. We may be looking at a future arsonist of America. And, what's that candle doing on the floor in the first place? It's a fire hazard, people! (Eric)

When the reading of these new versions of nursery rhymes winds down, Bob reads aloud *The True Story of the 3 Little Pigs by A. Wolf* (Scieszka, 1989), a children's book that retells the familiar tale from the point of view of the wolf. It begins: "Everybody knows the story of The Three Little Pigs. Or at least they think they do. But I'll let you in on a little secret. Nobody knows the real story, because nobody has ever heard *my* side of the story." And it ends: "So they jazzed up the story with all of that 'Huff and puff and blow your house down.' And they made me the Big Bad Wolf. That's it. The real story. I was framed."

Amid giggles and chatter, Jessie blurts out what many of his classmates were thinking, "Why did we do this, Mr. B? It was fun, but it seemed pointless."

"We did it to demonstrate one very important point—that the same story, even a simple story such as Little Miss Muffet, can take on very different meaning depending upon who is doing the telling. So, when we read, the meaning depends on who's doing the reading. Meanings are constructed; we create meanings that are influenced by who we are and what we are culturally, historically, psychologically, and, in the case of the Baker version of Miss Muffet, vocationally. If we can construct and change the meaning for something as simple as Little Miss Muffet, can you imagine the changes, the variations in meaning that occur among us as we read poems, short stories and novels?"

"What if," Bob wonders aloud, "*Adventures of Huckleberry Finn* were told from the perspective of Tom Sawyer or Jim; *To Kill a Mockingbird* were told from the perspective of Boo Radley or Tom Robinson; *The Diary of Anne Frank* from the point of view of Peter, Miep Giess, or Anne's father? How does a story change when the narrator changes? How are the basic elements of that story transformed? Is it the same story, or narrative, told from a different point of view, or does it become, at some point, a different story?"

Bob raises some questions fundamental to the study of literature, questions he would like to pursue with his students through the use of literary theory. How can we read a narrative from a single perspective and be able to trace the influences of that perspective on how the text is shaped? Given one perspective, how might we be able to imagine how other perspectives might change the telling of that narrative? In other words, how can we see the wolf's side in the pigs' story? Further, how can we deconstruct the singular vision that is represented by one story? And, how can we extrapolate from that single tile of vision to the mosaic of other human experiences and perspectives?

Imagine! All this from fairy tales and nursery rhymes!

FAMILY STORIES

Rachel is in her first year of teaching in a small rural community. Overall, her teaching has been going fairly well—she feels well planned and well prepared, and, for the most part, she's been able to maintain the interest of her 9th- and 10th-graders. Each day brings her a greater understanding of the different sensibilities between her small-town students and her own adolescence in a large, metropolitan city. Rachel admires the feeling of community and camaraderie among her students. There seems to be more unanimity about issues than she ever imagined possible in the diverse urban high school she attended. While she embraces the harmony of her students' common outlook, she finds the homogeneity of opinion tends to stifle class discussions. Like today.

After reading *The Scarlet Letter*, Rachel held a final discussion that she hoped would arouse some controversy. Throughout their reading of the text (mandated by the district's curriculum), Rachel tried to present a variety of contestable issues. What is a moral code? Who were the characters they most and least admired? Did Hester deserve her fate? What motivated the townspeople—cruelty, morality, both? What is innocence? Who was using whom? Do we have absolute moral codes in today's society?

On a variety of occasions, she threw out several provocative statements, playing devil's advocate and even offering some possible interpretations that she knew her students would find implausible. But her playful questioning was returned by either silence or half-hearted acquiescence. She tried extending one student's commentary by asking if anyone disagreed, but there were no takers. Finally, in desperation and in probably what was not her finest teaching moment she cried, "Isn't there *any* other way to see this? Do we have only one point of view out there? How can that be? Counting me, there are 31 of us. There has got to be more than one opinion among us!"

Rachel wants her students to be able to understand there is usually more than one side to any issue. Events, in literature and in life, are multifaceted and have different sides, cast different light, depending upon the viewer. She wants to change the monochrome of students' vision; she wants them to see other perspectives. She hopes that by the end of their year together, students will be able to do more than walk around in someone else's shoes. They should be able to see things from other viewpoints, heartily argue positions that they don't believe in, inhabit other ways of being or habits of mind. She wants her students to analyze their lives and texts, not just from the inside out but from the outside in. Eventually she hopes that the students will be able to take different theoretical stances to literary texts as well as other things. But now, at the very least, she wants them to see that every story, every position has more than one side. But, where should she begin?

She decides on a lesson on family perspectives. She tells a story about a little black puppy that came to her family as a stray. She says that when she compares notes with her siblings and her parents, each person has a different memory of who found the dog first, who named it "Pickles," and how long it was in the family. She asks students to consider a retelling of The Three Little Pigs from the wolf's perspective. Then she asks students to tell a family story from their own perspective (see Appendix, Activity 3). Finally, she asks them to have another family member tell his or her version of the story when they go home that evening.

The next day, Rachel leads a discussion on the different versions and introduces the concept of "perspectives." She tells her class that the notion of perspectives is very important to consider as one reads literature. She begins with the idea of being able to consider a story from perspectives other than that of the protagonist. For Rachel, this is not simply an important step in interpretive reading; real life also means looking beyond one's own point of view to understand the point of view of someone else. Rachel chooses a story by John Updike called "Separating." It's a typical Updike story, set in suburbia, told from the husband's point of view—and told as if there were no other point of view that mattered. This myopic narration is particularly relevant to the story line (as well as Rachel's larger purposes); the husband has decided to leave his wife, but neither his wife nor his children are aware of the decision.

After her students read the story, Rachel asks them to consider the plot of the story from the perspective of the other characters, such as the wife or the children (see Appendix, Activity 2). Rachel and her students move the discussion of point of view (something they've done since 7th grade) into a discussion of worldview or stance. She tells her students that stories are often told from a vision as singular as the husband's; it's just not always so painfully obvious to us. She tells them that for every text they read, there is another tale wanting to be told. Our job is to invoke those other voices, always on the lookout for the betrayed wife, the neglected child, the overarching commentary about manicured lawns and cul-de-sacs. She tells them to think about how tales could turn on the teller as they read their next book together, *Catcher in the Rye*.

STAR WARS AND MULTIPLE PERSPECTIVES

It is a crisp September morning and the school year is only 2 weeks old. The students in Martha's 12th-grade Advanced Placement class have just finished reporting on their summer reading. They are beginning to get to know one another and their teacher, and trying to figure out how this last year of high school English, how this Advanced Placement class, may be different from their previous study of literature. Or will it be? In *Literature in the Secondary School,* Arthur Applebee (1993) reports on how little has changed in curriculum and instruction in most high school literature class-rooms, especially among the upper-track classes. Are Martha's students simply in for more of the same?

On this particular day, the classroom is darkened and the students absolutely cannot believe their good fortune. The teacher plays *Star Wars,* and students watch the screen intently. She asks them to jot down a few things that strike them as particularly interesting or important as they view the film. Despite the block scheduling, the film spills into the next period and Martha feels a little guilty. After all, this *is* Advanced Placement, and the students' parents and administrators seem to impose a different level of accountability on the class.

When the film is over and the lights come on, Martha waits for the students to piece back together their location in the classroom world of fluorescent lights and chalk dust, literally light years from the intergalactic battles they've been cheering on. Martha distributes a discussion sheet entitled "Theory Wars" (see Appendix, Activity 7). Together they discuss the first two questions. They discuss the relative merits of seeing a movie and of reading a book more than once. They weigh the advantage of the surprise and spontaneity of a first reading or viewing to the ability to see things you didn't see the first time during a second, more considered reading. They also discuss the relative inequities that often exist in most classroom settings when students are encountering a text for the first time and the teacher may be encountering it for the tenth or thirtieth (Rabinowitz, 1987).

Martha leads the students through a brief discussion about archetypes, and the students are visibly gleeful about how easily the archetypes they learned last year in British Literature seem to fit the characters of *Star Wars.* Martha takes a deep breath and hands out a sheet called "Literary Theories: A Sampling of Critical Lenses" (see Appendix, Activity 5 or, for alternate definitions, see Activity 4), as well as a stack of theory cards, index cards with short definitions of literary theories (see Appendix, Activity 6). This handout contains brief synopses of some of the major literary theories she hopes to include during the rest of the year. It is a dynamic document, changing each year with a collective reconsideration of theory by Martha and her students. At this early stage of their time together, Martha does not want to either overwhelm or overfeed the class; she simply wants to give them a preview or taste of the theories to come. She will reintroduce them later, weaving them into the curriculum as the year progresses.

Generally, none of Martha's students has heard of literary theory before. Even though, as discussed in Chapter 1, many of them have been in classrooms that favor either a New Critical or a reader-response approach, those responses have never been explicitly articulated or "named." Their study of literature has, to this point, been atheoretical. One could argue that, even for this upper track, their entire education has been atheoretical. That is, the biases that frame the particular perspectives of their learning—be it scientific paradigms, historical school of thought, or approaches to literature—have never been admitted. To be sure, however, they are at play in the presentation of knowledge as truth. The students deserve to know that. They also need the tools that will help them recognize and evaluate the ideologies through which their education has been funneled. As Stephen Bonnycastle (1996) points out:

> The main reason for studying theory at the same time as literature is that it forces you to deal consciously with the problem of ideologies. . . . If you are going to live intelligently in the modern world, you have to recognize that there are conflicting ideologies and that there is no simple direct access to the truth. (p. 19)

Martha knows the dangers of teaching didactically; she tends to prefer a more inductive or a discovery approach, but this brief but explicit introduction of a sampling of literary theories is part of her grand plan. She hopes to briefly introduce all of the literary theories at once, to let them simmer in the students' minds as she introduces the readings and the texts one by one over the course of the school year. Martha and her students will return to this sheet again and again as they reframe their reading into the multiple perspectives that are suggested by the theories. Herein lies the optometrist's gold—the treasure trove of different colored lenses that can alter our vision. Martha and her class have taken the first step into their theoretical odyssey, an odyssey that is at the very center of her curriculum for her Advanced Placement students and the center of this book.

WHAT'S NEW ABOUT THEORY

The previous five classroom scenes, although they take place in separate classrooms distinguished by significant differences in teachers, students, and curriculum, provide the opening salvos to the concept of multiple perspectives. The activities themselves can be used individually or they can occur consecutively in any classroom. I tend to use all five when I introduce the topic of multiple perspectives and do them roughly in the order in which

I present them in this book. Encouraging multiple perspectives provides a conceptual introduction to considering the different "readings" of a text that literary theory can provide.

Taken together, these activities help students understand that literature can be read from a variety of perspectives. This pluralistic approach indicates that the sources of these different perspectives do not always spring from personal experience. It encourages students to hold texts up to the light, like a prism, just to see how many colors might be cast. Or, to return to the opening metaphor from the prologue, it introduces readers to a variety of tinted lenses through which they can view things differently.

At first blush, the experienced literature teacher may wonder if we are really offering anything new. For example, many teachers may have used "My Papa's Waltz" to teach tone. Activities such as rewriting nursery rhymes or considering other characters in the John Updike story help teachers convey age-old literary devices such as point of view, protagonist, or characterization. Similarly, archetypes, such as those embedded in Martha's *Star Wars* activity (see Appendix, Activity 7), have formed the anatomy of our literary criticism for years.

Further, the notion that there are several critical stances or perspectives from which texts can be viewed is not new in the language arts curriculum, especially a literature curriculum that has been duly influenced by Louise Rosenblatt, Robert Probst, and other notable proponents of reader response. Reader response clearly claims that the meaning of texts changes from reader to reader, that there is no single "correct" interpretation, that it is created by the transaction of reader and text, and that every reader may create a different interpretation of a text, given our different backgrounds and orientations. Yet all reader responses, regardless of how they may vary from student to student and reader to reader, are really variations on a single theoretical theme: Personal experiences provide the lens that colors the reading of the text. There is, of course, some unassailable truth as well as pedagogical promise to this claim. But most contemporary theoretical approaches, other than reader response, are rarely used in secondary literature classrooms. Additionally, as literature teachers we may want to move students beyond their own personal response into the perspective of others. As Pirie (1997, p. 23) points out, "At some point, examination of their own meaning-making will probably lead students to recognize limitations in their current perspectives—that's a characteristic of growth, after all—and engender new appreciation of many things, including perhaps Shakespeare."

Teaching multiple approaches to literature through contemporary literary theory promotes what many in the field of literacy education have come to regard as a constructivist approach to literature. As Applebee (1993) defines constructivism, "Instruction becomes less a matter of transmittal of an objective and culturally sanctioned body of knowledge, and more a matter of helping individual learners learn to construct and interpret for themselves" (pp. 200–201).

Applebee goes on to say that "The challenge for educators is how in turn to embed this new emphasis into the curricula they develop and implement." When teachers introduce literary theory into their literature classes, they invite students to construct both interpretive method and literary meaning into their study of literature. No longer will students respond within a preselected theoretical paradigm. They construct the theoretical context as well as the content of their meaning-making.

THE END OF THE BEGINNING

After these initial introductory activities, some teachers might want to offer students some straightforward explications of literary theory, such as Steven Lynn's (1990) "A Passage into Critical Theory," an essay in which he interprets a story by Brendan Gill about working at *The New Yorker* from a variety of theoretical perspectives. The essay nicely iterates the structure of the Baker piece but pushes students more firmly into the direction of theory. Excerpts from *The Pooh Perplex* by Frederick C. Crews (1965) provide a more elaborate variation on the same theme. These pieces whimsically demonstrate how different theoretical perspectives cast light differently on the same text, even an "innocent text" such as *Winnie the Pooh*. And, they remind all of us of the potential absurdity that can result when we overreach with our criticism:

> The fatal mistake that has been made by every previous Pooh-ologist is the confusion of Milne the writer with Milne the narrator, and of Christopher Robin the listener with Christopher Robin the character. These are not two personages but four, and no elementary understanding of Pooh is possible without this realization. We must designate, then, the Milne within the story as "the Milnean voice" and we must call the Christopher Robin who listens "the Christopheric ear." With these distinctions in mind, Pooh begins to make perfect sense for the first time. (p. 6)

The presence of humor and grace are important in this enterprise, for the introduction of theory needs to be approached gently and with care. Students already suspect that we English teachers meet together at conferences and make up terms like tone, symbol, and protagonist just so we can trick them on the next test, wreck something that was just starting to seem like fun, or complicate something that was just starting to get more simple. If theory is going to be believed and used by students, if it is somehow going to become an integral part of their repertoire of reading, then it needs a chance to make a case for itself, even if that means beginning slowly and subtly with activities such as the ones used by Joe, Bob, Rachel, Martha, and me.

Clearly not every theory should be used with every text. Reading with theory can become as mechanistic and arbitrary as some of the other kinds of literary apparatuses we've been collectively guilty of overusing in the past. Applying theory should be neither mandatory nor automatic. In fact, as Susan Sontag (1969) has argued, the reading of some texts should be done without any theory or interpretation at all. I sometimes go weeks without directly applying theory, letting it lie fallow as we go about our reading in the usual way. More often than not, as we read together, a student may bring up a particular lens. When that happens, I know that their theoretical journey is progressing, that it is they and not I alone who help construct the theoretical framework of the classroom.

While a teacher may chart the theoretical journey anywhere and with any theory or combination of theories, in this book we begin our study of theory with the one with which students may have the most practice— reader response. Although in many classrooms students have become well-socialized into sharing their personal responses to texts, rarely have they heard of Louise Rosenblatt or have any idea that their responses lie within a particular theoretical framework. Additionally, reader response is often unconditionally presented to students as the most comfortable and familiar way into a text, even though many teachers like Rachel have some understanding of the limitations and perhaps even dangers of this particular pedagogical approach, what Pirie (1997) calls "the cult of the individual." It is time to pull back the curtain on the workings of reader response.

CHAPTER THREE

The Lens of Reader Response
The Promise and Peril of Response-Based Pedagogy

> What a poem means is the outcome of a dialogue between the words on the page and the person who happens to be reading it; that is to say, its meaning varies from person to person.
>
> —W. H. Auden

> We must keep clearly in mind that the literary experience is fundamentally an unmediated private exchange between a text and a reader, and that literary history and scholarship are supplemental.
>
> —Robert Probst, *Response and Analysis*

> A poem is the map of a dream.
>
> —Kevin, Grade 12

> This poem has no meaning to me. Because I get no meaning, it is not poetry.
>
> —Jesse, Grade 12

A few years ago I served as an outside examiner for an International Baccalaureate (IB) program in an urban high school in Minneapolis. My role as an "invigilator" was to help students demonstrate their understanding of several canonical texts (*Oedipus Rex*, *MacBeth*, *Hamlet*, *The Grapes of Wrath*, *The Scarlet Letter*) by asking them first to prepare a brief explication of the text and then to respond to a series of questions.

Particularly memorable was one discussion I had about *The Scarlet Letter* with a 16-year-old student named Leah. Leah spent about two or three sentences on plot summary and then exclaimed, "You know, if my man ever treated me the way Hester's man treated her, he'd be out of my life before you could say 'The Scarlet A.' I can't believe the crap Hester took. Actually, last week my boyfriend Rob and I almost broke up. Okay, well, it all started when . . ."

Try as I might, I couldn't move our conversation back to Hester or to anything specifically textual about *The Scarlet Letter* or any of the other texts she had read for her IB English course. I felt that she had dived off the springboard of personal response into an autobiographical wreck (apologies to Adrienne Rich). Leah's inability to craft a response that was textual in any way might have been inadvertently facilitated by her skilled and well-meaning teacher who encouraged personal responses to literature and de-emphasized more traditional forms of textual analysis. While this anecdote may exaggerate the "worst case scenario" of the personalized approach to literature, it does point out some of the potential weaknesses in how that approach has come to be practiced in secondary schools.

This chapter reviews some of the basic tenets of a *reader-centered* approach, discusses some of the many advantages of this particular lens, and explains how its practice may have diverted from its intentions. I then explore some of the limitations to the approach that have emerged as both students and canon have become more diverse. Finally, a close look at reader-response activities in two different classrooms reveals that we can use reader response with our students more fruitfully by (1) teaching it more explicitly, and (2) teaching it as one of a variety of theoretical approaches rather than as the only possible approach. This multiplicity of approaches will be further explored in subsequent chapters.

THE BENEFITS OF THE READER-CENTERED APPROACH

There can be no denying the power and purpose of a reader-centered approach to literature and the degree to which it has positively informed our practice. It has made the enterprise of literature teaching more relevant, immediate, and important. It has forced us to rethink what we do when we teach literature, why we do it, and who we do it for. There is ample evidence of the soundness of the reader-centered approach; its advocates are influential and articulate—from Louise Rosenblatt's efferent to aesthetic reading to Judith Langer's engagement with literature to Robert Probst's elegant and elegiac meditations on the importance of personal response. The value of the lens of reader response to literature study in secondary classrooms simply cannot be denied. And no one would want to.

As we look back at literature instruction over the last 60 years, it is easy to see how reader-centered teaching fit perfectly with the goals of constructivist education and with the progressive education movement. At the center of the educational enterprise was the student. No longer was the text itself or the author the most salient part of literature study. No longer could students' individual responses to texts be considered "mnemonic irrelevancies," as I. A. Richards had claimed. Instead, the reader was the creator of meaning through a "never to be duplicated transaction" between the reader and the text (Rosenblatt, 1976, p. 31).

This new focus on the reader indisputably enlivened and irrevocably altered the teaching of literature. It changed or supposedly changed the power dynamics in the classroom and the role of the teacher, and it clearly changed what it was that we asked students to do when they read texts. The paradigmatic shift from a text-centered to a reader-centered pedagogy also changed our consideration of the kinds of texts we used. We found ourselves sometimes considering whether a particular text was teachable by the degree to which it might invoke personal responses from our students. From the point of view of most observers, at least, these were all changes for the better.

Five-paragraph themes gave way to reading logs; recitations of genre or structural aspects of the text gave way to recitations of personal connections to the text; and the traditional teacher-in-the-front formation gave way to the intimate and misshapen circles with which many of our students and many of us are familiar. Of course, knowledge of the text was still important, but personal knowledge seemed in many cases to be privileged over textual knowledge. Rather than seeking out biographical information about the author or historical information about the times in which the text was written or took place, teachers began to spend time finding personal hooks into the texts they chose and frequently began literature discussions with questions that began "Have you ever?"

A CAUTIONARY TALE

We met Rachel in Chapter 2. Rachel was an enthusiastic, if relatively inexperienced, practitioner of reader-centered pedagogy, and had become increasingly frustrated as she watched her students measure, by their own limited experiences, the predicaments and decisions of Hester Prynne, George and Lenny, Daisy Buchanan, and Atticus Finch. On one hand, Rachel is grateful that they can find connections between their own lives and the lives of these literary characters. She knows that personal experience often provides the coattails students ride into a book. She also knows enough about reader-response approaches to the teaching of literature from her college methods class to realize that using one's personal experiences to connect to the text can be a fruitful way for students to make meaning. She knows that personal response is the hook that many teachers favor for good reason. In fact, some of her colleagues contend it is the only way that really works.

And still . . . there is something about this personal approach to literature with which Rachel feels uncomfortable. Yes, she wants her students to read literature to gain insight into their own lives, to gain perspective into their own situations. Yet there is, Rachel believes, something limiting about that position, something that might trivialize the importance of the real differences that exist between the students' world and the world of the text. Are we *really* all the same? Is the purpose of studying literature only to clarify our own existence and underscore our unique personal attributes? We know the personal connection and engagement with literature that is gained when students measure the relationship of Hester and Chillingsworth through their own dating experiences, or issues of adultery with contemporary scandals involving American politicians. But what is lost?

Rachel is not the only one who has been reconsidering the relative merits of reader response. Perhaps one of the most biting reappraisals of an individualized reader-centered approach is offered by Bruce Pirie in *Reshaping High School English* (1997). In a chapter tellingly titled "Beyond Barney and the Cult of the Individual," Pirie reflects on the practice of valorizing individual responses in the literature classroom and the inherent dangers and complications of that approach. He argues that our focus on individuals may be overly simplistic. Even our definition of *individual* may be flawed; it does not acknowledge the contextual factors that help to make us individuals. As English teachers we may have been guilty of over-privileging and romanticizing the individual at the expense of considerations of context. Pirie warns, "We now need to question the limits of the doctrine of individualism before our classroom practices harden into self-perpetuating rituals" (p. 9). This is, in part, what James Marshall (1991) refers to when he calls reader response our new orthodoxy.

Pirie notes Applebee's (1993) observation that we shuttle between valorizing personal response as an end in itself or using it as a hook or motivation to get students interested in more serious literary analysis. Pirie (1997) also questions whether a personal-response approach to literature is justifiable from the perspective of academic rigor: "I am, however, suspicious of the suggestion that just expressing your personal response is a satisfactory educational attainment, or that such a response could be evaluated for its authenticity" (p. 120).

This failure to critique readings is also lamented by Michael Smith (Rabinowitz & Smith, 1998) when he says, "I think it's important for readers and teacher to have a theoretical model that allows them to critique readings" (p. 121). In their provocative book, *Authorizing Readers*, Rabinowitz and Smith remind us of the importance of authorial intention. If reader response is a transaction, at the very least we need to acknowledge that the text is an equal partner in that transaction. Meaning is a result of a kind of negotiation between authorial intent and the reader's response. It is not simply the question "What does this mean to me?" that Smith says captures the essence of reader-centered theories. How can literature foster a knowledge of others when we focus so relentlessly on ourselves and our own experiences? Without some attention to authorial readings, Rabinowitz and Smith remind us, we give up the power of the text to transform.

BE CAREFUL OF WHAT YOU ASK FOR

Perhaps the excesses that alarm even some of the originators and strongest supporters of reader-centered pedagogy have to do with how atheoretical its practice has become. Students are not exactly sure what it is they are supposed to do when they respond to a text; they just know they are supposed to respond *personally*. A cynical 10th-grader once confided, "My teacher likes it when we get gooey and personal—the gooier, the better." They sometimes even overreact by saying things like Nathan did in an 11th-grade discussion of *Snow Falling on Cedars*, "You really can't tell me anything about this book since my *personal* response is the only thing that counts." We may have "balkanized" the response-based classroom, thus preventing the ability to discuss or share our personal experiences. Since our responses to literary texts are particularly and uniquely ours, then what is it that anyone, teacher or classmate, could offer that would either enrich or contradict it? Perhaps it is this phenomenon that frustrates Rachel so much when she tries to get a discussion going. Her students' attitude seems to be, "If my response is uniquely mine, then what can anyone else tell me about it?" This also leads to the sort of autobiographical diving that Leah did with *The Scarlet Letter* in the anecdote that opened this chapter. Bonnycastle (1996) addresses this issue of reader response when he writes: "If each of us only pays attention to individual experience, the communal basis for the discipline will disappear and literature classes will have nothing to hold them together" (p. 174).

Then, of course, there is the matter of students who may be uncomfortable with personal response. This may be more than a question of learning style; it is in some ways a privacy issue or perhaps a cultural issue. The sharing circle that characterizes much of our practice is also culturally determined (Hynds & Appleman, 1997). It makes assumptions about the amount of trust that students have in each other and in their teachers. It makes some assumptions about their relationship to the institution of schooling and whether they have experienced school as a safe place. Perhaps most importantly, it also makes some assumptions about the degree to which students' lives are in "sharable shape." And, of course, underlying all of these assumptions is our belief that the sharing of personal responses in the public sphere of school will bring students to a greater understanding of themselves and one another rather than underscore the depths of the chasms, of the inequality, that often divide us. This is the essence of the false promise of democracy in the literature circle.

CONFESSIONS OF A TRUE BELIEVER

As a high school teacher during the 1970s and 1980s, I was an enthusiastic practitioner of reader response. I tirelessly sought the personal connections that would engage my students with a text, whether it was *To Kill a Mockingbird*, Of *Mice and Men*, *Ordinary People*, *Black Boy*, *The Hobbit*, or *The Great Gatsby*. Like the teachers I described above, I began more than my share of literature discussions with that "Have you ever . . . ?" opening. I have to admit, however, that while I considered myself to be a true-blue reader-response teacher for about 10 years of high school teaching, I never once explained to the students that what we were doing was called *reader response*. While I'm sure I explained or paraphrased the concept of a "transaction" with a literary text in general terms, I never was explicit about what exactly we were doing and why.

Sometimes the students themselves, noticing the tone of our classroom yet not being able to name the difference they felt, would refer obliquely or disparagingly to Mrs. Engstrom's sophomore American Literature class or Mrs. Debarge's 11th-grade British Literature class where there was clearly *one* meaning to a passage or even an entire text, and feelings were *never* discussed. The students would reminiscence bitterly about memorizing quotations, preparing for nit-picky objective tests, and embarking on wildly elusive symbol hunts. Even then I wasn't clear about what was different in this class. Neither did I name the competing traditions of literary study nor admit to myself and to my students the validity and potential advantages of a more text-centered approach. As I prepared my reader-friendly lessons, journal assignments, and essays, I vilified the New Critics, making them the evil straw people of single-minded interpretations. Ben Nelms (1988) stated it well in this description:

> I learned to think of the literary text as an edifice. Almost as a temple. Complete, autonomous, organically whole, sacrosanct. We approached it with reverence. We might make temple rubbings and we were encouraged to explain how its arches carried its weight and to speculate on the organic relationship between its form and function. But it was an edifice and we were spectators before its splendors. (p. 1)

I congratulated myself that I could never treat my students as "spectators" or the texts as "temples." I felt comfortable and confident—superior, even—in my reader-response pedagogy. Looking back, from the viewpoint of multiple perspectives, I realize I was guilty of imposing a theoretical framework with no room for deviation. In my own way, though I could never see it or admit it then, I was as narrow-minded and singular in my theoretical vision as Mrs. Engstrom or Mrs. Debarge and their single-answer worksheets and symbol hunts.

I would like to be able to claim that I somehow saw the light and eventually learned to teach explicitly and theoretically while I was a high school teacher, but that is simply not the case. It was only when I began teaching about teaching that I started making response-based teaching explicit with my own version of "the naming of parts." For those preservice and inservice teachers who had never been pricked by the needles of "porcupines making love" (Purves, Rogers, & Soter, 1990), I began to think strategically about how to make the lens of reader response explicit. In other words, I didn't simply want to encourage my students to respond to literature within a classroom context that was never articulated; I wanted to teach them about the theory of reader response and then encourage them to respond to literary texts with those responses enriched by their metacognitive awareness of that theory.

PULLING BACK THE CURTAIN

I began to pull the curtain back on reader response with my secondary pre-service teachers and realized, as I had with many other instructional strategies, that I had been withholding from the high school students themselves the power of being able to name what it was they were doing. It was rather like wanting students to reach the upper levels of Bloom's taxonomy but never teaching them about the taxonomy itself. I sometimes felt like I had been teaching high school like the Wizard of Oz, trying to create magic and illusion, asking students to ignore the man behind the green curtain when all the time it would have been more illustrative and perhaps even more magical without the illusion, if I had only trusted them enough to take them backstage.

Taking them backstage wasn't very hard. While there are many different forms and variations of reader response—as Beach (1993) categorizes them: textual, social, psychological, cultural, and experiential—I decided to focus primarily on a version of Louise Rosenblatt's transactional approach. It is, in many ways, the most straightforward, sensible, and comprehensible to secondary students. And, thanks to the wonderful "translations" of Robert Probst, it seems to be the version of a reader-centered approach to literature with which most secondary teachers are familiar. Rosenblatt views literary reading as a transaction between reader and text. She views responding to literature as an "event." As Richard Beach (1993) explains:

> In contrast to the textual theorists who are interested in the competent or ideal readers' knowledge in general, Rosenblatt focuses on the uniqueness of a particular momentary transaction. While the textual theorists are concerned with achieving interpretation consistent with knowledge of appropriate literary conventions, theorists adopting Rosenblatt's transactional model are open to exploring their responses as reflecting the particulars of their emotions, attitudes, beliefs, interests, etc. (p. 51)

In his useful volume, *A Teacher's Introduction to Reader-Response Theories* (1993), Beach illustrates some of the principles of reader-response theory by using the poem "Mushrooms" by Sylvia Plath, a poem already discussed in Chapter 2. The poem is so oblique and ambiguous that it can nicely illustrate some of the basic tenets of reader response to secondary students. It can become an important part of a lesson designed to help "pull back the curtain."

As Beach reports, readers respond with marked variety to this text and construct a wide range of interpretations. When the poem is presented to students without its title, even more interesting variation can result. For example, some students divine that the poem is about some kind of vegetation (from moss to trees) while others, especially female students, have mentioned that they think it's about unborn babies. Some students have suggested that it's about people who are oppressed—either people of color or perhaps women. One student ingeniously suggested that the poem was about rabbits and provided a line by line explication using words like *multiply*, *silent*, and *edible* to prove that it was so. A few others reported magical and mysterious walks in the woods with their fathers or mothers. A few even noted a trace of mental illness in the poem.

Here are some of the responses of 11th- and 12th-grade students after they were asked to write their responses to the poem on index cards:

> This poem is about conformity and how it jeopardizes our individuality.

> This poem is about an oppressed group of people. They are beaten, ignored, abused, used. There is some hope of things being OK for them. It comes in inheriting the earth. They are almost there.

> These are slaves, escaping from plantations. They were just mindless tools before; now they are individuals.

> Snow.

> About a class of un-noticed underdogs who will come together silently and rise against the present power.

> White carpenter ants.

> I think this is a dream. A dream is the uninhibited imagination and a poem is the same thing put to words. A poem is the map of a dream.

> Insects, cockroaches. . . . It made me think of how they say that if there is ever a nuclear war, it would just be cockroaches left to cover the earth.

> Mushroom-rotting fungus plaguing the earth.

> It's about woodland mice.

As these statements demonstrate, the range of responses to this poem is extraordinary, although some kind of cohort pattern can sometimes be detected—more women tend to see the unborn babies, college students seem to be more likely to see oppression. Students are usually amazed at the diversity of responses, and the activity itself makes the case for the notion that our responses to literature are almost as individual as a kind of literary fingerprint.

It is at this point, after they've responded to "Mushrooms," that I introduce the reader-response diagram to secondary students (see Figure 3.1). This diagram graphically illustrates the principles of Rosenblatt's transactional theory of reader response in the following ways. First, students are asked to consider what personal characteristics, qualities, or elements of their personal histories might be relevant to their reading of a particular text. We stress that the relevant personal qualities or attributes they choose are dependent upon the particular text. For example, it is obviously relevant that I have red hair when I consider my response to *Anne of Green Gables*. However, the fact that I have red hair is irrelevant when considering my responses to *A Separate Peace, All Quiet on the Western Front,* or *The Awakening*.

On the right side of the diagram, students are asked to consider the textual properties that might affect their reading or response and to list those properties. They might, for example, list the presence of vernacular or other aspects of vocabulary, the length of sentences, use of punctuation or italics, or the narrative structure. I point out to the students that all of these factors do contribute to a reader's response to a particular piece, but they are characteristics of the literary work, not of the individual reader.

In addition to considering both textual and personal characteristics, students are also asked to consider what contextual features may have influenced their reading. In some respects, adolescent readers seem to have a difficult time differentiating between the contextual and the personal, a fact that would not surprise most observers of adolescents. The lack of boundaries between self and other typify the kind of adolescent egocentrism that

Figure 3.1. Reader-Response Diagram

Context

Reader ⟶ Meaning ⟵ Text

Context

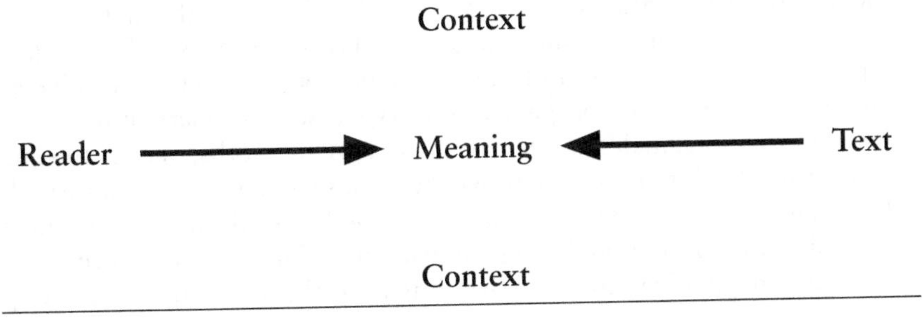

David Elkind (1986) has described. In this case, the word *context* is used in a fairly narrow sense, not the sociocultural context, which may indeed be imbedded in all three of the other categories, but the context or conditions under which the book was read. For example, people read differently under the fluorescent light of the classroom or on an airplane in close proximity to a stranger than they do when they are in the comfort of their own home and their favorite reading place. The amount of homework, what one has been required to do as part of reading, and what else may be occurring at school or at home are all factors that contribute to the reading context.

Next, we apply the reader-response diagram to the students' responses to the poem "Mushrooms." On the left or reader side of the diagram, students often list their affinity or lack of affinity for nature, their comfort and experience with reading poetry, awareness of being part of an oppressed or marginalized group, and whatever prior knowledge they might have about the poem. On the right or textual side of the diagram, students may list the following textual properties: There are only one or two words per line, the language is very concrete, the poem doesn't rhyme, it's "modern" and imagistic. Sometimes they mention that the poem is written by Sylvia Plath and offer some biographical information or insights (just the kind of thing that drove those New Critics crazy).

After we describe the mechanics of the transaction or dialectic between reader and text, we further discuss how that dialectic created individual responses for the readers that enabled them to construct their own personal meaning for the text. Given the range of responses to "Mushrooms," it is easy for students to see how they have imprinted their own experiences and understandings onto the text itself and rendered interpretations as diverse as their own life experiences. At this point, the case for reader response generally makes itself. Now, let's see how pulling back the curtain plays out in two different classrooms with two different texts.

READER RESPONSE AND *RUNNING FIERCELY TOWARD A HIGH THIN SOUND*: "I AM NOT A LESBIAN; I AM NOT A JEW"

Carolyn Bell's Advanced Placement class quickly forms the large circle that is the de rigueur formation of their class. Located in one of the most diverse high schools in the city of Minneapolis, the class of 30 doesn't fully reflect the heterogeneity of the overall school population, but it is more diverse than many of the AP or college preparatory classes elsewhere in the state. Juniors and seniors, males and females, preppies and goths, White students and students of color, those with brown hair, those with blue hair, those with yellow hair, jocks and poets, gays, straights, and bisexuals, they all assemble in their delicious and unpredictable individuality. Their regular teacher is a skilled and imaginative veteran with a taste for offbeat literature and a deep faith in her students' ability to be engaged and adventurous readers. When she is called to jury duty, she generously allows me to have her class for a week. The novel they will be reading has already been selected, since a visit from the author, who lives in Minneapolis, had been previously scheduled.

Never one to teach only the canon, Carolyn had introduced her students to a variety of literature, mixing some predictable AP or college-bound choices with more surprising ones. They have read *As I Lay Dying, Beloved, Stones from the River,* and now this, *Running Fiercely Toward a High Thin Sound,* a first novel about a Jewish family that is divided by the mental illness of one sister and the jealousy of the mother. Mental illness, family dysfunction, lesbian relationships, and Jewish family history and values are all salient themes of the book set in New England in the mid-1970s. Its uniqueness of theme, form, and content make the discussion of this novel particularly suitable for a reader-response approach, since students are bound to have visceral and highly individualistic reactions to the work.

While Carolyn's taste in literature is contemporary and unconventional, her pedagogy is a bit more traditional and highly effective. The class itself generally focused on some of the more traditional forms of literary analysis that they would be expected to use on the year-end AP exam. The class had been briefly introduced to reader response by a student teacher, but the students seemed to prefer a more text-centered, teacher-led approach to literature. To deepen their collective repertoire of ways of interacting with literary texts, I decided to spend my week with the students using a reader-centered approach.

We began by reviewing some of the basic tenets of reader response with a handout (see Figure 3.2 and Activity 11) adapted from an article by Lee Galda (1983). Then I introduced the transactional diagram described in the previous section and very slightly adapted for the novel. I asked the students to fill out the diagram at home and to bring a completed diagram to class the next day. I then asked them to write some "meaning statements" on the back of the handout—one or two sentences that described the meanings they constructed as a result of the transaction between themselves and the text.

We discussed the reader diagrams the following day. Under the reader heading, students listed some *reader characteristics* (or lack of characteristics) they felt were important to their reading of the novel:

I have a pushy mommy.

My family has communication problems.

My father is not always present in my life.

I have friends who are gay; I know lesbians, how they live and what they are like.

I am morally opposed to homosexuality.

I feel completely exasperated and helpless with my mother.

I am not Jewish.

I am not a lesbian.

I don't like reading about any kind of sex.

Interestingly, on the diagrams most students seemed to focus more directly on what they were not rather than what they were, a case of negative identity. I wondered whether this would have been true with any text or

---

Figure 3.2. Reader Response

What Is Reader Response?

"A reader makes a poem as he reads. He does not seed an unalterable meaning that lies within the text. He creates meaning from the confrontation." Louise Rosenblatt

Philosophy or Rationale

Reader-response advocates stress the interaction between the reader and the text. Reading is recognized as a process in which expectations operate to propel the reader through the text. Readers bring to the text their own experiences, morals, social codes and views of the world. Because readers bring their meanings to the text, the responses are different. Response-based teaching pays close attention to the reader, respects the reader's responses, and insists that the reader accept responsibility for making sense of personal experiences.

Response to Literature: Theory

In *Literature as Exploration* (1976), Rosenblatt presented her alternative to the belief that a text carries a precise meaning which readers must try to discern. She proposed that a literary text was simply symbols on a page and that the literary work, or "poem" as she later designated it, existed only in the interaction of reader and text. She defined the literary experience as a "synthesis of what the reader already knows and feels and desires with what the literary text offers" (p. 272). This transaction between reader and text consists of a reader's infusion of meaning into verbal symbols on a page and the text's channeling of that meaning through its construction.

The realization of a literary work of art requires an active reader who constantly builds and synthesizes meaning, paying attention to the referents of the words being processed while aware of the images and emotions experienced. The text does not embody meaning but rather guides the active creation of meaning. Thus, within this theory, it becomes impossible to discuss literature without reference to the reader.

Adapted from Galda, L. (1983). Research in response to literature. *Journal of Research and Development in Education, 16*(3), 1–6.

whether the students were particularly interested in disassociating themselves from being Jewish or lesbian.

The following *textual characteristics* were most commonly offered:

The book contains a lot of Yiddish words.

Explicit and graphic lesbian sex.

Going through mirrors, a surrealistic quality to the prose.

All the stereotype of the radical lesbians.

Magical worlds.

Multiple narratives or perspectives.

After the students listed both the reader traits and the textual characteristics, they were asked to compose several *meaning statements* that arose
from their "unique transactions" with *Running Fiercely Toward a High
Thin Sound*. These meaning statements were impressive in their range as
well as their gravity:

Books don't have to have redeeming, happy endings because a lot of
lives don't.

Sometimes what you perceive is not always the truth.

Mothers do not innately love their children. Society only thinks they
should.

Homosexuality is real and important but it is not the book's most
important theme.

You can't force your children to be what you want.

Forgiveness is not always possible.

Accepting other people for who they are instead of what you want
them to be is important in family relations.

You really have to love someone before you can hate them or truly be
cruel to them.

I found little meaning in this book at all as it didn't apply to me.

CONTRAST OF TWO READERS

What then happens in the reading of a literary work? Through the medium
of words, the text brings into the reader's consciousness certain concepts,
certain sensory experiences, certain images of things, people, actions,

scenes. The special meanings and, more particularly, the submerged associations that these words and images have for the individual reader will largely determine what it communicates to him. The reader brings to the work personality traits, memories of past events, present needs, and preoccupations, a particular mood of the moment, and a particular physical condition. These and many other elements in a never-to-be-duplicated combination determine his response to the peculiar contribution of the text.

—Louise Rosenblatt, *Literature as Exploration*

If we are to give credence to Rosenblatt's account of what happens in the reading of a literary work, we would expect that the individual characteristics of students would really come into play as they read a novel like *Running Fiercely*, one that is so clearly marked by definitive personal qualities, unusual lifestyles, and unique family history. We might, for example, expect students to have a wide range of responses to such an unusual text, given the diversity of the class. In addition, we might expect students whose "personality traits, memories of past events, present needs, and preoccupations" bear some resonance and similarity to the characters and events of the text to have a markedly different response from those students whose life experiences and memories stand in stark contrast to those that are represented in the novel. The student-response diagrams seem to call these assumptions into question. Though the text is not at all obviously theme driven, many students seem to have similar transactions with the text, not at all like the never-to-be-duplicated combination that Rosenblatt predicted.

While most of the students enjoyed the book, let's take a look at two students who seemed unable to make meaning or to have a positive transaction with the text. Of course, it is not particularly surprising that some students failed to respond to the book; as English teachers, we know that happens all the time. What is surprising, however, is how different these two students are. Their personal qualities are almost diametrically opposed and yet they experienced a similar response to the novel. Their shared resistance seems to call into question some of our assumptions about the relationship between personal qualities and their relevance in terms of how they might influence our responses to a literary text.

Mark

Mark is perhaps the most recalcitrant student in Carolyn's class. He is intelligent and competent if somewhat surly. His air of passivity and lack of emotion didn't seem to waver during the reading of the text, even when the author herself came to visit our classroom in all her radical lesbian splendor. Like many of his classmates, Mark listed the relevant reader characteristics in the negative. As a reader he described himself: "not Jewish, heterosexual, introvert, small family." In terms of the textual features that would influence his response he mentioned: "technique: metaphor, social ideas, Yiddish, and sexual content." See Figure 3.3.

Mark speculated that the novel might be about what he called the "inevitable conflicts between introverts and extroverts" and acknowledged the possibility that the author was telling a metaphorical story that meant something to her, that she was trying to educate the reader about an issue. Yet, in the end Mark came up relatively empty-handed in his transaction: "I found little meaning in this book at all, it does not apply to me."

It would be easy to dismiss Mark's inability to find meaning in this text as having something to do with how different he is from the characters in the book and his difficulty in relating to them. But Mark's classmate Ellen's reaction to the same text cautions us against making such a simplistic, if superficially sensible, explanation.

Ellen

Unlike all of her classmates, Ellen is Jewish and speaks Yiddish. Further, she believes that her parents are very much like the selfish, jealous, and woefully imperfect parents of the protagonist. Ellen doesn't find the family dynamics of the novel strange; she recognizes them as being very much like her own family. Ellen claims that the mother is bitter, jealous, and mentally unstable. One might think that Ellen's shared characteristics with the characters and situations would make the text especially relevant for her. At the very least, we might expect that her response would be significantly different from a

Figure 3.3. Mark's Reader-Response Diagram

Context

Reader ⟶ Meaning ⟵ Text

(What personal qualities or events relevant to this particular book might influence my response?)		(What textual features might influence my response)
not Jewish, heterosexual, introvert, small family	I found little meaning in this book at all, it does not apply to me	technique: metaphor, social ideas, Yiddish, and sexual content

Context

classmate who was as dissimilar from the characters as she was similar. This is not the case. (See Figure 3.4.)

As did her classmate Mark, Ellen seems to have an unfulfilling transaction with the text. Like Mark, she dismisses the author's motive as being more writer-based than reader-based: "I think Judith Katz wrote this as therapy. I could tell it was based strongly on her life. She wanted to pull out everything that pissed her off and write about it." Ellen fails to map her own experiences onto the text and instead concludes, "I don't think there is a good meaning for this book," a response remarkably similar to Mark's. It may, in fact, be the first thing they have had in common.

The contrast of these two students helps make two points about the use of reader-centered pedagogy in the classroom. I am not suggesting that Rosenblatt argued that students would map their own personal qualities into the text, and the better the match the greater the response would be. For the record, she never claimed anything like that. Our individual qualities, she asserted, would inform our responses to a text but would not necessarily dictate what they were. In practice, though, we have tended to select texts

Figure 3.4. Ellen's Reader-Response Diagram

Context

Reader   ⟶   Meaning   ⟵   Text

(What personal qualities or events relevant to this particular book might influence my response?)

(What textual features might influence my response)

- I'm Jewish
- my mother is bitter & jealous
- I'm mentally unstable

Yiddish & Jewish references
Fay is just like my mom
they ALL are.

Context

Meaning statement: I don't know that there is a good meaning to this book. I think Judith Katz wrote this as therapy. I could tell it was based strongly on her life. She wanted to pull out everything that pissed her off and write about it—the stereotype lesbians, the good girls, and the crazy ones. Some people shouldn't have kids, just because they can get pregnant. Having kids doesn't void you of jealousy. Books don't have to be redeeming, happy endings because a lot of lives don't. Not all mothers are good. Almost any nutcase can get pregnant. A smart person would give that some thought.

that in provocative ways provide matches between our students' worlds and the worlds of the characters. While in many ways it may be fruitful to do this, it may also be dangerous, which this contrast points out.

First, we may misinterpret how a student's shared experiences and characteristics with the characters' may affect her response. In some ways, as Ellen's case illustrates, the closer the students' own experiences are to the text the more likely they may be to reject the text. For example, adolescents dealing with suicide attempts of friends or family members might find *Ordinary People* too excruciatingly close to home to read. Second, we may be inadvertently giving students a dangerous message: If you can't "relate" to the book, you may not be able to find meaning in it, or, as Mark so succinctly claimed: "I found little meaning in this book; it doesn't apply to me."

In *Authorizing Readers,* Michael Smith (Rabinowitz & Smith, 1998) addresses some of the issues that arise in what he calls "the pedagogy of personal experience" (p. 119). He claims that an emphasis on the personality of the reader, what is at the heart of many reader-centered theories and pedagogies, may cause students to ignore the differences and respect for those differences that is ironically one of the goals that is at the heart of our attempt to diversify the curriculum.

We also trivialize some of the profound and perhaps irreconcilable differences between us. As Smith points out, we may be able to appreciate a character's situation but we never will be able to fully understand it; and we reduce the power of literature and the representations of those experiences by pretending that we have such understanding. Smith claims that the pedagogy of personal response can make it difficult for students to realize that one doesn't necessarily have to be able to relate to a character to respond to a literary text. He believes it is unrealistic to expect the paths of our lives to map meaningfully onto the lives of characters. Our pedagogy of personal response, he claims, limits students' ability to derive meaning out of texts that describe worlds and experiences far different from their own, a reason, ironically, why many of us began to love literature in the first place.

Smith quotes a student who feels she cannot respond to Toni Morrison's *Beloved*: "I felt alienated by how their family interacted. I had no basis on which to relate or empathize" (p. 124). Smith agrees that perhaps Toni Morrison is counting on exactly this to make her point—that you can never understand, and that's exactly a part of what you need to understand. This point is especially important in the next section, as we consider the responses of a different literature class to Richard Wright's *Native Son*.

READER RESPONSE AND *NATIVE SON*

Unlike Carolyn's classroom, Martha's 12th-grade English class is located in a suburb, filled with white-collar families and three-car garages. As part of her AP curriculum, Martha has introduced her students to critical theory. They have read a variety of works, both canonical and nontraditional, including *Beowulf, Much Ado About Nothing, The Things They Carried, Hamlet, Frankenstein,* and *Snow Falling on Cedars.*

Martha's students are familiar with the term *reader response.* In fact, they have completed Activity 8 (see Appendix) on the poem "Mushrooms" and discussed some of the factors that influence their responses to particular texts. They also seem to understand that there are several approaches to a literary text, of which reader response is just one. On the other hand, they do have a tendency to oversimplify the concept of reader response as simply meaning: What does this book mean *to me?* That is, they conflate the concepts of personal meaning with the identification of personal characteristics that may affect their responses. They need to clarify their understanding.

Martha has decided to teach Richard Wright's *Native Son* and wants to approach the novel through a variety of critical lenses—social class (a natural for this novel), gender, and reader response. Martha also hopes that the distance between her mostly White, mostly middle-class students and the novel's African American and sometimes violent protagonist Bigger Thomas will help her students see that literary responses are not dependent on one's similarity to a character. She believes as Smith argued that, in fact, the differences are sometimes precisely the point.

Martha and her students spend about 2 weeks discussing various aspects of the novel. Then she divides the class into four groups and has them complete an activity called Theory Relay (see Appendix, Activity 36), where they visit a reader-response station, a historical/biographical station, a gender station, and a social class station. The students are asked to describe how each of the four theoretical perspectives informs their understanding of *Native Son.* Each station includes some supporting documents such as biographical information on Richard Wright, explications of social class and gender literary theory (see Chapters 4 and 5), and some quotations from the text that are particularly relevant to each theoretical perspective. Students move around the room from station to station as they listen to the blues.

When students arrive at the reader-response station, there is a description of reader response and a reader-response diagram tailored for *Native Son* (see Appendix, Activity 12). As did Carolyn's class, the students first listed what relevant reader characteristics came into play as they read the text. They then listed the textual characteristics that influenced their responses to the text. Finally, they listed the meaning statements that they derived from their reading transaction. Here is how Martha's students characterized those transactions with *Native Son* from the perspective of reader response.

Reader Characteristics

My religious background tells me that killing is wrong.

I think the death penalty should be applied in some circumstances.

I have strong views on justice and on taking responsibility for your actions.

I don't believe in the death penalty.

The fact that only women are murdered would have an effect as well. I seem to be very sympathetic to remorseful criminals.

I know that it is wrong, but sometimes I am racist and sometimes others are racist against me. I was picked on by a group of Black girls when I was in 6th grade.

I am Black in America.

I'm reading the book in a class full of White students with a White teacher.

Text Characteristics

The way the book is set up from the beginning of White versus Black.

How gory Mary and Bessie's deaths were.

The descriptive nature in which the author describes the murders and the racist treatment of the Black people; the detailed arguments of the lawyer, who tries to give reasons for why things are the way they are, also influences my response.

Reading the closing statements from the prosecutor and just that whole side of the case is really appalling, especially when Bigger is referred to as a beast and other things, which flat-out classify him as not being human simply because he is Black—not even because he killed two women—I was quite shocked.

Meaning Statements

Even with oppression, free will can exist.

There will always be the resistant or rebellious element in human beings as long as they are oppressed.

Because I am a White female, Mary Dalton's case is just as tragic as Bigger's, if not more so, because of her brutal death without any responsibility. Because I am educated, Bigger Thomas owes much of his demise to his lack of education and could have done something, if only a bit, about this. Prejudice: Bigger Thomas was under tremendous emotional stress because he was targeted on the basis of his race alone and we should all sympathize with him.

I feel Bigger Thomas was made into who he is by his society.

Racism used to be much worse in society than it is now. Segregation is no longer legal, but people still segregate themselves.

Being female I understand the discrimination Bigger faced every day and sympathize with his feelings of rage and helplessness.

DISCUSSION

The reader-response diagrams helped Martha's students isolate the features of the text as well as the personal characteristics that influenced their responses to *Native Son*. As we might expect, many of those responses clustered around issues of race, gender, and class. Students thought about not only their own race but also their own feelings about race relations. They also confronted the intersection between race and gender. White females in particular felt torn between their sympathy for Bigger as an oppressed person and their disgust for his violence. Violence also affected students' responses in terms of their feelings about the death penalty as well as in terms of their visceral reaction to the violence in the story. The reader diagrams forced students to think explicitly about the mechanics of their responses and to map those factors in terms of what belonged to them and what belonged to the text. They made their transactions explicit to themselves, to their teacher, and to their classmates.

Sometimes, completing the diagram forced them to confront the degree to which they were unable or unwilling to have an emotional reaction to the book. For example, one student wrote: "My response as a whole has been quite unemotional. I read Wright's work with interest, see his points, and it raises interesting questions, but I am quite uninvolved, probably largely as a result of my boredom with my life, especially school, and a number of distractions in my mind."

Under the "reader characteristics" she wrote, "As a young White, middle-class female, I feel I am perhaps better furnished to sympathize with Mary than with Bigger. It is difficult to truly understand the factors in a life leading to such an end, as such pressures and oppression have happily been completely absent from my life." Under the "text characteristics" she wrote: "The brutalities Bigger commits are atrocious and while Wright succeeds in explaining Bigger's condition, it does not justify Bigger's actions. Wright intentionally makes his book confusing and therefore disturbing, raising questions about the collective versus the individual in racial issues."

The reader-response station helped to make the mechanics of the reader response explicit and helped students locate the sources of the factors that contributed to their responses. Many students were able to empathize with Bigger Thomas despite the profound differences they named between their situations and Bigger Thomas's. Others, like Mark in Carolyn's class and the student Michael Smith quotes as she reads *Beloved*, were unable to construct meaning because the text bore no relevance (or so they thought) to their protected and privileged suburban, middle-class lives. Hence, the frequency of meaning statements such as: "This book was not relevant to us." "One's White, middle-class background makes it hard to relate to the text." "This is obviously very difficult for me to personally relate to."

This dismissal because of difference is often where a reader-centered discussion ends: The text was not relevant to me; therefore, I found no meaning in it. As Smith points out, this is the inherent irony and limitation in a pedagogy of personal experience, especially when we read multicultural literature or other texts that portray worlds far different from our students'. Martha's students could not simply come up empty-handed because of an unsatisfying personal transaction with the text. Because their reader-response exercise was situated within a multiple perspective approach, they were invited to find meaning in other ways.

In addition, the fact that reader response was part of a multiple-theory relay allowed students to critique the relative usefulness of the reader-response lens. Martha asked her students to compare and evaluate the four theoretical approaches. She then asked which lens seemed to be most consistent with the intention of the novel, which lens was the most difficult to apply, and which lens was the most informative. Not surprisingly, most students found the social class lens among the easiest to apply or the lens that seemed most consistent with the intention of the novel. Most students found it to be particularly difficult to apply the gender lens.

While there was some general agreement about the relative usefulness of these two lenses in terms of *Native Son*, they seemed much more divided about the usefulness of the reader-response lens, with some student reporting that it was the hardest lens to apply and others reporting that it was the most applicable.

Difficulties Students Reported as They Applied the Reader-Response Lens to Native Son

I'm so used to having to write great statements of theme that when I was presented with an opportunity to simply state my opinions on meaning, I had great difficulty.

The lens that was most difficult to apply for me was the reader-response lens because I questioned what exactly I brought to the text.

One lens I found surprisingly hard to relate to was reader response. I feel like I haven't had enough experiences with oppression or racism to relate at all to this book. I can't relate to Bigger's feelings because I live in a world that has never limited my options . . . also the feelings of hate the Whites have for Bigger is incomprehensible for me.

Successes Students Reported as They Applied the Reader-Response Lens to Native Son

The reader-response lens seemed to be the most attractive to the text. I liked it because it was open-ended and I can use it to interpret *Native Son* as I wanted to.

The reader-response lens seems to be the most consistent with the intention of the novel. Richard Wright is a Black man who writes about Blacks' points of view for White people. The Blacks already know what he is trying to say; it is the White people he is trying to make an impact on. He wants his White audience to think about their own lives and do the best they can to try to relate to the Blacks.

It seems that with the novel, as with any work of art, the artist (author) is most interested in the individual effect each reader experiences. Hence, it seems logical that the lens most consistent with Wright's intention would be reader response, gauging what one has personally gained from reading the novel.

TOWARD A SOLUTION: MULTIPLE VISIONS AND THE NAMING OF PARTS

The reader-response movement was a friendly antidote to the tyranny of the text that characterized some of our earlier approaches to the teaching of literature. It provided students with a way to engage personally with literature, opened up the possibility of multiple interpretations of individual texts, and made our students the meaning-makers of texts. In fact, to some the reader actually became more important than the author. But when reader response becomes not just *a* way of reading, but *the* way of reading texts, it is an ideology, regardless of how appealing that ideology might be. We need to challenge the overly simplistic notion of the individual that has characterized our "pedagogy of personal experience." As I have argued in this chapter, we can do this by directly teaching the elements of reader response.

Martha's and Carolyn's classes demonstrated the value of making our reader-response teaching more explicit. In addition, we've seen that by recontextualizing reader response within a multiple theoretical framework, we can create a critical and comparative context that can help us use what is best about the lens of reader response and, at the same time, guard against its excesses by not having it be the only way we encourage students to respond to texts.

Martha's students did indeed consider their reading of *Native Son* from a reader-response perspective, but they did so as they concurrently considered three other theoretical perspectives as well—Marxist/social class, feminist/gender, and biographical/historical criticism. The students considered the viability of those other perspectives as well as their relative effectiveness in helping them make sense of the text. This multiple theoretical or comparative perspective can help keep our practice from veering into dogma. The next two chapters deal with the social class and gender lenses and how they can contribute to the larger systems that are at play as we read texts and learn to interpret our world through critical encounters.

SUGGESTED NONFICTION SELECTIONS FOR THE READER-RESPONSE LENS

Zora Neale Hurston, "How it Feels to be Colored Me" (pdf available online)

Annie Murphy Paul, "Your Brain on Fiction" (*New York Times*)

Keith Dorwick, "Getting Called Fag" (*Oxford Reader for Writers*)

Peggy Orenstein, "The Way We Live Now: I Tweet, Therefore I Am" (*New York Times*)

N. Scott Momaday, "Excerpts from The Names: A Memoir" (pdf available online)

Amy Tan, "Mother Tongue" (pdf available online)

Sherman Alexie, "Superman and Me" (*New York Times*)

E. B. White, "Once More to the Lake" (pdf available online)

Gary Soto, "The Pie" (pdf available online and from *A Summer Life*)

Plato, "The Allegory of the Cave" (pdf available online)

CHAPTER FOUR

What's Class Got to Do with It?

Reading Literature Through the
Lens of Privilege and Social Class

> It is *not* that we shouldn't care about individual students and texts. We should, and I do. We also recognize, however, that students and texts are embedded in huge, living, sometimes contradictory networks, and if we want students to understand the workings of textuality, then we have to think about those larger systems.
>
> —Bruce Pirie, *Reshaping High School English*

> There is, in fact, no need to drag politics into literary theory; as with South African sport, it has been there from the beginning. I mean by the political no more than the way we organize our social life together and the power relations which this involves.
>
> —Terry Eagleton, *Literary Theory*

> The Philosophers have only interpreted the world in various ways; the point is to change it.
>
> —Karl Marx

A THEORY BY ANY OTHER NAME?

Many teachers who are eager to invite students to consider the ideological underpinnings of class in both texts and their lives have been reluctant to introduce the Marxist lens, so named. Some schools may confuse the introduction of Marxist literary theory with the practice or indoctrination of Communism, and teachers may receive negative reactions from parents, community members, administrators, and other teachers. Indeed, discussing the differences between Marxism and Marxist literary theory is a difficult but necessary element to introducing students to this critical lens. Those discussions may indeed help diffuse some community resistance. On the other hand, that very resistance may be the strongest proof that we need the vision the Marxist lens provides to read our ideologies and to teach our students of literature to do the same, regardless of what we call it. While one might be tempted to suggest that it is precisely that kind of timidity that teaching with theory is designed to combat, it would be cavalier and unfair to underestimate the political pressure that is brought to bear on teachers, or the degree to which certain terminology can imperil an innovative curriculum.

So, after conferring with dozens of teachers across the country, I will refer to *the Marxist lens* as *the social class lens* for the rest of the book. Given the broad range of critics and scholars who do this work, I think it is a fair expansion and hope that theoretical purists will forgive this generalizing move. As one 10th-grader put it, "you could call it the who's-got-the-cheese lens and we think we'd know what you mean." In places within the chapter, especially when quoting the works of others or quoting student-teacher interactions in the past, the term *Marxist literary theory* will appear as well.

Marxist lens = social class lens

WHY DO WE NEED A SOCIAL CLASS LENS?

While the study of literature in the secondary schools has shuttled somewhat uneasily between text-centered and reader-centered approaches (Applebee, 1993), cultural studies and political approaches to the teaching of literature have moved through our profession like a brush fire. At many colleges and universities the inclusion of social class and gender lenses (see Chapter 5) has become the rule rather than the exception. In fact, some have been left to wonder whether the subject of English as we have known it is actually dead and we shouldn't rename our enterprise something like cultural studies (Boomer, 1988; Pirie, 1997).

interesting

Critical theory in college-level literary studies has become something of a lightning rod, a conduit of contention about our goals, purposes, and methods of teaching literature (Graff, 1992, 1995; Slevin & Young, 1995). For some, critical theory has energized a once staid and quaint field on the verge of becoming anachronistic. For others, cultural criticism and postmodern theories have drawn us away from what they believe should be at the center of our study—great books—and into a morass of subjectivity, relativity, and political correctness.

While most high school classrooms are clearly far removed from this frenzied state of affairs, more and more secondary teachers have begun to consider using social class and gender lenses with the texts they teach. Slowly, yet palpably, more secondary teachers have recognized the potential richness and utility of introducing cultural criticism to their students and encouraging them to view literature through political prisms. Several secondary literature textbooks have begun to include chapters on cultural criticism. For example, both Harper and Row and Prentice Hall have published anthologies that now include critical tables of contents and chapters on literary theory (Guerin, Labor, Morgan, & Willingham, 1992; Guth & Rico, 1996). The 12th-grade level of the College Board's *Springboard* has an entire section on multiple perspectives. Holt, Reinhart and Winston's 2009 *Elements of Literature, Grades 6–12* includes a grade-appropriate strand of literary perspectives, including the "political" perspective. Further, high school teachers have begun with increasing frequency to adapt critical materials prepared for college students, such as *The Bedford Reader*. This series provides commentary on such well-known works as *Heart of Darkness, Hamlet, The Tempest, Gulliver's Travels, The Secret Sharer*, and *Frankenstein* from a variety of critical perspectives, including psychological criticism, gender and social class lenses, and reader response. It appears that the time may be just right to encourage secondary teachers to integrate political literary theory into their literature instruction.

In some respects, there is a great deal of similarity between the social class lens and the gender lens. Both are political, both interrogate textual features with considerations of power and oppression, and both invite us to consider the kinds of prevailing ideologies that construct the social realities in which we participate, sometimes unwittingly. However, the kinds of questions that undergird those lenses—as well as the texts, activities, and student responses to those lenses—differ significantly enough that we will explore them in two separate chapters, this one and Chapter 5.

Social class & gender are similar lenses but not the same

WHY TEACH THE SOCIAL CLASS LENS NOW?

This is a particularly appropriate moment in the history of literacy education to introduce the lens of social class into our classrooms. There are numerous reasons why this is so, among them our increasingly diverse literary canon as well as the changing nature of our students.

Our evolving canon has caused us to consider the cultural and historical factors inherent in looking at a work of literature. Teachers feel compelled to teach background knowledge, including cultural and historical aspects, especially when dealing with multicultural literature. Faced with new literary and cultural territory, teachers find themselves rethinking their approaches to literary texts (Desai, 1997). For example, they may find themselves considering particular aspects of the political content of the text, the author, and the historical and sociocultural context of the work. They may also find themselves thinking about how their students as readers are situated culturally, politically, and personally in relation to the content of the text (Willis, 1997).

Of course, as new historical critics might assert, one could argue that these careful contextual considerations are relevant for all works of literature. Yet, when teaching multicultural literature, teachers seem to have a more acute need to fill in their own knowledge and provide the context for their students. Many teachers express discomfort or a kind of insecurity that springs from their unfamiliarity with the cultural background of the author, the issues that underlie the text, or even of the structure of the narrative itself in cases such as Morrison's *Beloved* or Silko's *Ceremony*. This quest for additional knowledge helps set the stage for cultural criticism or for political/social class and gender lenses.

Besides our evolving and more inclusive literary canon, the increasing diversity of our students, even in primarily White suburban school districts, underscores our need to integrate cultural criticism into our literary study. In classrooms across the country, teachers have been called upon to heed the different cultural backgrounds of their students and to anticipate how those differences may come to bear on the reading of the literary texts they choose to teach, be they canonical or multicultural. As we acknowledge the diverse backgrounds and perspectives of the students who will read and discuss literary texts together, we might also acknowledge the need to consider particular issues of race and class deliberately and thoughtfully (Hines, 1997). In *Loose Canons: Notes on the Culture Wars*, Henry Louis Gates, Jr. (1992) argues that race *is* a meaningful category in literary studies and the shaping of critical theory. He writes:

> Ours is a late twentieth-century world profoundly fissured by nationality, ethnicity, race, class, and gender. And the only way to transcend those divisions—to forge, for once, a civic culture that respects both differences and commonalities—is through education that seeks to comprehend the diversity of human culture. (p. xv)

For Gates, of course, that education is both a literary and a theoretical one that challenges the centrality of what he calls "our master's pieces" and urges us to consider "the politics of interpretation" as we encounter literature with our students.

This new knowledge is requisite not only for the reading and interpretation of literary texts but for the development of a kind of classroom community where students begin to understand each other and their perspectives (Hines, 1997). This kind of knowledge extends beyond the personal and anecdotal; it extends beyond the individual into the community. For students to be able to understand themselves and each other, they need to be able to contextualize their knowledge in terms larger than themselves; in other words, they need to be able to place their own particular situations and the texts they read into a larger system or set of beliefs. It is for precisely this reason that the particular lens of social class can be useful.

WHAT THE SOCIAL CLASS LENS HELPS US SEE

The social class lens offers several approaches for literature instruction. One approach is to consider the political context of the texts themselves.

Gerry Graff presents the issue of the political content of texts in *Professing Literature* (1987) as well as in *Beyond the Culture Wars* (1992). He quotes George Orwell: "No book is genuinely free from political bias. The opinion that art should have nothing to do with politics is itself a political attitude" (Graff, 1992, p. 144). Graff and others argue that politics has always been inextricably woven into our literary tradition; like all art, it provides both a representation of ideology and a way to resist it.

Theory, then, helps us pose those political questions, thus reframing what it is we do when we read literature. Bonnycastle (1996), for example, advocates the use of Marxist literary theory because "it places the study of literature in the context of important social questions" (p. 199). This rationale has long been one aspect of what Applebee (1993) calls our "competing traditions" (p. 3) in the teaching of literature. Engagement in important ideas or social issues has clearly been a goal that has shaped our canon, curriculum, and classroom practice. Political lenses such as social class and gender ask us to interrogate rather than simply acknowledge the texts that comprise our cultural heritage.

Using this perspective, students can consider the issues presented in the text through the lens of the prevailing ideologies of the author's political and historical context. For example, in reading *Of Mice and Men* or *The Grapes of Wrath*, students might consider the plight of migrant workers, John Steinbeck's motives as muckraker, and even Tom Joad as an emblem of the pursuit of freedom (Greene, 1988, p. 49). The lens of social class may make possible such readings as the following:

- "The depiction of the sterility of European bourgeois capitalism in the early twentieth century in T. S. Eliot's 'The Wasteland'" (Bonnycastle, 1996, p. 202)
- The axis (centrality) of class in the worlds portrayed in the novels of Jane Austen or the Brontes
- The plight of African Americans as seen through the eyes of Bigger Thomas in Richard Wright's *Native Son*, and Wright's eventual indictment of American society as racist.

In addition to examining the political content of texts, the lens of social class also encourages students to consider the ways in which literary texts and the reading audiences for those texts—including themselves, their classmates, and their teachers—are socially constructed. As McCormick (1995) argues, using culturally situated theories such as the lens of social class is important

> so students can see that they, as readers, are socially constructed subjects, that texts are also constructed in particular social contexts—which may be quite

different from their own and which they may need to study—and that different ways of telling stories have consequences. (p. 307)

Pirie (1997) also underscores the importance of students' awareness of audience construction and the role that theories such as social class and gender can play in facilitating that awareness:

For any text we can ask students what kind of ideal audience is being constructed. Who does this story think its readers are? Who would it like them to be? What does it assume about the reader's attitudes, values, and prejudices and about the best ways of trying to change those attitudes? Or is it trying to change the reader at all? We can then compare our responses as actual audiences: Do we willingly allow the text to construct us in the shape of its ideal reader, or do we find ourselves resisting at some points? Should we? Marxist/social class and feminist/gender critics have for some time enacted the possibility of audience resistance by constructing readings that expose and critique the ideologies of canonical works, but this form of reading is still uncommon in high school literature classes. (p. 30)

Mary Beth Hines (1997, p. 129) quotes a college teacher who uses social class and other forms of cultural criticism to promote his pedagogical priorities of social justice, "I want to stress that the text is a social construction, and if it's a social construction, then who constructed it, what's it doing, and what are the mechanisms that are at work here." This notion of construction is a central element of students' ability to learn to read and interpret literature, to read both resonantly and resistantly (Wolf, 1988).

It is not only the political content of the texts themselves or the ways in which audiences are constructed by those texts that can be read through the lens of social class; these theories make visible the idea that literature itself is a part of ideology. Bonnycastle (1996) writes, "A further role of Marxist [social class] criticism is that of pointing out and documenting the way in which literature and 'the literary' function as a part of ideology" (p. 203). He claims, "Theory is subversive because it puts authority in question. . . . It means that no authority can impose a 'truth' on you in a dogmatic way—and if some authority does try, you can challenge that truth in a powerful way, by asking what ideology it is based on" (p. 34).

Selden (1989) explains Terry Eagleton's assertion of the relationship between literature and ideology this way:

The text may appear to be free in its relation to reality (it can invent characters and situations at will), but it is not free in its use of ideology. Ideology here refers not only to conscious political doctrines but to all those systems of representation which shape the individual's mental picture of lived experience.

The meanings and perceptions produced in the text are a reworking of ideology's own working of reality. (p. 42)

In response to William Bennett, Henry Louis Gates, Jr. (1992, p. 35) writes, "The teaching of literature *is* the teaching of values; not inherently, no, but contingently, yes; it is—it has become—the teaching of an aesthetic and political order in which no women or people of color were ever able to discover the reflection or representation of their images, or hear the resonances of their cultural voices."

Secondary teachers can use the lens of social class to help bring into greater visibility the issues of power, class, ideology, and resistance that are embedded in the texts they read with their students. When paired with canonical texts, the lens of social class can be especially useful in revitalizing texts that seem tired or anachronistic. This is in part what Graff (1995) refers to in his now famous argument on "How to Save Dover Beach": "I concluded in my *Harper*'s essay that the best way to rescue poems like 'Dover Beach' was not to try to protect them from the critical controversies about their value, but to use those controversies to give them new life" (Graff, quoted in Slevin & Young, 1995, p. 133). The lens of social class can help shape that debate, whether it centers on the literary merit of the text itself, on reading the text politically, or on recognizing the text as a cultural construction or part of our overarching ideology.

In the next section a secondary teacher uses the lens of social class with *Hamlet* to encourage students to consider ideology and social power as they read literary texts.

READING *HAMLET* THROUGH THE LENS OF SOCIAL CLASS, OR, "WHY DO THE GRAVEDIGGERS SEEM TO KNOW MORE ABOUT LIFE THAN ANYONE?"

In a suburban classroom, where the student parking lot is filled with cars far nicer than those their teachers are driving, an AP English class is studying *Hamlet*. With few exceptions, the students in this class have lives that are privileged and full of possibilities. Nearly all of these students, sons and daughters of white-collar professionals, will go to college. They think nothing of dropping hundreds of dollars on prom night. They are the envy of the rest of the students in the school: the beautiful people—smart, popular, and affluent. They're basically good kids, motivated learners, and engaged students, but they hardly ever think beyond the boundaries of their own comfortable world.

Michael, their teacher, has ambitious goals. He wants to engage his students in great literature. He wants to teach a college prep English course rigorous enough to help his students sail through the year-end AP test. He wants to help his students create some provocative links between Hamlet's world and their own, links that extend beyond the connections of personal response, as powerful as those responses might sometimes be. Somewhat hesitantly Michael explains, "I've always worked on getting kids to respond to whatever we read on a personal level, to relate to the characters and their situations by thinking of similar situations of their own, to find a way into the text through their own personal experience. But lately I've been thinking, I don't know, more politically. I want my students to think about the worlds these texts both represent and invoke. I want them to think about what set of beliefs drive these characters and, in some cases, help seal their fate. I want them to think about the author's relationship to those sets of beliefs. I think I sometimes forget to help them see the big picture. And lately, I've been doing all this reading on contemporary criticism and I found myself thinking that these suburban kids never talk about class or privilege, even though, or maybe because, they're surrounded by it. So, I thought I'd try the social class/Marxist lens with *Hamlet* this time and see what happens."

On a drab winter morning colored only by the bright blue classroom carpeting and a bulletin board full of senior class pictures, Michael begins class by asking his students to consider the role of power in *Hamlet*. "What kinds of power do you see operating in the play?" asks Michael. There is a virtual cacophony of response.

"Power about who rules."

"Power about who's king."

"Power about property."

"Power over other people's lives, like Rosencrantz and Guildenstern."

"Power over whether certain countries go to war and who gets to fight them."

"Personal power. Like Hamlet over Ophelia."

"OK. Let's think about power in a particular way today," says Michael, "who's got it, who doesn't, and why. And, let's think about where power comes from, both now and in Shakespeare's time. I understand that some of you took Russian history with Mr. Murphy last semester. What can you guys tell me about Karl Marx?"

"Father of Communism?"

"Power to the Proletariat!"

"What's the Proletariat?"

"Power to the people!"

"Same thing!"

Michael distributes a handout titled Key Ideas of Marx (see Appendix, Activity 13) and quickly reviews it with the students. In addition to Marx's beliefs about the stages of history and dialectical materialism, the class discusses capitalism, class struggle, working-class misery, and class consciousness. Then Michael says, "In addition to the Marxism we've been talking about, there is also something called Marxist literary theory. Marxist literary

theory is a kind of political lens through which we can read works of literature. Marxist literary theory asks us to consider the social structures that are
portrayed in a particular work and how power is allocated among different
social groups. Many Marxist critics believe that we cannot understand individual people or literary characters, or even authors without understanding
their social positions and the larger systems in which those social positions
operate. Marxist literary theory also asks us to notice in the texts we read
what is the dominant view of the world, a prevailing set of beliefs, or ideologies. What are some ideologies or sets of beliefs that you've come across?"

"Freedom of Speech."

"Equality."

"Democracy."

"How the world was created. I think there are a bunch of ideologies
about that!"

"Anyone can succeed if they try hard enough."

"That's crap."

Michael smiles and says, "Hmmmm. We'll be getting to that later. Now
what seems to be the prevailing ideology or ideologies that operate in the
world of *Hamlet*?"

"The divine right of kings."

"That women are powerless."

"Yeah, they couldn't even play themselves."

"We are born into our lot in life."

"Royalty are better than other people and have the right to rule other
people."

"Gravediggers have a much different view of the world from the bottom than Claudius does from the top."

"Great, Alex. You bring me to my next question. Aren't we in some way
thinking about society as a social ladder, kinda like we do with things here
at this school? Take a look at this." Michael then distributes a handout entitled "Reading *Hamlet* through the Marxist/social class lens" (see Appendix,
Activity 14). He directs them to a drawing of a "social ladder." Then, after
a spirited discussion about the social ladder of their particularly cliquish
school, the students consider the social ladder of the play. Michael designed
the vertical diagram to demonstrate graphically the existence of hierarchy—
something that is important not only in the discussion of Marxism/social
class but in laying a conceptual foundation for a discussion of patriarchy,
which will come during a discussion of gender that Michael has already
begun to think about.

Michael next asks his students to consider pairs of characters in terms
of who has power and who does not. He asks students to indicate which of
the sets of power struggles they listed might be considered class conflicts.
Michael wants his suburban students to be able to read the text with a

heightened awareness of class and privilege—their own and the characters'. He encourages his students to examine the agency of social class in the play as well as in their reading of it. In fact, when asked to consider where they would situate themselves relative to issues of power, their responses are telling. Michael asks students to place a mark on a concentric circle graph that indicates where they are in relation to the center of money and power. There are five concentric rings: one is the closest to the center of power and money, and five is the most distant (see Appendix, Activity 14).

More than 75% of the students place themselves in the second or third circle closest to the center of money and power. One student places himself in the fourth circle and one places herself in the fifth circle, the one farthest from the center of power. By contrast, one student actually places himself right in the center!

Even though Michael carefully constructed this part of the activity so that students would reflect privately upon their own economic status, his usually compliant students seem a bit uncomfortable with this exercise; in fact, some are overtly hostile. "What does our social status have to do with reading *Hamlet*?" asks Tim, an Ayn Rand fan. "Social status isn't that important. People make too much of it. And besides, Marx wasn't born until after Shakespeare died, I mean, like, way after? Marxism wasn't around then. So, how can we use it to read the play?"

Michael isn't quite prepared for this resistance. He finds himself challenged and feels even more strongly about the importance of pursuing this line of inquiry. He asks his students to try to consider how issues of class might have affected their reading of *Hamlet*. He also asks them, "What characters in *Hamlet* do you feel most closely represent where you are socially?"

The student responses are varied. They struggle desperately to discover a Shakespearean middle or upper-middle class, one that would mirror their own location. Many students think that characters such as Laertes, Polonius, Horatio, and Ophelia somehow make up that middle class:

I am an average middle-class person. Closest to Ophelia.

Polonius and his family. I guess they were right in the middle.

For the students, the middle class represents people with some resources and power but with a reasonable perspective that neither royalty nor the lower class seems to possess. These middle-class characters, according to the students, allow them to understand both groups—those more and those less fortunate than they. It is clear that students feel this is a perspective they have, not only on the characters in the play but on their own lives:

I think being in the middle of things I can be pretty open-minded about the class structure on the whole.

Being in-between having the power and having no power, I am able to sympathize with all groups.

Many students express affinity for Horatio—neither rich nor poor, not quite a commoner, not quite royalty—a sort of Everyman with class:

I'm like Horatio. Being in the middle, it's easier to be unbiased. I can see both ends of the spectrum—those with money and power and those without.

Horatio seems most like me. He's in the middle of the ladder but sort of near the top.

I identify with Horatio a great deal. He is involved with the upper class but not because he's vying for a place in circle #1. He focuses on his friends, not on their social and economic worth.

This "Horatio affinity" characterizes the responses of most of the class, both in terms of character identification as well as economic identification. Students seem comfortable marking themselves as being close to power through either money or friends, like Horatio, but not totally within the epicenter of the prevailing power structure, like Hamlet.

While most of this suburban AP class is solidly middle to upper-middle class, there are a few students in class whose social status is quite different from that of their more wealthy classmates. These students marked the fourth and fifth circle out from the center of power and seemed eager to claim affinity for a different set of characters as well as to announce their less fortunate economic status:

I have more in common with the lower social characters; I root for the underdog.

Probably the lower-class servants. They have to work pretty hard and can't advance right now anyway because of circumstances. I live with my mom because my parents were recently divorced and there is no child support coming.

Interestingly, many female students felt they related most closely to Ophelia. For them, issues of gender seem to be more salient than issues of class. A few noted the conflation of gender and class. Here are a few illustrative comments:

I feel closest to Ophelia because although she is high-class (because of family, like me), she is a woman and doesn't get much consideration for her own well-being.

I probably feel I am most closely represented by Ophelia. Ophelia is one of the few females in the book and she does not have a lot of power, money, but she's not near the bottom of the social scale.

And, of course, several students unabashedly related most to Hamlet. These students (all male) self-identified in either the second or the first circle of power and privilege.

It may sound egotistical, but it is hard not to identify, at least a little bit, with Hamlet.

Hamlet is the character that I most identify with, since his positions and responsibility force him to distance himself socially.

I *am* Hamlet. I am not going to be king, but how Hamlet thinks and acts I can definitely relate to.

Many students reported that they had never seriously considered issues of class before and didn't feel that issues of power and class affected their reading of Hamlet. These students seemed almost offended or apologetic by the suggestion that considerations of power and privilege might have affected their reading:

If my social status affected my interpretation of Hamlet in any way, I honestly was not aware of it.

I really did not feel like it affected anything.

When I read Hamlet, I did not feel the class struggle applied to me in my life.

In summary, most students reported that issues of power and class clearly affected their response to the play, though they might not have been aware of it as they read. These students crossed all divisions of class—some saying that it affected their reading because they had power, some saying that considerations of status affected their reading precisely because they did not have power, and some who were in that middle "Horatio" position.

tool to determine reader's prior lens, really
& how it impacts reading

THE BIG QUESTIONS

Marxist literary theory [the social class lens] encourages us to look at big questions, and it has developed impressive tools for doing that. The main use of Marxism in literary studies rests in adapting those methods, especially those dealing with ideology, to help us talk about and resolve the smaller problems, which occupy most of us most of the time.

—Bonnycastle, *In Search of Authority*

For the most part, Michael felt he had accomplished a good deal by having his students try on the Marxist/social class lens, in however simplistic a version. They had discussed the concept of ideology and read the text for evidence of it. They had discussed power and class structure in terms of how it affected the characters and the play and considered the characters not just as individuals, but as players in a large social and economic system. Michael also felt that students had, for perhaps the first time, considered their own social status and had explored the possibility that their own position in the prevailing social structure may have influenced their reading of the text as well as the level of affinity they felt for any particular character. Finally, Michael felt that reading *Hamlet* through the Marxist/social class lens had enabled students to do precisely what Bonnycastle claims Marxism is particularly good at doing—encouraging us to ask both the big and the small questions. On the last question of the Marxist/social class lens handout (see Appendix, Activity 14), Michael asked his students to think of such large and small questions grounded in the Marxist/social class lens. He encouraged them to think of some questions that were concerned with the world of the text and questions that concerned them on a more personal level. Michael was gratified by the range and depth of questions and by the evidence that they had actually been peering at *Hamlet*, and at themselves, through the Marxist/social class lens. Here are some of their questions:

About the text:

- Is having so much power good for human nature?
- If Ophelia was so high up, why was her only point in the story to go crazy?
- Do women really have any power—even in the highest classes?
- Why does Hamlet feel he can dismiss the lives of Rosencrantz and Guildenstern?
- Why is it that the gravediggers seem to know more about life than anyone?

About themselves:

- Why can the middle class be fooled so easily by the upper class? Does the upper class have the right to use the underclass like they do? Does social position justify treating someone as if they are inferior?
- Does power mean you can do anything, even if it's illegal?
- Are all people created equal? Darwinian evolution suggests they are not. By resisting class differences does one destroy human nature?
- Why should society be based on rank? Are you a better person because you have power and/or money?

As he and his students discussed these questions, Michael knew that the social class lens enriched and complicated their reading of *Hamlet* and highlighted some details that might not have otherwise been heeded. He was glad that, in addition to the personal response strategies and the textual and new critical strategies they brought into the class with them, they now had social class literary theory as part of their interpretive repertoire or tool kit.

CHALLENGES IN TEACHING THE SOCIAL CLASS LENS

Teaching social class literary theory in secondary schools is a complicated enterprise. Some students may be resistant to the whole notion of the social class lens. As one student wrote in response to the Marxist handout: "I found this question to be offensive and pointless. My perception allows me to imagine myself at any point in the circle." Another said, "The social ladder is an arbitrary construct and I don't choose to think of myself in those terms. Therefore, the question is meaningless." One student wrote, "Thinking about the Marxist ideology makes me realize how Marxism undermines morality. Morality consists in making choices that respect the rights of others. By focusing on class conflict, Marxism obliterates the idea of personal responsibility and implies that any action is justified to help one win the class conflict, and thus no morality is possible." As Bonnycastle (1996) points out:

> There is an unconscious hostility to some Marxist ideas in most students, especially if they are consciously trying to "improve themselves." One way to measure how you are improving is to see how you are rising on the social scale; and if you feel you have moved yourself up to a new level, that is a clear indication of success. But this measuring stick entails a class system, with many of the unattractive features inherent in such a system, such as competition and the victory of the winner paid for by the suffering of the loser. (p. 200)

It is difficult for all of us, and especially for students, to critique and resist the prevailing ideology as we participate in it. Many of the students in Michael's suburban AP class found this perspective to be alienating and uncomfortable. And yet it was this very discomfort and students' obliviousness of their location in educational and economic privilege that contributed to Michael's desire to introduce them to the social class lens.

In addition to this lesson on *Hamlet,* we also used the lens of social class with *The Great Gatsby* (see Appendix, Activity 17) and with the powerful Sharon Olds poem "On the Subway" (see Chapter 9 and Appendix, Activity 24). In each case students found that the direct consideration of class and power significantly enhanced their interpretations of the texts. In each case the prism of social class seemed to invite students into the central issues raised by each text. And in each case students were also encouraged to view the text from other perspectives as well, thus decreasing the likelihood that teachers would be perceived to be privileging one particular political perspective or reading over another. We have also used the class lens to read nonfiction (see Appendix, Activities 15 and 25). We've discovered that, as with fiction, the lens helps bring issues of privilege and social class into sharper relief as students apply it to nonfiction texts.

Now let us turn to another political prism, the gender lens. It too encourages us, as Bonnycastle (1996, p. 205) said, to name and resist ideology, and to "look at the big questions," which in this case, are the "questions" of gender as they relate to the reading and interpretation of literary texts.

SUGGESTED NONFICTION SELECTIONS FOR THE CLASS LENS

Julia Baird, "How the Recession is Redefining Failure" (*Newsweek*)

Lars Eighner, "On Dumpster Diving" (pdf available online)

Malcolm X, "Learning to Read" (pdf available online)

David Leonhardt, "Students of the Great Recession" (*New York Times*)

Christian Williams, "This, That and the American Dream" (*UTNE Reader*)

Mike Rose, "I Just Wanna Be Average" (pdf available online)

Mike Rose, "Blue Collar Brilliance" (*American Scholar*)

Stephen Marche, "We are not all Created Equal: The Truth about the American Class System" (*Esquire*)

Robert Reich, "Why the Rich are Getting Richer and the Poor are Getting Poorer" (*A World of Ideas*)

Jeremy Brecher, "The 99 Percent Organize Themselves" (*The Nation*)

CHAPTER FIVE

The Social Construction of Gender

A Lens of One's Own

The study of gender, within literature, is of general importance to everyone.

—Judith Spector

We don't know what women's vision is. What do women's eyes see? How do they carve, invent, decipher the world? I don't know. I know my own vision, the vision of one woman, but the world seen through the eyes of others? I only know what men's eyes see.

—Viviane Forrester, *New French Feminisms*

I have a male mind with male experiences. Therefore I see things through the perception of a man. I couldn't relate to some of Virginia Woolf's views and I despised the way she pushed her viewpoint on the reader. This was brought on by my masculinity, I feel.

—Bill, Grade 12, after reading *A Room of One's Own*

Being a feminist is not a gender-specific role.

—Erin, Grade 11

Martha's 2nd-hour 11th-grade literature class is reading *Death of a Salesman*. In previous classes they've discussed the contemporary literary called the feminist lens, and frankly, they're a bit wary. The boys generally groan, steeling themselves for what they assume is another session of male bashing. The girls seem astonishingly anachronistic in their positions toward feminism. Many of them make disparaging comments about militant females who hate men. They seem to reflexively equate feminism with unfemininity. Their reflexive attitudes sometimes provide a roadblock to productive conversations about literature. Still, Martha views their collective reluctance to discuss the feminist lens as all the more reason to do so. She realizes that her students evoke socially sanctioned and reified constructions of gender, constructions that can hold them hostage, in adolescence and beyond, to limiting social expectations of behavior.

"I'm tired of this feminist lens backlash," Martha says. "I wonder what would happen if we focus on the issue of gender." "Feminism does focus on the issue of gender," I reply in a slightly exasperated tone. "I know," Martha

says to me conspiratorially, but let's see what happens if we call it gender."
"Okay," I say, remembering all the times teachers have told me this very
thing. "Let's give it a try," I agree.

We begin by offering the following explanation to our students: "Our
ability to assign gender to words or constructs has to do with what some
people call the social construction of gender. Using the feminist lens is one
way to examine gender construction, but the notion of the social construction of gender broadens the lens to more fully consider how both men and
women are affected by this social construction." We give the students a
handout beginning with a series of words (see Appendix, Activity 20): *fash-
ion, football, breadwinner, pilot, strength, flower, ambitious, perseverance,
compassionate, bossy, helpless, thoughtful, soft, brassy, dangerous, perpe-
trator, victim, attractive, opinionated, hostile, emotional.*

We then tell the students, "Using your first instinct and without over-
thinking, write them in the column that seems most appropriate." The students work on their table:

Male	Female	Both	Neither

They scribble furiously, sometimes bursting out in giggles. The results of
this simple and seemingly benign exercise were astonishing (see Figure 5.1).
While there was some bleeding between categories with words such as *attractive*, there were other examples of gendered constructions. For example,
not a single student categorized the words *emotional, victim,* or *thoughtful*
as male. Not a single student categorized the words *pilot, football,* or *per-
petrator* as female.

"Whoa, this was too easy," Scott says. "I agree," echoes Leah. "I didn't
realize these categories were so fixed in my mind."

Indeed!

WHY TEACH GENDER/FEMINIST THEORY NOW?

Viviane Forrester's (1980) acknowledgment of the dominance of men's vision, or "what men's eyes' see," provides an explicit rationale for teaching
contemporary feminist/gender literary theory to adolescents. Throughout
this chapter, I will be using the terms *gender* and *feminist theory* inter-
changeably. While theoretical purists may rightfully object to the renaming,
the change seems consistent with the calls of feminist theorists in the last
25 years to make certain that feminist theory is not limited to only women
writers or women's experiences. As Nelly Furman (1988) writes:

Figure 5.1. Student Assessment of Gender Traits

Death of a Salesman and the Social Construction of Gender

Word Options	Male	Female	Both	Neither
Fashion	0	33	4	0
Football	38	0	0	0
Breadwinner	10	2	20	3
Pilot	24	0	12	0
Strength	27	1	11	0
Flower	0	36	0	2
Ambitious	3	1	31	3
Perseverance	2	2	31	5
Compassionate	1	23	12	1
Bossy	5	12	18	2
Helpless	1	11	3	21
Thoughtful	0	10	22	4
Soft	1	25	4	8
Brassy	12	4	1	17
Dangerous	19	0	9	9
Perpetrator	15	0	4	13
Victim	0	17	13	6
Attractive	2	18	18	0
Opinionated	3	11	24	0
Hostile	10	2	11	13
Emotional	0	27	8	0

Since, for the textual reader, literature is not a representation of experience but something that is experienced, from a feminist viewpoint the question is not whether a literary work has been written by a woman and reflects her experience of life, or how it compares to other works by women, but rather how it lends itself to be read from a feminist position. (p. 69)

Gender theory provides us with a way of recognizing and naming other visions while promoting our own ways of seeing. It helps us recognize the essential quality of other visions: how they shape and inform the way we read texts, how we respond to others, how we live our lives. Theory makes the invisible visible, the unsaid said.

Theory asks us to treat the text and our responses to it as cultural objects. Rather than removing us farther from the world, feminist/gender theory asks us to invoke our world as we read, interpret, and evaluate texts. As Eagleton (1983) remarks:

> Literature, we are told, is vitally engaged with the living situations of men and women; it is concrete rather than abstract, displays life in all its rich variousness, and rejects barren conceptual enquiry for the feel and taste of what it is to be alive. (p. 196)

Feminist/gender literary theory invites us to consider a wide variety of issues of gender, of "the living situations" of men and women as we read. Feminist/gender literary theory asks us to attend to the cultural imprint of patriarchy as we read. We do this by heeding features of language, of canon formation and transformation, of the nuanced voices of female and male writers, and of the portrayal of masculine and feminine experience. As noted critic Sydney Kaplan (2000) explains:

> I desperately needed a method of study that might help me shape my life and extricate it from the patriarchal forces I confronted both at home and in the university. I quickly discovered that I could explore the issues that many of my contemporaries were approaching through consciousness-raising by transferring the formalist methods I was learning in class to texts that had personal meaning for me—texts by women writers. Yet, I should emphasize that this early work, contrary to some of the myths about the evolution of feminist criticism, neither focused on a critique of male writing nor was part of the "images of women" genre. It was *already* concerned with the intersections of literary form and the structure of gender relations—with how literary conventions embodied societal values and unconscious levels of ideology; in other words, it was, from the outset, a cultural critique. (p. 1168)

As Kaplan points out, theory attempts to capture the complexities of human existence as it is portrayed in literary texts. In Bruce Pirie's (1997, p. 97) recent plea to shift our notion of literary studies to a broader vision of cultural studies, he calls for a high school literature program that would "treat texts as constructions within intertextual webs, sponsored by institutions and interacting with audiences and would also encourage a study of our own situation as readers." Political literary theories such as gender and social class require readers to ask questions about the construction of culture, of texts, and of meaning as they seek to construct their own interpretations.

There are, of course, as many "feminisms" as there are "Marxisms," and it is easy for both teachers and students to become confused about feminist/gender theory, or even feminism, for that matter. As Elaine Showalter (1985,

p. 127) writes, "not even feminist critics seem to agree what it is they mean to profess and defend." Two of the classroom activities in the Appendix (Activities 15, 17) reflect a working definition of feminism. In a true feminist tradition the definition continues to evolve.

As with Marxist (social class) criticism, the point of reading with feminist (gender) theory, of course, isn't to transform unsuspecting and largely apolitical high school students into feminists (or Marxists); the point is to help adolescent readers read texts and worlds more carefully as they become aware of the ideologies within which both are inscribed. Bonnycastle (1996, p. 194) writes, "Feminist literary criticism has a political and moral dimension. It doesn't need to be revolutionary, but, like Marxism, it does aim at changing the world and the consciousness of people in the world."

Like the Marxist theories we discussed in Chapter 4, feminist/gender theory provides a lens through which students can interpret literature and life. As students read and interpret literary texts, feminist theory can help them to notice salient issues of gender—the portrayal of women in the world of the novel, the gender of the author and what relevance it may bear on how the work is both written and received, the ways in which the text embraces or confronts prevailing ideologies of how men and women are situated in the "real world," and the ways in which our own interpretations as individual readers are gendered.

WHAT STUDENTS CAN SEE WITH FEMINIST/GENDER THEORY

There are at least four dimensions in which using feminist/gender theory can transform students' reading—how students view female characters and appraise the author's stance toward those characters, how students evaluate the significance of the gender of the author in terms of its influence on a particular literary work, how students interpret whole texts within a feminist framework, and finally, and perhaps most importantly, how students read the gendered patterns in the world. To explore how feminist theory can inform the literary experience of adolescents, I developed some activities to use with a variety of texts. Working with teachers in both urban and suburban classrooms, I introduced students to the feminist/gender lens and chronicled their attempts to adopt gendered considerations of texts, of authors, of characters, of themselves as readers, and of the world around them. Four of these literary transactions follow.

1. What Color Are Your Walls? Changing the Way We View Female Characters

One way the feminist/gender lens can inform how students make meaning of texts is by refocusing their reading of female characters. As some feminist critics assert (Showalter, 1985), readers should learn to recognize what happens to female characters under the "male gaze" of authors. How does the fictional portrayal of female characters reflect the reality of women's lives? How does the creation of female characters reinforce or resist certain social attitudes toward women? And, finally, how are we as readers implicated in what is essentially a gendered act as we read and interpret the lives of women who people the pages of the works of literature we read?

In previous work (Appleman, 1993), I illustrated how students' interpretive vision adapted easily to the lens of feminism as they considered characters from *Of Mice and Men*, *Ordinary People*, and *The Great Gatsby*. We asked students to make traditional descriptions of these female characters and then to make a different sort of statement in light of our discussion of feminist theory. Here are some of the resulting examples:

Curley's Wife

Traditional Statement: She was a bad girl, a tease, and a flirt.

Feminist Statement: She's just been treated poorly by her horrible, selfish, chauvinistic husband. She is not bad.

Beth

Traditional Statement: She's the great American bitch.

Feminist Statement: She's a repressed woman who is trapped by society's expectations of what a wife and mother should be.

Daisy

Traditional Statement: She was a "beautiful little fool" who depended on her husband to take care of her.

Feminist Statement: Her husband took control of her and wouldn't let her think for herself. She was doing her best within the limits of women's role in society.

I decided to explore feminist theory with Martha Hargrove's students, who had just finished reading *Hamlet*. (We met Martha in Chapter 3 as she introduced her 12th-grade students to multiple critical approaches to *Native Son*. We'll spend even more time with her in Chapter 8.)

As part of our introduction to the feminist lens and as part of our larger purpose of demonstrating that different classical or canonical texts can be viewed from more than one theoretical perspective, we asked students to read Gertrude and Ophelia through a feminist lens. Note that these students had already considered *Hamlet* from a Marxist/social class perspective (see Chapter 4). In addition to encouraging multiple perspectives, we also wanted to emphasize the intertextual nature of interpretation. That is, a critical lens is not an artifact of interpretation suitable to only a particular text but rather is a flexible tool that can be used with a variety of texts.

After a brief explication of the feminist lens (see Appendix, Activity 18), we asked students to consider Gertrude and Ophelia from the perspective of the feminist lens and to contrast that with statements using a "traditional" perspective, one that didn't consciously incorporate any considerations of gender into its interpretation. Here are some of the resulting descriptions:

Gertrude

Traditional Statements:

She is an adequate woman of the times, and she plays her role of loyalty and servitude toward the men in her family.

Gertrude is the queen who lost her husband and immediately married another.

Wife of two kings.

She is a queen who lives how she wants to live.

Feminist Statements:

She is more of a plot device than of thematic importance herself.

She's defined by her husbands and her son.

Despite the illusion of power, she is actually powerless. She is not allowed to advise on matters of importance but must be advised in all she does. She is not really trusted to take care of herself.

Ophelia

Traditional Statements:

Sheltered and devoted to those who love her; always tries to please her family while following her heart.

Emotional, young, innocent, weak, fragile; she needs protection.

Ophelia was a girl of reasonable status in the kingdom which implanted a daring notion that she may someday marry the prince, Hamlet.

Feminist Statements:

Her feelings and identity have been repressed by the male figures in her life. When her father is killed, she is separated from that control and goes crazy with the release of her pent-up identity.

Trapped in her traditional role, she's always being told what to do by a man—her father, her brother, Hamlet.

Any woman of sound body and mind like Ophelia had, at least to begin with, should have the power and right to pursue life as she pleases without the restraint of society's rules and arranged marriages.

She is forced into insanity by the forces of the men in her life. All of her emotions depend on Hamlet's actions.

This exercise enabled students to cast two characters they already knew well in the light of a feminist interpretation. They seemed to be able to do so with ease. The contrast of the traditional perspective with the feminist perspective helped underscore some of the more salient features of a feminist interpretation. In addition, it helped students exercise a kind of mental flexibility, one of the goals of the multiple theoretical approach to literature advocated by this book. That is, rather than viewing things from a rigid—or dualistic, as cognitive psychologist William Perry (1970) might call it—perspective, students have the opportunity to develop a kind of theoretical pluralism from which they can consider characters from more than one point of view. Here is an incident from one of Martha's classes that reveals the students' ability to view female characters from the feminist perspective:

We are discussing Virginia Woolf's *A Room of One's Own* during first period. Ever since we began discussing the feminist lens and *A Room of One's Own*, there's been a kind of edge in the air, especially with the male students, who are outnumbered by the female students by almost two to one. Adam and Tom look even more bored and contemptuous of the day's activities than usual. Kevin, an outspoken member of the alternative theater crowd, is sporting a new hair color (bright yellow) and seems particularly feisty.

"I'm, like, so over this Virginia Woolf," he says. "I think she goes way overboard; she overgeneralizes. She takes her argument too far, plus, she nitpicks."

Belinda asks, "What do you mean 'nitpicks' and 'overgeneralizes'? How can she be doing those two things at the same time?"

Kevin looks a bit taken aback. "She just takes things a bit too far."

"Like what?" Belinda persists. "Can you think of anything from the text?" (This kid has been well-trained!)

"Like that part about Shakespeare," Kevin finally answers.

"What about it? Be specific." Belinda now seems to be doing a full-out imitation of her teacher.

"Well, you know. She says that Shakespeare writes for men and writes all these strong roles only for men. But in my opinion, when it comes right down to it, there are a lot of good women in Shakespeare. I mean, take Beatrice in *Much Ado About Nothing*, for example. I mean, need I say more? I mean, who could be a stronger role model than Beatrice? Didn't you just *admire* her? I mean, I did, and I'm a guy. Just think about Beatrice and you'll see. Virginia Woolf is whacked," Kevin concludes with a flourish.

"Yea, Beatrice *is* something," Belinda concedes. "You've got a point there."

This classroom episode is illustrative of the lively and engaged discourse that was engendered by the introduction of the feminist lens. In addition to the students' evocation of the lens, this episode is also notable for the intertextual nature of the argument. That is, Kevin uses Shakespeare to support his point about Virginia Woolf. These students seem to be thoroughly in charge of their own interpretations. They use the feminist lens to cajole each other into reconsidering a character from another perspective. How encouraging to think that they may be able to view their peers, teachers, and families from other perspectives as well!

2. Changing the Way We View Texts, "Feminist" and Otherwise

Analyzing female characters is only one way the feminist lens can inform students' reading; the sociocultural context of texts can also be viewed through the feminist lens. This holistic view can illuminate classic texts, as it did in our reading of *Hamlet*, or more contemporary texts, as it did in our reading of *Native Son*. While the feminist lens can be fruitfully applied to any work of fiction, it may have different purposes when applied to texts authored by men and texts authored by women. As Elaine Showalter (1985) points out:

> Feminist criticism can be divided into two distinct varieties. The first type is concerned with woman as reader—with woman as the consumer of male-produced literature and with the way in which the hypothesis of a female reader changes our apprehension of a given text, awakening us to the significance of its sexual codes. Its subjects include the images and stereotypes of women in literature, the omissions and misconceptions about women in criticism, and the fissures in male-constructed literary history. . . .The second type of feminist criticism is concerned with woman as writer—with woman as the producer of textual meaning, with the history, themes, genres, and structures of literature by women. (p. 128)

While the feminist lens can be used profitably with a variety of texts, as I demonstrated with the re-rereading of *Hamlet, Native Son, The Great Gatsby*, and *Ordinary People*, among others, many feminist critics point to some seminal (excuse the expression) literary texts that serve as flashpoints for feminist scholarship and virtually demand a feminist reading. These texts include *The Awakening, A Room of One's Own*, "The Yellow Wallpaper," and "A Jury of Her Peers." (See Selected Literary Texts for a complete list of texts and authors.)

Whether to use these "feminist" texts or traditional texts in the teaching of the feminist/gender lens is an interesting question for teachers. Texts that, for the purpose of this discussion at least, I have labeled "feminist," help make the case to doubters or skeptics and broaden the discussion to larger considerations of women writers, women's ideology, and even whether there is such a thing as a "feminist text." On the other hand, the "eureka moments" of unexpectedly altered vision through the power of critical lenses can sometimes occur more dramatically with texts that don't seem "loaded" or predisposed to a feminist treatment. In this case, as in many others, I promote the notion of "both and" rather than "either or" and try to include several different kinds of texts as I help students peer through the feminist lens.

Two classic texts that deal directly with feminist issues are "The Yellow Wallpaper" by Charlotte Perkins Gilman and *A Room of One's Own* by Virginia Woolf. I have used both to introduce the feminist lens to high school students and offer both strategies and examples of student responses in the next section. While the previous lesson focused on student responses to female characters using the feminist lens, the following activity is a consideration of an entire text from the feminist perspective.

I introduce the idea of a whole text interpretation by presenting a concrete poem (see Figure 5.2). This lesson gives students the opportunity to create an interpretation of an entire work with a contained and literally concrete text. It gives them an opportunity to interpret a text as a cultural object. In addition, students are asked to consider a text about which they have not been able to form any investment, defensiveness, or prior expectations. The students in small groups note some of the physical features of the poem, for example, the serpentlike "S" that makes he into she, the "h" for homo sapiens and the "e" for Eve.

Figure 5.2. From "Epithalamium—II"

—Pedro Xisto

They then try to regard the lens from a feminist perspective in light of the basic tenets of the definition that they were given (see Appendix, Activities 15–18). In other words, they attend to features of gender, to what statements this poem might make about the relationship between the sexes, about the prominence of the letter S and the cultural encodings about the relationship between men and women. Here are some samples of the students' readings of this concrete poem:

She is better than he because the S creates a more developed, more aesthetically pleasing he.

She is encompassing he.

Women are strong and bold but still bound by the central power of men. He is ever-present inside a woman controlling all of her actions and thoughts. He is the center of she.

It's useful for students to see that they can disagree on the implications of a feminist reading of this poem—that is, for some it represents a feminist victory over male dominance; for others, it's just the opposite. Both interpretations rely on a feminist lens to provide meaning. Reading with theory doesn't necessarily lead one to particular conclusion about texts; it is not a prescription for dogma. Rather, it suggests a framework in which a variety of interpretations can be articulated. There is no one single feminist reading of a particular text, and this exercise seems to illustrate that plurality of possibility fairly well.

After students discuss this initial foray into "reading feminist" with the concrete poem, we move to a consideration of "The Yellow Wallpaper," which, for a variety of reasons, is an important starting point for our exploration of the feminist lens. Annette Kolondy, for example, remarks on the significance of Charlotte Perkins Gilman's short story to feminist literary scholarship. First, "The Yellow Wallpaper" is an example of "previously lost or otherwise ignored works by women writers" (Kolondy, 1989, p. 144) that have returned to circulation as a result of feminist literary scholarship. Originally published in 1892, Gilman's short story was reprinted in 1973, and in the ensuing decades has become something of a feminist sensation, both widely anthologized and widely taught.

Kolondy (1989) remarks on the difficulty Gilman had initially publishing her piece as well as on the resistance it met with readers after it finally saw print. Readers could easily, as Kolondy points out, have found resonances with Edgar Allen Poe's work in Gilman's. Yet, they did not display the same willingness to follow the interior tour of the disturbed mind of Gilman's trapped protagonist as they apparently had with Poe's counterparts. Kolondy views "The Yellow Wallpaper" as a kind of metacommentary on the sexual politics of literary reading and production. Kolondy points to the significance of the female protagonist whose imagination is limited by her proscribed activities and confinement, and whose experience as described in the text cannot be accurately read or interpreted by her male audience.

"The Yellow Wallpaper," then, presents multilayered aspects of feminist meaning. It seems, therefore, to be a natural place for students to use the feminist lens. As a follow-up to the reading of the concrete poem, I asked students to apply the feminist lens to write a brief analysis of the narrator in "The Yellow Wallpaper," her situation, and perhaps Perkins Gilman's intent in writing the piece. In addition, they were to consider Perkins Gilman's audience and, finally, what meaning(s) they derived from the text. Here are some of their resulting analyses:

> It shows the effects of the repression of woman's will by what men saw as care and protection. John won't allow her to write or care for her child, two important expressions of who she is, because he doesn't want her to get tired. She is the toy that can't be played with because it will decrease in value; that has no personal value because it can't be put to its use.

> Charlotte Perkins, it seemed, was writing for her own struggle. The woman was trapped within the wallpaper while maybe Perkins was trapped in her words, thoughts, and positions. The woman was trapped, and the expression in her writing presents the struggles with her husband as a "Nora" (*A Doll's House*). They don't know her exact sickness or ailment but she is to stay in bed, cooped up to be better. But she needed to get out.

> This woman is treated as if she were no more important than the wallpaper. Her husband has no regard for her well-being because, as she states early in the journals, she hated the wallpaper. By her husband forcing her into that room, telling her she is okay, he metaphorically pushed her into the wallpaper, a nonexistence. I believe Perkins wrote this story to help the women see their helplessness and inability to control their own destiny, although most probably, though, Perkins was crazy.

> I would like to look at this through a mixture of lenses. In order to do this story justice, I must mix historical and feminist lenses. The feminist lens may show an idea of oppression, but the addition of the historical lens shows triumphant behavior. Around the time when this was written and many years after, women were controlled by their "male figures." These figures could be fathers, brothers, husbands, or even sons. By showing how she is able to make a small step toward her own decisions, this woman has made a statement to the community of women readers.

These are complex and perceptive responses to a fairly difficult text. Perhaps some of these themes of entrapment, manipulation, helplessness, and the veritable psychological war between the sexes (at least as represented by the narrator and her husband) might have emerged from students' readings if the feminist lens had not been a part of their interpretive repertoires. But the students' ability to view the text as a cultural artifact, as a challenge to a prevailing ideology, to amplify the struggles of the narrator to include all women, including Gilman's struggle as a writer, to understand the dialectical role the piece plays (e.g., "maybe to have *us* discuss it in class")—all these seem to demonstrate the influence the feminist lens had on their reading.

3. "Men Have Gender, Too!" *Death of a Salesman* and the Social Construction of Gender

As one can see from the previous examples, classic feminist texts such as "The Yellow Wallpaper" and *A Room of One's Own* can help adolescents inhabit the gender lens. Many teachers reported that studying the feminist lens in combination with the use of literary texts that can be read as "feminist tracts" made the reading experience too overtly feminist for comfort, especially for many male students. This is precisely why in this chapter I encourage the use of the more inclusive term *gender*. In addition, in order to help students see that issues of gender affect males and male characters as much as they do females and female characters, I developed a lesson on the gender lens with *Death of a Salesman*, a classic work widely used in secondary classrooms and one that clearly illustrates the entrapment of men in the gender regime of contemporary American society (see Appendix, Activity 20).

The lesson begins with an examination of the gender of particular words, the activity described in the opening of this chapter. Following that is a consideration of the fact that masculinity is socially constructed just as femininity. Next is an examination of representations of the characters in *Death of a Salesman* as they appear in a reader's guide as well as in a film adaptation of the play. Finally, students consider the ways in which the characters are "held hostage" to social expectations of gender. Here are some of their responses:

> Willy is expected to be the breadwinner of the family and provide more than he is physically able to. He is expected to be a respected salesman and not a carpenter. He is expected to raise his sons to be successful. He is expected to be confident and all-knowing. The combination of these is too harsh for Willy to handle—he becomes suicidal. This led me to see that Willy was confined by expectations— he couldn't be who he wanted to be.

Linda is held captive not only to the restrictions accompanying being a stay-at-home mother but also captive to the need for success that binds Willy. Since Willy is the measurement of *her* success in society, she feels the need to keep his fragile world from breaking because it is hers as well. When Willy's world falls apart there is no hope for her—in the movie her hair is gray and her life feels meaningless. For this reason she fights against Biff and Happy when they try to accuse the man to whom her identity is bound.

Willy struggles deeply with the gender expectations of males and how he is unable to meet some. He fails to be a wealthy and successful man, and psychologically that is really hard for him. Where he fell short, he pushes his sons harder to excel, such as sports and with women. Because he never made an overwhelmingly good salesman, he increasingly became obsessed with it until it took over his mind and drove him to suicide. He also felt forced to not openly share his emotions, struggles, and shortcoming with the rest of the family. In the movie Willy was played as a man who was very distraught and almost frantic, he definitely lacked real stability.

Biff Loman is constrained by both his father's expectations and society's expectations. His father's expectations stem from the societal expectations that a man must work in a respectable job with a solid salary after achieving athletic glory as a youth. The contrast between Biff's high school and adult experiences highlights the fact that Biff does not wish to conform, and his relationship with his family has been ruined as traditional male roles are forced upon him.

As these responses indicate, the students were able to use the gender lens to read the social construction of conceptions of both masculinity and femininity. Now, I wondered, could they transfer these awarenesses from the classroom to the world outside of school? Could they apply this gendered way of reading the ideologies inscribed in texts to the ideologies that are inscribed in our world? After all, isn't real-world relevance central to reading with critical lenses?

4. Reading the World: From Text to Context

There is a quiet revolt that seems to be gathering steam in Martha's 5th-hour literature class. They have just finished discussing Charlotte Perkins Gilman's "The Yellow Wallpaper" and are in the throes of their consideration of feminist literary theory. They are trying the feminist lens on literary characters they have previously met such as Curley's wife from *Of Mice and Men* and Daisy Buchanan from *The Great Gatsby*. They apply the feminist lens to *Hamlet*'s Gertrude and Ophelia, and to a concrete poem (see Appendix, Activity 18).

David, seated near the front of the room, is absolutely bursting at the seams. For weeks he has fumed silently through the explanation of the feminist lens and through class activities that applied feminist theory to various literary texts, but now he seems unable to restrain himself.

"All this stuff is *construed*," David suddenly exclaims. "It's BS! Isn't there a *masculine* lens? This 'feminist lens' just isn't working for me."

"Of course it's not working for you!" Maria interjects from across the room. "You're a man. *You* can't see it, but *I* can see it because I live it." She continued firmly, "Besides, I was watching your face when we were reading about feminist literary theory. You were already shaking your head." (David shakes his head.)

"Yes, you were, David. You are so closed-minded."

A spirited discussion ensues between David and the other female students in the class who come quickly to provide unnecessary but welcomed support for Maria. The other male students listen in stony silence, refusing to rescue their self-appointed spokesperson who is besieged by his frustrated female classmates. David doesn't seem to mind.

"I just don't buy it," David continues. "Just because a man writes a book doesn't mean he disses women."

"Oh, yeah?" says Robyn. "Let's take your favorite book—of course by Hemingway. What about Lady Brett Ashley? How does Hemingway portray her?"

"Yes, as a sex object, of course," David concedes.

"See?" says Robyn triumphantly.

"Wait a minute," replies David. Now he's angry. "You mean, women *never* do that to men? Women authors *never* portray men as sex objects? You mean, there's no such thing as reverse sexism?"

"David," Maria is almost pleading. "Don't you realize you can only see things one way? It's because you're a man!"

"Well, you can only see things one way because you're a woman."

"No, that's not true. I have to see things from the masculine perspective because that is the perspective that dominates our society. And I also have to see things from a feminist perspective because I'm a woman." (I can't help but think of DuBois's concept of "double consciousness" as Maria speaks.)

David shakes his head and tightens his jaw.

"Just try the lenses on, David! You can always take them off if they don't work for you!"

"I know, I know. But I still think it's construed."

This exchange, difficult though it was in many ways, indicates that, for these students, feminist theory has begun to move from the pages of their assigned reading to the foundation of their world. This notion of reading the

world and culture against the grain is, of course, one of the primary goals
of introducing students to literary theory. While many students move from
textual to personal on their own, others need encouragement and practice in
reading culture against the grain, and resistantly, as feminist theory encourages us to do.

To help facilitate this movement from textual to personal, I created
an activity to encourage students to read the world through feminist eyes
(Appendix, Activity 37). It begins by asking students to look at some cultural artifacts such as Mount Rushmore; the Miss America pageant; vice-
presidential candidate Sarah Palin; Hillary Clinton's bid for the Democratic
nomination for president; and the immense celebrity of such personalities
as Paris Hilton, Lindsay Lohan, and Britney Spears. The students are then
asked to write two sentences about those objects or situations that contrasts
a traditional perspective with the feminist perspective. Here are some of the
responses:

Mount Rushmore

Speaks to the fact that we had founding fathers and not founding
mothers. And why? Because at the time, women weren't allowed to
participate in society as leaders.

Let's face it! History glorifies men and excludes women. Period.

These are all presidents. A woman should have been president by now.

Behind each of these men there is a woman who helped this country.

The Miss America Pageant

Women walk around parading on heels and dressed up like dolls for
the benefit of the male public.

It is a tribute to our obsession with the physical appearance of women.

It's a parade of women who starve themselves so that a bunch of
ignorant men can drool at them.

Hillary Clinton's Bid for the Democratic Party Nomination for President

Would she be where she is without her husband?

I notice that she always wears pants—is she trying to de-feminize
herself?

I can't believe how she was pounced on when she cried—they would
never have done that to a man.

These responses are indicative of the students' ability to cast these cultural artifacts in the interpretive light of feminist literary theory. Yet the goal of teaching theory is not to produce discrete interpretations of individual artifacts; it is to help interpret, understand, and respond to our lived experiences. To encourage students to expand their interpretive skills from texts to objects to actual events, the final section of this activity asks: "Can you think of anything that has happened to you or to a friend of yours in the last 2 weeks that could be better explained or understood through a feminist lens? Pick a partner and share stories." Here are some of their resulting narratives:

Gender Tales: Reading the Texts of Our Lives

I am a waitress and the other night I received a very large tip from two men. When I told one of my male coworkers about it, he made a very obscene remark along the lines of "What did I have to do for it." It was a very dirty, nasty thing to say, and even though it was a joke, it was not right. Feminist lens: He disrespected me.

Yesterday in gym we were picking teams for handball. There are only two girls in the class and, as always, they were picked last. Everyone is okay with that because we all assume they are just bad at sports.

Being a cheerleader, I am subject to stereotypes every time I step into uniform. People joke about us; they automatically assume we spend more time doing our hair than practicing. They do not consider us athletes and believe the only reason we are cheering is to be close to the boys. Through the feminist lens, cheerleaders would be a part of a male-dominant society, only there to cheer the males to victory.

Last week I tried to help a girl carry a set of lights that were obviously too heavy for one person to try to carry. She did not want any help and almost dropped all the lights. A feminist would applaud the girl for trying to show that women can do jobs usually assigned to males. Even if the lights might have broken, it was okay. Women have to take risks in order to gain complete equality. The way I approached it was completely colored by gender. I was easily offended and very defensive. I feel I always have to be defensive nowadays. I am a Man.

As Judith Fetterley (1978) starkly reminds us, reading and teaching literature is political.

Feminist criticism is a political act whose aim is not simply to interpret the world but to change it, by changing the consciousness of those who read and their relation to what they read. (p. xxii)

Learning to read with feminist theory means learning to attend to the ideology of patriarchy, to the gendered nature of textual worlds, and to the significance of our responses as male and female readers. Gender theory provides a critical lens that can transform students' visions as they interpret individual characters, as they evaluate the cultural significance of particular texts, and as they read and respond to the gendered patterns in the world. Finally, they are also able to see how their own gender affects their response to literary texts.

When the students were asked how their gender affected their reading, they offered comments like the following (see Appendix, Activities 15 and 31):

> I was not really affected by it despite my being male. The book itself seemed to be, for the most part, indifferent towards men; it dealt mostly with the women. (Justin)

> I think my gender did affect my reaction because I could directly relate to some of the things she complained about. I have run into people with the opinions that women can't be as smart as men. I have never believed that, but I have felt the shock of people when I do well in math and science, traditionally male fields. Things are nowhere near as extreme for me as they were back in 1928, but that occasional feeling of being an oddity is much easier to relate to as a woman than I think it would be for a man. I think men are pretty aware of the big issues but sometimes I think they might miss the importance of little things such as looks and tone of voice. As a woman I felt much more connected to what Virginia is talking about. (Shannon)

> My gender definitely did play a role in my reading of A Room of One's Own. It was difficult for me not to feel a bit defensive when it seemed that Virginia Woolf was attacking my fellow males and me. Still, after the initial impulse to defend myself and my gender, I was able to evaluate Woolf's ideas a bit more objectively. I believe that if I had been a woman, my reading would have been a bit different; I probably would have been a bit quicker to identify with Woolf. (Eric)

> Yes, I think being a female somewhat influenced my reaction to A Room of One's Own. In many ways, I can see Woolf's arguments and problems because I can see them for myself in everyday situations. She talks about how men had all the freedom and women had none. Although this is, I believe, taken to an extreme, it is easy to understand these things because of my experience as a female. Also, I think it is easier to side with Virginia Woolf because I am a female and she is too. It's sort of like rooting for your own team because you are a part of it. (Jenny)

I think my gender affected my reading of *A Room of One's Own* slightly. I noticed myself paying attention more to the successes (or at least what Virginia Woolf saw as a success) of women. I read those passages and felt proud of the individual women and of women in general. When Woolf talked about the injustices against women, it didn't affect me as much because I haven't experienced it. I sort of looked at those with a sense of "look at what women have accomplished," but from a third-person sort of way. (Jessica)

Understanding the role one's gender plays as a reader is a significant step to understanding one's gender role in society at large. Through texts such as *Death of a Salesman*, *The Great Gatsby*, "The Yellow Wallpaper" and *A Room of One's Own*, adolescent readers become acutely aware of gender and how it is socially constructed. Gender/feminist literary theory provides a way for young men and young women to make meaning of their reading, their schooling, and their gendered place in the world. The process of recognizing textual politics and taking a stand with or against the authors and characters enables students to begin to articulate a more generalized sense of their places as women and men who create, out of necessity, gender readings not only of texts but of their lived experience as well.

SUGGESTED NONFICTION SELECTIONS FOR THE GENDER LENS

Deborah Tannen, "There is No Unmarked Woman" (pdf available online)

Jill Filipovic, "Why Should Married Women Change Their Names? Let Men Change Theirs" (*The Guardian*)

Stephen Jay Gould, "Women's Brains" (pdf available online)

Dave Barry, "Lost in the Kitchen" (pdf available online)

Sojourner Truth, "Ain't I a Woman?" (pdf available online)

Alice Walker, "In Search of Our Mothers' Gardens" (available online)

Wendy Kaminer, "Let's Talk about Gender, Baby." (*The American Prospect*)

Elizabeth Cady Stanton, "Declaration of Sentiments and Resolutions" (pdf available online)

Virginia Woolf, "Shakespeare's Sister" (pdf available online)

Germaine Greer, "Masculinity" (pdf available online)

CHAPTER SIX

Columbus Did What?

Postcolonialism in the Literature Classroom

Until lions have their own historians, tales of hunting will always glorify the hunter.

—African Proverb

In early March, Peter's 11th-grade World Literature class is deep into its reading of Conrad's *Heart of Darkness*. A skilled and resourceful teacher, Peter is already planning to show Francis Ford Coppola's dark film *Apocalypse Now*, which follows the basic plot outline of *Heart of Darkness*. Peter has also provided opportunities for the students to find intertextual connections, with Chinua Achebe's *Things Fall Apart*, which the class read in the fall. Yet something seems to be missing from the discussion of this complex work. Discussion of characters center on obvious comparisons, no one mentions the hierarchy embedded in the text, and while Peter offers some brief historical and biographical background information, the discussion has remained largely apolitical.

The texts we read in literature classrooms reflect our evolving history. One potent example is literature that was "produced in the crucible of colonization and its aftermath of independence and postindependence movement and struggles" (Dimitriadis & McCarthy, 2001, p. 3). While the teaching of literature need not always be both historical and political, Peter's eager students seem to be circling around the heart of *Heart of Darkness*.

WHY POSTCOLONIALISM?

As school populations become more diverse, the task of helping students see themselves in the literature they read becomes more challenging for teachers. As more immigrants and refugees enter our classrooms, we must consider a broader range of literary texts in order that they may see themselves and their circumstances in the works they read. In addition, we need to consider the perspectives and identities of populations who historically have not seen themselves as part of the American mainstream. If we can successfully demonstrate for them that alternative ideologies belong within the

American imagination, we will demonstrate as well the liberating power of literary interpretation. Direct attention to postcolonial literature provides a means for this understanding of our national imagination.

We should also think of the benefits that postcolonial perspectives provide for majority students as well. Colonialist worldviews serve as the underpinning for much of the ideology that pervades mainstream American culture. If we set as one of our goals the ability of our students to read the world in multiple ways—to see things through a variety of lenses—we need to acquaint them with the lenses of colonialism and postcolonialism. Those of us raised in the United States have experienced a world shaped by traditional Western values and beliefs. While many of these values serve us well, we have to distinguish those that drive us toward the highest ideals of democracy and equality from those that provide advantage to us and adversity to others. In her very helpful primer on critical theory, Lois Tyson (2006, p. 417) remarks that postcolonial criticism helps us see "connections among all the domains of our experience—the psychological, ideological, social, political, intellectual, and aesthetic—in ways that show us just how inseparable these categories are in our lived experiences of ourselves and our world." Postcolonial theory, in other words, makes better readers of us all.

Studies in postcolonialism often begin with the work of the literary critic and professor of English and comparative literature Edward Said. His memoir titled *Out of Place* (1999) details the experience of leaving the Middle East to study in the United States. The title of this work might well name the feelings of many new Americans. His major work, *Orientalism* (1979), describes what he thought to be incorrect assumptions about "the East," based on Western cultural presuppositions. This cultural worldview, as Said saw it, reduced the Arab world to a few stereotypical characteristics, ignoring the complexity, diversity, and humanity that its people represent.

An understanding of postcolonial viewpoints is crucial for students if we are to educate new generations of Americans who are willing to move beyond Western stereotypes and biases. It is also an essential component of literary study that moves beyond universal standards of judgment and allows diversity of opinion in literary criticism, especially a criticism that reflects the multiplicity of the United States today (Bonnycastle, 1996). Whatever ideologies postcolonial theory might challenge, its most important benefit is that it empowers students to reflect upon their own cultural knowledge as they build interpretations of literature. It thus becomes an essential component of inclusive literary pedagogy.

Perhaps most importantly, postcolonial criticism provides an opportunity to level a playing field that has been tilted since the beginnings of Western identity. In her explanation of colonialist ideology, Lois Tyson (2006) summarizes the origin of the problem—the construction of a worldview that inherently privileges the perspectives of those who constructed it.

The colonizers believed that only their own Anglo-European culture was civilized, sophisticated, or, as postcolonial critics put it, *metropolitan*. Therefore, native peoples were defined as savage, backward, and undeveloped. Because their technology was more highly advanced, the colonizers believed their whole culture was more highly advanced, and they ignored or swept aside the religions, customs, and codes of behavior of the peoples they subjugated. So the colonizers saw themselves at the center of the world; the colonized were at the margins. (p. 419)

This colonialist ideology constructs a world that imprisons both sides. It precludes any ability for Western peoples to learn from histories and cultures of the colonized, to incorporate ideas and values that have successfully sustained non-Western societies for centuries, often with less detrimental effects than Eurocentric cultural practices. Most importantly, it provides an opportunity for our students to employ their imaginations to the fullest extent.

LITERATURE AND COLONIALISM

For a very long time, authors, poets, critics, and scholars have made the case that literature reflects cultural heritage. Largely as a result of this understanding, literature study has traditionally been divided into historical periods and national literatures. We established historical and cultural contexts for literary study to help provide a map of our cultural history, and for many decades this practice went unquestioned. We saw literature, then, as a public celebration of human advancement, the apex of our linguistic accomplishment, and the most beautiful expression of our sentiments. Dominant societies created images of themselves by publicly recognizing what they thought to be the best representations of their arts and sciences. Featured among these representations were literary masterworks thought to capture the essence of who we were and what our societies stood for at various points and places in the past.

In time, however, it became clear that the images created within our national literatures provided less than a complete understanding of our history and our heritage. Only those people who had historically participated in the construction of our cultural imagination found themselves fairly represented, and their voices were predominantly White, male, and of the upper social classes. Members of racial and ethnic groups who were not part of the mainstream found themselves and their cultures represented from the outside. They themselves became the creations of a cultural imagination that neither understood nor sympathized with them. The same was true for women. The source of this misrepresentation was a cultural predilection that reflected the products and processes of Western civilization. Foremost among these processes was colonization—an ostensibly benevolent expansion of our best cultural principles.

Among the cultural themes represented in Western literature are conflicts that pit Civilization against "savages," peoples generally defined by non-Christian and non-European values and practices. Within literary representations of these conflicts, Western supremacy in technology quickly translates into superior power, principally in navigation and weapons. As Joseph Conrad's *Heart of Darkness* shows us, industrial and economic superiority are culturally transfigured. They justify colonization, imperialism, and even genocide. Kurtz's closing exclamation in his treatise captures the worst sentiment of Western hegemony: "Exterminate all the brutes!" The colonialist worldview thus imposes upon other landscapes and peoples its own images of the colonized as it wished them to be. Competing worldviews were summarily dismissed.

THE ORIGINS OF POSTCOLONIAL READING

In the late 20th century, with the ascendancy of civil rights, equal rights for women, and an expanded understanding of cultural sovereignty, literary critics attempted to broaden the scope of cultural exploration through their study of literature. Thus they began their exploration of an expanded literary canon: a more varied list of works and authors representing diverse cultures. The underlying idea was that the colonized needed to have their stories heard. In many cases their stories had already been written, but they had not been included in the literary canon of their colonizers. They were not recognized as a part of the whole. The movement that we now call postcolonialism was both an invitation and a recognition. Those who had not yet told their stories had the opportunity to write themselves into the literary record. Those who had already written their stories could be included in the literary conversation.

Postcolonialism focuses on literary works from and about countries that formerly had been colonies of Western nations. It also calls attention to propensities of the Western world: the privileging of science over custom, the imposition of economic structures into societies that had already developed their own, and an understanding of Western causes and effects that rendered Western institutions powerful and others powerless. Christianity frequently served as both a motivation for colonization and a means for defining the colonized. European commerce prompted a search for resources and riches that, in Western eyes, lay unclaimed among the uncivilized. In general, it was the perspective of more developed nations that their cultural, commercial, and religious superiority gave them license to take what they needed for their own advancement. The results were often violent.

From the 16th to the 20th century, the voices of colonized peoples were largely unrecognized. Political, economic, and military superiority provided a platform for European literary art, which carried the ideology of the colonizers forward. The literatures of the colonized, to the extent that they were allowed to exist, were dismissed. The hallmark of the postcolonial movement today, then, is found in its opposition to imperialist cultures and the identities they constructed for those they had colonized. Africa and East Asia, the primary geographic targets of European colonialism, are sites today for rich postcolonial literary expression. The Caribbean is another area of contested cultural identity in both literature and music.

QUESTIONS OF CULTURAL IDENTITY

A consistent outcome of colonialism is the inability of colonized people to determine their own cultural identity. Their religious practices are frequently replaced, most often by Christianity. Rituals that create unity and cultural continuity are discouraged. Languages are supplanted by the tongues of their conquerors. Colonized people are robbed of distinctions they hold dear—the traits and heritages that separate them from their neighbors—by a European worldview that sees no point in differentiating them one from another.

In European inscriptions of history and culture, colonized people lose not only their ability to construct their identities in the present, but the power to represent their cultural achievements in the past. Their histories are suppressed, their secrets are revealed (a grievous fault in traditional societies) to a world that has no context for understanding them, and their values are denigrated. Chinua Achebe's *Things Fall Apart* tells a story set in Nigeria about the impact of Christianity and of a European justice system that humiliates and imprisons those who resist its orders. Ngugi Wa Thiong'o's *The River Between* sets up a conflict between Christian missionaries and traditional tribal practice in Kenya that is seemingly irreconcilable. Derek Walcott and V. S. Naipaul each won the Nobel Prize for Literature while investigating the ideologies that established European dominance in the Caribbean. By telling their stories to the world they recapture a history that had been stolen from them, along with the dignity and identity that had long been reserved for the colonizers alone.

American Indian cultures—to the extent that they are preserved—are frequently misrepresented and idealized by a Western society that wishes to make peace with its own history but is unwilling to acknowledge its own exercise of ideological suppression. These themes of colonization also play out in American history: Christianization of the native people, suppression of indigenous languages, and the imposition of economic practices such as farming by way of what we now know as the Dawes Act. Such laws were intended to "civilize" Native Americans by forcing a Eurocentric culture on their well-established ways of life. The effect of the Dawes Act was to remove them from the lands that had supported and defined them. Since the late 1960s, a rich literary tradition has sprung up among American Indian writers who now have the opportunity to reclaim their history and identity by writing about it. Frequently, as in the case of Leslie Marmon Silko's *Ceremony*, this recovery takes the form of a return to tribal customs and beliefs. A common theme is the reclamation of cultural identity.

In the colonial mindset, the colonized come into existence when they are "discovered" by the colonizers. This explains, for example, the colonialist claim that "Columbus discovered America," a statement we will revisit later in Peter's classroom. Prior to this "discovery," it is as if Native Americans did not exist, or they existed in a state that had little meaning or significance for people from the "civilized" world. To the extent that American literature represents the discovery and conquest of the North American continent, its Western biases reflect the perspectives of the "civilized," even to the point of justifying colonization and westward expansion. Thus, a particular aim of postcolonial theory is to reclaim a history and cultural identity for Native Americans.

WORKING AGAINST A
"UNIVERSALIST" UNDERSTANDING OF LITERATURE

It has been common in the past to suggest that the study of literature leads us to understand that which is universally shared within the human experience. As Peter Barry (2002, p. 192) points out, "If we claim that great literature has a timeless and universal significance, we thereby demote or disregard cultural, social, regional, and national differences in experience and outlook, preferring instead to judge all literatures by a single, supposedly 'universal' standard."

This approach necessarily privileges the standards and perspectives of the dominant culture. Postcolonialism, by contrast, recognizes the differences that give peoples their identities, their uniqueness, and their histories. Through this approach, English teachers create more inclusive classrooms. It validates the experiences and perspectives of readers from outside the mainstream.

Because the manner of our inquiry determines the ways in which we create meaning, we need to think clearly about the questions we ask about literary works. As Bonnycastle (1996) suggests, this means questioning cultural supremacy and the literature that it favors. Reading literature with a postcolonial lens does just that.

Interpretations traditionally break down along the line that separates colonized from colonizers. A postcolonial lens, on the other hand, allows for the possibility of interpretations that cross this line because it provides a basis of historical and cultural understanding. These will not be universal interpretations, but rather interpretations based on new understanding of political and historical contexts and the cultural identities they acknowledge for the peoples they represent.

Another important point to keep in mind is that multicultural treatments of literature must not turn their subjects into objects. They must instead accurately represent the values, ideas, customs, and beliefs of the non-Western world as they would be seen through non-Western eyes. Edward Said (1979) characterizes the conflict in this way:

> Consider how the Orient, and in particular the near Orient, became known in the West as its great complementary opposite since antiquity. There were the Bible and the rise of Christianity; there were travelers like Marco Polo who charted the trade routes and patterned the regulated system of commercial exchange . . . ; there were the redoubtable Eastern conquering movements, principally Islam, of course; there were the militant pilgrims, chiefly the Crusaders, although an internally structured archive is built up from the literature that belongs to these experiences. Out of this comes a restricted number of typical encapsulations: the journey, the history, the fable, the stereotype, the polemical confrontation. These are the lenses through which the Orient is experienced, and they shape the language, perception, and form of encounter between East and West. . . . Something patently foreign and distant acquires, for one reason or other, a status more rather than less familiar. (p. 58)

The aim of postcolonial study, then, is to restore the history, the dignity, the validity, the cultural contributions, and the global significance of those whose experiences have been represented within a worldview that provided no way to include "the Other" except through direct contrast with itself. This manner of binary construction—Western/non-Western, civilized/uncivilized, Christian/non-Christian, democratic/nondemocratic—necessarily reduces everything and everyone it encounters. It diminishes not only the complexity of the colonized world, but its legitimacy as well.

Including a non-Western perspective in American education also provides a means for moving students outside of their familiar patterns of thinking as they try to understand the larger world, and in order to successfully read the world they must have this larger perspective. Gayatri Spivak (1988), who was born in India but has spent years teaching in American universities, relates this challenge that she put to a group of her honors students concerning their own ideological indoctrination:

> Suppose an outsider, observing the uniformity of the mores you have all sketched in your papers, were to say that you had been indoctrinated? That

you could no longer conceive of public decision-making except in the quan-
tified areas of your economics and business classes, where you learn all the
rational expectations theories? You *know* that decisions in the public sphere,
such as tax decisions, legal decisions, foreign policy decisions, fiscal decisions,
affect your *private* lives deeply. Yet in a speculative field such as the interpretation of texts, you feel that there is something foolish and wrong and
regimented about a public voice. Suppose someone were to say that this was a
result of your indoctrination to keep moral speculation and decision-making
apart, to render you incapable of thinking collectively in any but the most
inhuman ways. (p. 99)

The point she makes is that her students seemed to want to under-
take sociocultural analyses as unique individuals. To broaden their sphere
of understanding in addressing social issues, they needed to think of themselves as public individuals as well. This need, she said, came from the fact
that their "historical-institutional imperatives [were] proving stronger than
[their] individual good will" (p. 98). As their teacher, she trusted their intelligence and their positive motivations, but she could not trust that they had
a broad enough view to see the world that their own decisions as future
leaders would bring into being.

TEACHING THE POSTCOLONIAL LENS: COLUMBUS DID WHAT?

Although he might not state it quite the same way, Peter, like Spivak, wants
his students to be able to see the world broadly and interpret texts like
Heart of Darkness with both private and public awareness. Peter's 11th-
grade World Literature class is lens savvy and theory rich. They've worked
through reader response, the social class lens, and the lens of gender. As
Peter anticipates teaching the next book in his curriculum, Joseph Conrad's
Heart of Darkness, he decides that in order for his students to fully understand the novel, they need to add another tool to their interpretive toolkit,
this tool being the postcolonial lens. Peter believes that, although both the
social class and the gender lenses have helped students see how the dynamics of power and oppression are often inscribed in the texts we read, the
dynamics of the colonized and the colonizer need to be underscored in a
separate lesson.

Peter begins his lesson on postcolonialism with a few introductory explanations (see Appendix, Activity 21). After he explains the basic premises
of the postcolonial lens, he asks students to rephrase, from a postcolonial
perspective, the following sentence: "Christopher Columbus discovered
America." At first, the students giggle nervously, the weight of a decade of
historical misunderstanding seems to paralyze their pens. Then, they begin
to write. Here are some of the resulting rephrasings:

Columbus took control of land inhabited for centuries by native people, and in the process stripped them of their independence and unique culture.

Columbus was an explorer who arrived at the North American continent already populated by several different societies and facilitated the destruction of these cultures for profit.

Christopher Columbus landed in America.

Christopher Columbus exploited the natives of America and dehumanized them of their right to own land. In saying that he discovered the country, it is indicating that the people living there were inconsequential.

Columbus stumbled upon land unclaimed by other European countries, starting an epoch of oppression of Native Americans.

The students seem to take to the idea quickly. This simple exercise helps Peter's students see how the postcolonial lens quickly shifts the focus from the colonizer to the colonized. Peter then moves to a literary text and hands out the following poem by Native American poet Diane Burns:

Sure You Can Ask Me a Personal Question

How do you do?
No, I am not Chinese.
No, not Spanish.
No, I am American Indi-uh, Native American.
No, not from India.
No, not Apache.
No, not Navajo.
No, not Sioux.
No, we are not extinct.
Yes, Indian.
Oh?
So, that's where you got those high cheekbones.
Your great grandmother, huh?
An Indian Princess, huh?
Hair down to there?
Let me guess. Cherokee?
Oh, so you've had an Indian friend?
That close?
Oh, so you've had an Indian lover?
That tight?
Oh, so you've had an Indian servant?

That much?
Yeah, it was awful what you guys did to us.
It's real decent of you to apologize.
No, I don't know where you can get peyote.
No, I don't know where you can get Navajo rugs real cheap.
No, I didn't make this. I bought it at Bloomingdales.
Thank you. I like your hair too.
I don't know if anyone knows whether or not Cher is really Indian.
No, I didn't make it rain tonight.
Yeah. Uh-huh. Spirituality.
Uh-huh. Yeah. Spirituality. Uh-huh. Mother
Earth. Yeah. Uh-huh. Uh-huh. Spirituality.
No, I didn't major in archery.
Yeah, a lot of us drink too much.
Some of us can't drink enough.
This ain't no stoic look.
This is my face.

—Diane Burns

Peter asks the students to begin by writing down two or three sentences of personal response to the poem, as well as any questions or points of confusion. Then in groups of four or five, the students discuss their personal responses and their questions. Peter wryly comments that before he considered using literary theory, his lesson about the poem might end there. Peter then asks the students to consider the basic tenets of postcolonial theory from the handout. He instructs each group to construct a postcolonial reading in groups of three or four. Here are some of the group's postcolonial readings of "Sure You Can Ask Me a Personal Question":

The author feels like no one understands Native American culture, only the stereotypes surrounding it. She does not apologize or attempt to explain, only answers the question.

Instead of being proud of her Indian culture, the speaker seems to be offended at how the world sees her differently. She doesn't like that the world makes stereotypes about who she is. Through a postcolonial reading, one might say that the rest of society in fact destroyed her culture because things that they found beautiful are now looked at as ordinary.

The most striking idea in this poem is the binary approach taken in this discussion; there is clearly a colonizer (the questioner) and an "other" (the Native American). It appears that the questioner has no malicious intent; however, from the questions one can see that the speaker in the poem is nevertheless offended. By grouping all

Indians together with cheap Navajo rugs, liquor, and a past servant, the questioner inadvertently calls into play a number of derogatory stereotypes.

The conversation is between the oppressor and the oppressed. It shows the way White civilization destroyed the lives of the natives and uses their history, livelihood. The oppressed speaker had an indignant and retaliatory attitude [which] highlights [reaction to] the postcolonial attitude.

In these responses, Peter's students demonstrate that they are clearly "seeing" the poem from a postcolonial perspective. Peter is convinced that the themes of oppression and marginalization that the students uncovered are rendered much more visible through this lens. Peter concludes that his students are now ready to read *Heart of Darkness*.

The next day, after the students have read several chapters of *Heart of Darkness*, Peter asks them to list characters as colonized, colonizers, or both. He then asks students to list some questions that emerge from their postcolonial reading of this text, questions that will shape their future discussions of the novel. Here are a few of their questions:

- Would you consider Marlow a true colonizer? Or does he just follow along with what the company does?
- Who in this book is isolated and who does the isolating?
- What shapes the image of colonization in the West?
- How does Marlow's sympathy with the colonized alter his stance as either the colonizer or the colonized?
- What motivation is more detrimental in colonization: an economic motivation or a civilizing motivation?
- Why does Marlow describe the natives as animals?
- Who was more of a factor in Marlow's changed view: Kurtz or the cannibals?
- How can an "uncivilized" person resist colonization?

Peter is pleased with these questions. He sees that his students understand the pervasiveness of colonist ideology in this text and the degree to which it translates into a kind of colonial psychology in the novel's characters. He also knows that colonialist ideology has far from disappeared from American society. As Tyson (2006) writes:

White supremacist backlash, for example, as witnessed in the proliferation of racist hate groups; the persistence of covert racial discrimination . . . in housing, employment, and education; the othering of the homeless, indeed their virtual erasure from American consciousness and conscience; and all the forms of othering that still flourish in this country today make it clear that America's neocolonialist enterprises around the globe will be accompanied by versions thereof at home for a long time to come. For colonialist psychology and the discriminatory ideologies it supports are a part of our historical and cultural legacy. . . . And this is a reality that will have to be confronted anew by each generation of Americans. (p. 445)

Peter believes that by using the postcolonial lens in his literature classroom he has given his students an important interpretive tool. In doing so he has also introduced this generation of Americans to the insidious nature of the psychological heritage of colonialism.

SUGGESTED NONFICTION SELECTIONS FOR THE POSTCOLONIAL LENS

Bharati Mukherjee, "Two Ways of Belonging in America" (pdf available online)

Malcolm X, "Learning to Read" (pdf available online)

Edward Said, "The Myth of 'The Clash of Civilizations'" (pdf available online)

Frederick Douglass, "Learning to Read and Write" (pdf available online)

Gloria Anzaldua, "How to Tame a Wild Tongue" (pdf available online)

James Baldwin, "Notes of a Native Son" (pdf available online)

George Orwell, "Politics and the English Language"* (pdf available online)

Bassey Ikpi, "Why the Whole 'Poor Africa' Thing Isn't Cool"* (xojane.com)

Charles Kenny, "Haiti Doesn't Need Your Old T-Shirt" (foreignpolicy.com)

Judith Ortiz Cofer, "The Myth of the Latin Woman: I Just Met a Girl Named Maria" (50 Essays) (pdf available online)

*Suggested Common Core Anchor Texts

CHAPTER SEVEN

The Past Is Always New

Reading with New Historicism

We may each draw upon different discourses, and we may each draw upon them in different ways, but it is through the discourses circulating in our culture that our individual identities are formed, are linked to one another, and are linked to the culture that both shapes and is shaped by each of us.

—Lois Tyson

Meaning is contextual.

—Steven Lynn

There is a heated debate raging in Michael's 5th-hour 11th-grade English class. Michael has just announced that the next text they will be reading is Shakespeare's *The Merchant of Venice*.

"I don't think we should be reading that play," says Sam. "Everyone knows that Shakespeare was anti-Semitic." "Yeah, and a misogynist too," says Alicia. "We shouldn't be reading books that put people down based on race, gender, or religion, Mr. Richards. What about all that ideology stuff you taught us to think about when we were learning about the gender, class, and postcolonial lenses?"

"Calm down, everyone. I understand your concern and appreciate your references to the ideas we've learned as we've tried on those other lenses of literary theory. But there is a new lens we need to think about Shakespeare in light of your objections—new historicism."

"Aaaw, don't you think we have plenty of lenses already? This class feels like an optician's office." Giggles erupt all around. "Yes," Michael says, "but this lens is a very important one, and in some ways it calls some of the other lenses into question. New historicism asks us to look critically at how our culture influences how we read texts. It's obvious to state that our world is very different from the world that Shakespeare inhabited. But that means that some of the assumptions we make may not be able to be fruitfully applied across time. Or, at least we need to realize that we, too, are in the business of cultural production. The cultural productions of Shakespeare's text didn't stop in 1616 with Shakespeare's death. Look at the film interpretations, for example, or productions of Shakespeare plays in modern dress. They all require us to rethink the play and history."

"Well, what about Shylock?" insists Sam. Michael replies, "New historicism would ask us to consider Shylock within the context of the time it was written. It would require us to rethink the significance his occupation as a moneylender what, given the lack of other available professions for Jews in the 17th century. And, it would require us to think about how intervening historical events, such as the Holocaust have shaped and reshaped our considerations of Shakespeare's portrayal of Shylock."

"Here, let's begin our study of the play by reading the article by Stephen Greenblatt called, 'Shakespeare and Shylock,' which is a review of Al Pacino's performance of the role."

WHY WE NEED NEW HISTORICISM TO UNDERSTAND HISTORY

The relationship between history and literature has long been an intimate one. In the past, literary history viewed works of literature as representations of historical events, especially when the literary works in question featured historical settings and situations. According to this traditional understanding of both history and literature, history presented an accurate account of past events, while literature presented an impression of history. This relationship seemed to work to the benefit of readers and critics who sought meanings for literature in history. With history providing a stable, accurate, and concrete understanding of the settings within which literature happened, critics could count on historians to foreground their interpretations.

Most of us first encounter history as a certain and trustworthy narrative of past events. Because it is an object of study, and because it has factual roots in the cultures and events that are its subjects, history is believed to be not only accurate but to have explanatory strength as well. We take it to be a record of the thoughts and actions of people present at important moments in time. In many ways, this manner of history constitutes the memory of a society and its culture.

But what if—as cognitive science suggests about the human mind— memory is less a record than an impression? Impressions are susceptible to the influence of prior understanding, to cultural values, to manners of thinking, to political theories, to self-concept, to purported ideals—in short, to everything we bring with us into the world as we encounter it. Add to these facts that memory is changeable; the more frequently we activate memories, the more they are subject to alteration. If history, then, is an impression of the past rather than a record, then how do we discern its value, its accuracy, and its origins? And if history is culturally conditioned, then how do we understand its relationship to literature?

Within a larger understanding of the postmodern condition, we have come to see history as changeable, as subject to impression, and, perhaps most importantly, as a product of the culture that creates it. Contemporary historians recognize and acknowledge that history is subjective. The key to understanding history, then, is to understand the nature of its subjectivity. To the extent that literature informs our awareness of human events as representations of the world we know, it can have an influence upon history. Within this postmodern understanding of history, literature is less an outgrowth of its historical context than a source of cultural perception that shapes and reshapes history.

Using this new conception of the relationship of literature and history, we find a new set of tools for the construction of cultural meaning. In fact, within the practice of new historicism, history and literature share the same status as parts of a larger cultural text. And when we view all of culture as a "text," we recognize that history and literature are products of a common impulse: a need to explain what is meaningful about any society and its impact on our awareness of human experience. So, while historians and literary critics use different methods for exploring human experience, in a sense they use the same text: the cultures out of which their respective representations of human experience arise.

LITERATURE AS A SOURCE OF HISTORY

As a set of literary practices, the new historicism vastly opens up our possibilities for interpretation. At its core, this theory focuses on power relations in society, and so it overlaps Marxist theory in this regard. Its methods are more expansive, though, as its practitioners attempt to expose the historical origins of social concepts like culture, the state, the individual, the family, and religion. As power becomes an object of inquiry, history becomes more subjective because history as we have known it heretofore has been a product of the power relations it examines. To get at the sources of power in any society, new historicists would say, we need to see the complex relationships between a society's discourses and its sources and use of power.

Discourses of the kind new historicists study encompass all manner of texts and language practices. This definition of discourse draws primarily on the work of Michel Foucault, who viewed these language practices through social languages that grow out of historical circumstances. For example, there are discourses of environmental awareness, of free-market economies, gendered employment, prolife and prochoice politics, Christian family values, access to medicine, individual liberty, and American exceptionalism. Each of these discourses is socially and historically situated, and each lays claim to some manner of power. The key to understanding any of these discourses, new historicists would say, will be found in the relationship between these discourses and the cultural artifacts by which they are represented.

Another debt we owe to Michel Foucault (1982) is the notion that power is not so much a force to be imposed by the powerful upon the powerless as it is a force for the reproduction of cultural viewpoints. Within this framework, Foucault rejected the idea that power is repressive and argued instead that power works by organizing and channeling the forces that oppose it. As Gerald Graff (1989) says:

> [Power] triumphs over opposition not by negating it but by producing it according to its particular requirements. Thus, in Foucault's analysis, what passes conventionally for transgression or rebellion against power . . . turns out to be only another of the faces of power, another means by which power reproduces, distributes, and extends itself. (p. 169)

This understanding of power significantly shifts postmodern thinking about history away from the notion that history is a record of political causes and toward the idea that history is a cultural product. To the extent that literature provides conventional representations of historical power, it offers support for a cultural metatext—a conglomeration of all the representations that a culture produces. To the extent that it attempts to subvert a cultural paradigm, literature is likely to be co-opted by cultural histories that redirect its oppositional force. For example, when we read Ralph Ellison's *Invisible Man* as an indictment of a White American society that refuses even to see African American people and their experiences, the book seems subversive, a provocation to challenge the idea that America represents freedom and opportunity for all. When we place this same novel within a rewritten history that represents American cultural multiplicity, it becomes a source of evidence that prior histories were too narrow to represent American life as a whole. At that point, Ellison's work is co-opted by those who would channel the force of his literary work: Its force is redirected toward a new historical argument.

Within the framework of the new historicism, we understand literature as more than a product—more than an outgrowth of the social conditions from which it arises. Literature is a cause, a source of power: a shaping influence in the construction of social institutions and the power that derives from them. Within this framework all of culture can be read as a text, and because literature has a particular status as a discourse it has a particularly important role in revealing and reinforcing all manner of social power. For this reason, we find myriad examples of social sanction for literature, co-optation of literature, and literary censorship. Most importantly, though, the new historicists argue, literature is inextricably woven through the whole of our culture, and as such it becomes an immensely important source of cultural study.

THE CHANGING FACE OF HISTORY

Using history as a stable set of referents, for example, we could imagine Stephen Crane, in *The Red Badge of Courage*, and Ambrose Bierce, in short stories like "An Occurrence at Owl Creek Bridge" or "One of the Missing," to be telling us what the American Civil War was like. History conceived in this way fills in the big picture: the dates, the battles, the weaponry, and the goals of the opposing armies. Literature, on the other hand, adds a human dimension to the stories of war: the fears, the follies, the heroism, the personalities—the motivations of men in battle. Crane and Bierce show us portraits of soldiers who fought in this war and the landscapes on which they fought it. They tell us what it was like to experience loss of life and limb on a massive scale. They show us soldiers in action and inaction. In other words, they give us entry into a historical world—a world that actually existed and that has been chronicled by historians. The result is that we imagine the literature of Crane and Bierce growing out of its historical setting, as if there were a one-way street leading from history to literature.

But what if these historical perspectives were not the accurate accounts we imagined them to be? What if we were to see history as interpretation as well? The use of literary theoretical lenses supposes that literature develops its meanings in the mind of a reader enacting critical practice. If this is the case, then why wouldn't histories be subject to the same variations in perspective and ideology? In fact, doesn't it seem almost inherent that the past historians constructed meaning for historical events in exactly the same ways that literary critics did? If it is impossible to operate in the world without an ideology, then wouldn't histories be as subject to ideological interpretation in the same manner as literature? And if we return to Crane and Bierce's literature of the Civil War, how might we imagine their fictional stories reframing our understanding of the history of this era.

When we consider the relationship between the American Civil War and the growth of Northern industry during the war, for example, we might imagine that our Civil War was one of the first truly industrial wars. Weapons, especially rifles, were being mass-produced by machines. When Henry Fleming imagines how he will rejoin his unit after running from battle in *The Red Badge of Courage*, the novel's narrator tells us that the rifle he had dropped could quickly be replaced: "He had no rifle; he could not fight with his hands . . . Well, rifles could be had for the picking. They were extraordinarily profuse" (Chapter 9). While one interpretation of the novel might focus on the number of soldiers who were killed or had deserted, another focuses on the historical fact of the abundant manufacture of weapons and supplies. Crane's account of these weapons fuels a historical perception that the war was won less by soldiers and their bravery than by the success of Northern industry.

Likewise, *gun* and *rifle* are frequent metonyms throughout the novel, even replacing humans as a source of courage or actions. As Crane's narrator tells us, "The guns, stolid and undaunted, spoke with dogged valor" (Chapter 6). These descriptions reinforce our historical view of the rise of the industrial North, and in doing so provide a perspective for future historians. As the example above suggests, courage in war could literally be manufactured. Viewed through the lens of literature, these literary accounts of the North's supremacy in the Civil War provide testament to its industry. The war itself and the stories of it stand, at least in part, as a representation of the inception of the United States as an industrial nation. Whether for better or worse, in battle or in commerce, that war and the literature that immortalized it are part of our cultural understanding of American prosperity and industrialization.

CULTURE AS TEXT

As historiography changed with postmodernism to understand history as an interpretation of events, historians came to recognize that these interpretations grew out of a vast array of cultural concepts and products. In fact, the whole of any culture serves as a text. This idea is explained by Gallagher and Greenblatt (2000) in the following way:

> The notion of a distinct culture, particularly a culture distinct in time or space, as a text . . . is powerfully attractive for several reasons. It carries the core hermeneutical presumption that one can occupy a position from which one can discover meanings that those who left traces of themselves could not have articulated. Explication and paraphrase are not enough; we seek something more, something that the authors we study would not have had sufficient distance upon themselves and their own era to grasp. (p. 8)

In a way, this view of history works against a more selective representation by bringing to bear the whole of a culture and its representations. It also allows for multiple accounts of history—the writing of counterhistories—and the possibility of simultaneous and competing narratives. With more than one history in play at a time, the possible literary interpretations multiply even further.

Gallagher and Greenblatt (2000) explain how this happens and why it serves as a benefit to literary criticism: "The notion of culture as text has a further major attraction: It vastly expands the range of objects available to be read and interpreted. Major works of art remain centrally important, but they are jostled now by an array of other texts and images" (p. 9). Among these other texts, Gallagher and Greenblatt suggest, are lesser works of literature whose inclusion in our interpretive activities challenges the criteria by which we have judge literature in the past. A reevaluation of these criteria, in turn, challenges the foundations for our arguments about what is literature and what is not. At the same time, literature itself is subsumed within other art forms, especially advertising, which subverts the literary impulse by making it self-consciously commercial.

APPROPRIATING ROBERT FROST: A CASE STUDY

In January of 2000, a web-based employment service used much of the text of Robert Frost's poem, "The Road Not Taken." It is important to note that it also elided those parts of the text that create ambiguity. Monster.com, the company responsible for this advertisement, wanted to get its message across: By taking the less-traveled path and expressing individuality, a job-seeker can make a choice that retrospectively can be seen to have "made all the difference." While that phrase can also be read as ambiguous, our prevailing ideology attaches a highly positive interpretation to it. To "make a difference" is to do something of importance, and we need this cultural connotation to take the message of the advertisement.

The Monster.com advertisement was unveiled during the Super Bowl in that year—a context that by itself engages our critical sensibilities. This event commands the most expensive television time available to advertisers, and so the stakes are high. In a sense, then, Frost's poem becomes a key piece in a capitalist agenda to use art to promote commerce. By way of careful editing, the text of the poem presented in this ad is decidedly less ambiguous than is the full text of the poem. At the same time, its images almost confront the young woman who serves as its protagonist. Passersby, speaking lines from Frost's poem, seem to give testimony to the importance of making the right personal choice. Line by line, they construct a message. The images are in black and white—a color scheme that makes an additional argument against ambiguity within the poem—moving quickly past the protagonist as if to enhance the urgency of her choice. Near the end of the ad we see her standing at an intersection—a crossroads—as the seemingly prophetic last lines of the poem still echo around her. Here is the altered text presented by the advertisement:

> Two roads diverged in a yellow wood,
> And sorry I could not travel both
> And be one traveler, long I stood
> And looked down one as far as I could
>
> And both that morning equally lay
> In leaves no step had trodden black.
> Two roads diverged in a wood, and I—

I took the one less traveled by,
And that has made all the difference.

This advertisement, of course, is a cultural artifact, and arguably one of some significance. Its message to us all, as we imagine ourselves standing in for its protagonist, is that our choice of paths is purposeful, causal, and significant. The full text of Frost's poem, however, seems to resist that interpretation. After looking down one path, the narrator tells us that he "took the other, as just as fair":

And having perhaps the better claim,
Because it was grassy and wanted wear;
Though as for that the passing there
Had worn them really about the same,

These lines, which do not appear in the advertisement, suggest that the choice was somewhat random, that the two paths really weren't distinct. Also missing from the text of the ad are lines 16 and 17, which suggest both backward reflection and possible regret:

I shall be telling this with a sigh
Somewhere ages and ages hence:

While these bits of context for Monster.com's use of Frost's poem are clearly cultural, it is also clear that this cultural backdrop is historically located. Super Bowl XXXIV in January 2000 featured 16 dot-com companies that each paid over $2 million for a 30-second spot. The term "dot-com" was itself a historical referent. The following year there were only 3 dot-com ads. This particular rendering of Frost's poem, then, is used to create an image of history during the dot.com boom, but we can see how an interpretation of the poem absorbs the influence of a culture driven by economic prosperity.

In addition, this commercial is itself a text, a cultural representation of our perceived desire to find meaningful work. It incorporates within its images an American ideological belief in individualism. The actors appear to represent individual people who simply pass the focal character on the street, apparently on their way to something important. They do not stop to converse or to engage the young woman at the center of the narrative; they deliver their lines while continuing on their own paths. They seem to admonish the focal character to find her own way, presumably as they already have. Even the commercial's final image makes us of a cultural conceit, as a small group of schoolgirls actually lift off the ground, suggesting an upward movement that we can associate with work that gives us an individual identity. While clearly ambiguous, this final image ties to an image schema that cognitive linguists label "up-is-good," a schema that is also reflected in the notion of a career ladder. During the dot.com boom, this discourse of possibility seemed ubiquitous. Taken all together, these images find associations and coalesce within a collective cultural text that, at every moment, asks to be written into our understanding of "history."

COUNTERHISTORIES

Our previous definition of a history suggested a systematic narrative that accounts for past events and their influence on society and culture. Histories constitute grand narratives, stories that give structure and meaning to the events they describe and relate. The explanatory strength of histories gives them power, and the power of these narratives frequently serves as a unifying force for the societies that write and perpetuate these histories. For example, if we imagine that the United States is a nation forged by a national desire for liberty and justice, then any history of the United States should explain how these final causes were achieved by important figures in U.S. history. United States history, then, employs these final causes as its central theme, its unifying principle, and the measure of any isolated historical event.

The history of America's "discovery" and colonization might provide a prototypical historical narrative. As a story of national origin, it has power and appeal because it exemplifies the values that make America noteworthy among human societies. Its discovery required courage and faith in oceanic navigation. Its settlement required yet more courage, along with sacrifice, ingenuity, and hard labor. The development of its government constituted a grand experiment in democracy born of the age of enlightenment. Its westward expansion symbolized an embrace of possibility. And its ultimate prosperity speaks to its ultimate rectitude—or the providence of the divine—in the accomplishment of all the final causes that underlie its creation. This is the history that most American schoolchildren inherit.

Literary accounts of our early American history find expression in the works of James Fennimore Cooper and Nathaniel Hawthorne, but do these fictional works accurately present American life? If not, we need to examine the value and truth of our inherited historical legacy. Among the characters who people these stories—sometimes only as frightening shadows on the landscape—are Native Americans. When we encounter these Americans as fictional characters, we need to ask ourselves about the ways in which history has framed them as within the larger American story.

From a native perspective, one might see both fictional and ostensibly authentic histories as highly idealized, even whitewashed. European ethnocentrism gave shape to our previous historical accounts in which white colonialists gave shape and purpose to an amorphous landscape peopled by godless savages. The final causes of early White Americans have consistently been posited as progress, opportunity, self-determination, and democracy, and the narrative that follows from these causes glorifies the accomplishments of European colonists and settlers. In order to contest this general narrative, counter-historians needed first to provide a different set of final causes: the acquisition of land and wealth, the imposition of Old World values and cultural concepts including religion, ownership and commodity exchange, settlement of land and removal of natural resources, and the politics of war and conquest. Technological superiority—in the sense that White Europeans had more deadly weapons and military tactics, more efficient means for modifying the landscape, longer-range modes of transportation, and more broadly developed literacy practices—gave Europeans great advantage in the accomplishment of their ends. These advances and advantages provided a basis for European ethnocentrism, and European histories solidified colonial claims to power. No matter how ruthless or duplicitous, European land and resource acquisitions seem well justified in light of European claims of cultural superiority.

The counterclaims to this history can be easily posited. The Americas were not "discovered"; they were already inhabited. The mythology of Native Americans living on land that they neither modified nor improved has been largely debunked as a naïve overgeneralization that extends the social practices of a few Plains Indian tribes to the whole of American indigenous peoples. And if we see technological superiority merely as technological difference, with each set of people viewed through a lens of cultural relativity, then "superiority" loses its claim to cultural power. In the end, an indigenous counternarrative opens American history up for serious interrogation. To see how new historicism works, then, students of literature can create similar interrogations of our conventional histories. For example, historical investigation can open up new interpretive possibilities for the following works.

ACTIVITY: WRITING AND USING A COUNTERHISTORY

For teachers wanting to introduce their students to counterhistories, there are resources like James W. Loewen's *Lies My Teacher Told Me: Everything Your American History Textbook Got Wrong*. Among Loewen's examples are commentaries that question the role of Christopher Columbus, the first Thanksgiving, the historical representation of Native Americans, the whitewashing of endemic American racism and the omission of antiracism narratives, and the pervasive American myths of opportunity and progress. As general themes of American history, these concerns act as filters for historical considerations. Stories that don't align with these American mythologies are omitted from our histories.

Both literary works and historical documents exist, however, to cast doubt on our conventional explanations of our past. Books like Charles C. Mann's *1491: New Revelations about the Americas before Columbus* offer evidence about the lives and societies of Native Americans, noting that the realities of their lives do not align with those of the mythical Indians—neither the heathen savages presented in John Ford's film *The Searchers* (1956) nor the idealized guardians of American plains depicted in Kevin Costner's *Dances with Wolves* (1990). Books like Mann's can offer evidence and counternarratives to what too often become reductive, stereotypical, and mythologized accounts of pre-Columbian American culture.

To begin a counterhistory assignment, one might first identify historical events that appear to be the product of ideological bias—accounts of the kind that Loewen discusses in his book. Students can then be asked a series of questions about this event or historical theme:

- What has history previously told us about this event?
- What ideological values does this account privilege or advance?
- What is the general public's perception of the truth of this account?
- Has this account persisted even in light of counterevidence, and, if so, why?

The purpose of these questions is to frame a prior historical understanding of the event in question and to examine the bases for its construction. For example, the American myths of opportunity and self-determination serve as a justification for the displacement of Native Americans away from valuable and desirable natural resources and into reservations. As such, a genocidal conquest is disguised as "progress." The first task of the assignment, then, is to articulate the underlying ideological program of a historical event.

The second step in this assignment is to establish the basis for a counterhistory. At this point, students would address questions similar to the following:

- What do indigenous sources tell us about the events or westward expansion and White settlement?
- What evidence remains of Native American culture that might contradict Western accounts of Indian life?
- What historical events suggest unfair or illegal treatment of Indians by White Americans and their governments?

A third step in this exercise is to examine a piece of literature or other cultural text that relates thematically to the cultural and political conflict existing between White and Indian societies. Through an examination of a specific literary text, students can address a set of literary questions that illuminate its surrounding history. The following might illustrate the kinds of critical questions that students would have:

- What does a literary work like Louise Erdrich's *Tracks* tell us about attempts to preserve Native American culture, or about the contact zone between traditional Native beliefs and Christianity, or about the conflict between White and Native perspectives on land use?
- How do these accounts, told by Native and mixed-blood narrators, cause us to see both White and Native perspectives in ways that offer alternatives to the conventional White histories of the upper midwest in the early 20th century?
- In the end, how does this novel force a reexamination of previous histories of this time and place?

Students could begin a historical reassessment by discussing the ways in which history should be informed by this novel:

- What would happen if the history of White settlements in early 20th-century North Dakota were to privilege a Native perspective over a broader American ideological framework?
- What can a literary work, and especially its narrative structure, tell us about the shaping forces of history of U.S.–Native American relations?
- And what other cultural artifacts or representations might be brought forward for further examination of this historical inquiry? What might these artifacts reveal to us?

And finally, students can read historical documents alongside fiction, poetry, and art to create different interpretations of historical events (see Appendix, Activities 22–23).

CONCLUSION

As a result of this changing view of history, literary critics have looked at the relationship between history and literature as reciprocal. Literature may not change historical events, but it can change how we read history. In other words, in the same way that history shapes literature, literature shapes history. And while the traffic along this street may at first seem difficult to comprehend, there is good evidence that each brings its passengers to the other destination. If we understand history to be a cultural product shaped by a society's beliefs, values, and intentions, then we see that it is not as different from literature as we might at first believe. This means that in our literature classrooms, we are teaching our students to read history along with the texts we assign.

SUGGESTED NONFICTION SELECTIONS FOR THE NEW HISTORICISM LENS

Martin Luther King Jr., "Letter from Birmingham Jail" (pdf available online)

David Kamp, "The Way We Were: Rethinking the American Dream" (*Vanity Fair*)

Sara Rimer, "Gatsby's Green Light Beckons a New Set of Strivers" (*New York Times*)

Elie Wiesel, "Hope, Despair and Memory."* (pdf available online)

Frederick Douglass, "What to the Slave Is the Fourth of July?"* (pdf available online)

FDR's Executive Order 9066 (pdf available online)

Tim O'Brien, "The Vietnam in Me" (*New York Times*)

John Grey, "A Point of View: Gatsby and the Way We Live Now" (BBC)

*Suggested Common Core Anchor Texts

CHAPTER EIGHT

Deconstruction

Postmodern Theory and the Postmodern High School Student

Between the unspeakable world and the text that will never shut up, where are we?

—Robert Scholes

Deconstruction is dumb. It's people who want to feel important trying to destroy meaning.

—Tim, Grade 12

The words fall over themselves, trying to assemble into a meaning that even the author doesn't believe in.

Annie, Grade 11, on reading *The Things They Carried*

There is a music video that is relevant to the consideration of postmodern theory in the secondary classroom. The singer is Natalie Umbruglia, and the video is for the song "Torn," which was on the top 10 list for several weeks after its release in 1997. In the video, as in many music videos these days, the singer acts out a tortured and doomed relationship with a handsome male model pretending to be her boyfriend. They pace around a set designed to look like a 20- or 30-something's apartment right out of a TV sitcom.

The premise for the video is a familiar one—two young people trying to figure out what happened to their once passionate relationship. Familiar, too, are the sunken eyes, flat bellies (heroin chic), khaki pants, and a melodic lament. But something is very different about this particular video.

As the singer proceeds with her song, construction workers arrive and begin to disassemble the set, taking it apart, *deconstructing* the "apartment" piece by piece, revealing it to be nothing more than a bare sound stage. The viewer then realizes the pretense of the assumptions on which the video is based. Similarly, the singer and the actor playing her boyfriend step out of their respective roles, revealing themselves to be two disconnected and unrelated people pretending to care about each other for the purposes of selling a CD. In a remarkably self-reflexive move, the video dissembles and the layers of pretense and the artifice of the music business are stripped away.

The willing suspension of disbelief that readers and viewers willingly engage in as we enter a constructed world of a cultural artifact—be it a poem, a short story, a novel, a magazine article, a film, or a music video—is revealed, interrogated by the structure of the video itself. This re-examination of the constructs of the music video can serve as an interesting starting point for adolescents and deconstruction. After all, deconstruction invites us to "unravel" the constructs that surround us and to re-examine the relationships between appearance and reality.

DEFINING DECONSTRUCTION: AN EXERCISE IN FUTILITY?

Even those literature teachers who may be well versed in some of the other critical lenses we've discussed to this point may shudder at the notion of teaching deconstruction. Because it challenges the very iconic nature of the high school curriculum and the fixed meanings that have been assigned to canonical texts, it is a lens that most secondary language arts teachers have avoided. Another impediment: as Lois Tyson (2006) points out, major proponents of deconstruction—such as Jacques Derrida, as well as their "translators"—often attempt to explain the basic principles of the theory in language that is alienating and difficult. Finally, deconstruction has frequently been misunderstood as a destructive methodology, one that ruins our love and appreciation of literature with a superficial and trivial attack that amounts to nothing more than academic wordplay (Tyson, 2006).

What *is* deconstruction and why does it inspire both fear and loathing? Here is one deconstructionist's hypothesis:

> Perhaps deconstruction has fired fear in people because it is difficult to define, and what cannot be defined cannot be pinned down and labeled; yet here lies the productive energy of deconstruction. In the very difficulty of naming and defining deconstruction, in the slipperiness of language that refuses to be pinned easily, deconstruction demonstrates and represents an understanding of language as vibrant and creative, opening up possibilities for meaning making. (Leggo, 1998, p. 186)

Despite his claim that it is difficult to define deconstruction, Leggo (1998) proceeds to offer a clear and lucid explication:

> Deconstruction is a practice of reading that begins with the assumption that meaning is a textual construction. Perhaps even more useful than the noun "construction" is the verb "constructing" because deconstruction is a continuous process of interacting with texts. According to deconstruction, a text is not a window a reader can look through in order to see either the author's intention or an essential truth, nor is the text a mirror that turns back a

vivid image of the reader's experiences, emotions, and insights. Instead, deconstruction is a practice of reading that aims to make meaning from a text by focusing on how the text works rhetorically, and how a text is connected to other texts as well as the historical, cultural, social, and political contexts in which texts are written, read, published, reviewed, rewarded, and distributed. (p. 187)

Deconstruction seeks to show that a literary work is usually self-contradictory. As J. Hillis Miller (1989) explains, "Deconstruction is not a dismantling of the structure of a text, but a demonstration that it has already dismantled itself. Its apparently solid ground is no rock but thin air" (p. 199).

In other words, a reader does not destroy or "dismantle" a text. She or he uses the interpretive strategies of deconstruction to reveal how a text unravels in self-contradiction. The source of those contradictions lies in the instability of language, the "undecidability" of meaning, and the ideologies that are often unconsciously revealed in the text. Appignanesi and Garratt (1995) emphasize this aspect of unintended meaning:

Deconstruction is a strategy for revealing the underlayers of meaning in a text that were suppressed or assumed in order for it to take its actual form. . . . Texts are never simply unitary but include resources that run counter to their assertions and/or their authors' intentions. (p. 80)

As Barnet (1996) puts it, deconstructionists "interrogate a text and they reveal what the authors were unaware of or thought they had kept safely out of sight" (p. 123). Barnet also offers a definition of deconstruction that is accessible to high school students:

[Deconstruction is] a critical approach that assumes that language is unstable and ambiguous and is therefore inherently contradictory. Because authors cannot control their language, texts reveal more than their authors are aware of. For instance, texts (like some institutions as the law, the churches, and the schools) are likely, when closely scrutinized, to reveal connections to society's economic system, even though the authors may have believed they were outside of the system. (p. 368)

Here is another good explanation of deconstruction, an explanation that also appears on the deconstruction handout (Appendix, Activity 24) that forms the heart of the lesson described in this chapter:

Deconstructionist critics probe beneath the finished surface of a story. Having been written by a human being with unresolved conflicts and contradictory emotions, a story may disguise rather than reveal the underlying anxieties or perplexities of the author. Below the surface, unresolved tensions or contradictions may account for the true dynamics of the story. The story may have one message for the ordinary unsophisticated reader and another for the reader who responds to its subtext, its subsurface ironies. Readers who deconstruct a text will be "resistant" readers. They will not be taken in by what a story says on the surface but will try to penetrate the disguises of the text . . . . They may engage in radical rereading of familiar classics. (Guth & Rico, 1996, p. 366)

"Radical re-readings of familiar classics" and resistance to what a story says on the surface are consistent with the original aims of deconstruction. For example, Johnson and Ciancio (2008) offer a lesson on how to deconstruct the power relationships in *Othello*. Yet, it is easy to jump to an oversimplified conclusion that deconstruction means nothing more than to "take apart" or "analyze." The term is now stripped of its once radical sheen. *Deconstruction* seems to be used and overused by pundits and commentators and CNN reporters, as in "Let's deconstruct what happened during Hurricane Katrina," or, "Let's deconstruct this film." But these commentators don't unbuild or systematically examine the underlying constructs of, say, a political system or a leader or the ideology of a country or the motifs and conventions (binary or otherwise) that are presented in a film. They simply analyze their subject for its "deeper meaning," a move the deconstructionists abandoned. Deconstruction is a particular kind of unbuilding, one that takes into account the very nature, weight, and composition of the bricks or constructs it dismantles.

As Moore (1997) points out, many have confused *deconstruction* with *destruction*, a confusion that could be amplified by a careless use of the video that opened this chapter. Deconstruction is not a mindless dismantling; it is a mindful one. It is not destruction; it is de-*construction*. It is not, as Barbara Johnson (1981, p. xiv) has pointed out, "a kind of textual vandalism." While deconstructionists discount particular sources of meaning, such as the binary oppositions of the structuralist or the notion that a text can have a single, fixed meaning, it does not assert that literature, or the study of literature for that matter, is meaningless. Rather, it posits that a text will yield multiple meanings, depending on the ways in which an individual reader may attempt to resolve the ambiguities and inconsistencies in the text.

Murfin (1989) points out that, despite its difficulty, there is something almost irresistible about deconstruction:

Deconstruction has a reputation for being the most complex and forbidding of contemporary critical approaches to literature, but in fact almost all of us have, at one time, either deconstructed a text or badly wanted to deconstruct one. Sometimes, when we hear a lecturer effectively marshal evidence to show that a book means primarily one thing, we long to interrupt and ask what he or she would make of other, conveniently overlooked passages that seem to contradict the lecturer's thesis. Sometimes, after reading a provocative critical article that almost convinces us that a familiar work means the opposite of what we assumed it meant, we may wish to make an equally convincing case for our old way of reading the text. It isn't that we think that the poem or novel in question better supports our interpretation; it's that we think the text can be used to support both readings. And sometimes we simply want to make that point that texts can be used to support seemingly irreconcilable positions. (p. 199)

WHY ADOLESCENTS NEED DECONSTRUCTION

Despite the natural appeal of deconstruction that Murfin describes, the utility of deconstruction is fiercely debated even within literary circles. Even those who are firmly convinced of the usefulness of other kinds of literary theory readily dismiss deconstruction as both frivolous and difficult. Like a theoretical house of cards, deconstruction is easily dismantled. It is often accompanied or practiced with a cynical, dismissive, and even contemptuous tone. Barnet (1996) complains:

> The problem with deconstruction, however, is that too often it is reductive, telling the same story about every text—that here, yet again, and again, we see how a text is incoherent and heterogeneous. There is, too, an irritating arrogance in some deconstructive criticism: "The author could not see how his/her text is fundamentally unstable and self-contradictory, but _I_ can and will issue my report." (p. 123)

Others view deconstruction as passé, no longer a relevant or startling literary or theoretical enterprise the way it was when it crashed on the scene in the late 1960s and really took hold in the academy in the 1970s. In fact, in her _A Teacher's Introduction to Deconstruction,_ Sharon Crowley (1989, p. 24) quotes newspaper clipping declaring that deconstruction is in fact "dead."

So, why should something so peripherally relevant even within the esoteric world of literary criticism be seen as something important for today's adolescents?

As argued in Chapter 1, contemporary adolescents are faced with a bewildering and confusing world, one that presents them with a dizzying array of social and psychological constructs, some as benign perhaps as the "Torn" video, with which this chapter began, others more potentially destructive. Some have argued, in fact, that adolescence itself is a complicated and often cruel construct of our post-industrial society. As Moore (1998) points out, in an argument for the relevance of semiotics to adolescents:

In adolescence students read the world that is represented to them, but they also socially construct a world in which they want to live, one that creates the identity they desire in the difficult landscape between childhood and adulthood. (p. 211)

Moore quotes T. McLaughlin who emphasizes the necessity of theory in the classroom. It is "equipment for post-modern living" (p. 212), and he contends that students are ready for it. They are adept at reading the artifacts of their culture, a culture which "values image over reality, which has replaced product with information" (p. 218).

Reading this postmodern culture requires that we reconsider which artifacts or elements of culture actually can and should be read. In other words, we must refine "texts" to include a variety of forms, both print and nonprint, literary and nonliterary. While the expansion of the concept of text can clearly accompany any of the previous lenses we discussed, and is indeed a requisite part of these critical encounters, it seems especially useful to redefine the concept of text through the lens of deconstruction. The interrogation of the meaning of *text* is a requisite part of deconstruction:

> For many deconstructionists, the traditional conception of literature is merely an elitist "construct." All "texts" or "discourse" (novels, scientific papers, a Kewpie doll on the mantle, watching TV, suing in court, walking the dog, and all other signs that human beings make) are of a piece; all are unstable systems of "signifying," all are fictions, all are "literature." (Barnet, 1996, p. 124)

In his invitation to English teachers to rethink the school subject of "high school English," Bruce Pirie (1997) points out that English teachers must learn to redefine texts and refocus the objects of study in our classroom to include the artifacts of popular culture and to learn to read them as texts. As Garth Boomer (1988) argues, "if the profession of English studies and English [instruction] is to survive and have any relevance for our students at all, we need to expand our idea of texts to include the multivariate multimedia stimuli that surround them" (p. 102). Pirie quotes Boomer:

> Once "text" is conceived of as a cultural artifact, any text, past or present, classic or popular, fiction or non-fiction, written, oral or filmic, can be admitted to the English classroom for legitimate and regarding scrutiny, from the standpoint of "Who made this? In what context? With what values? In whose interest? To what effect?" (Boomer, 1988, as quoted in Pirie, 1997, p. 17)

It is not only for the survival of our profession but for the survival of adolescents as well that our students, now perhaps more than ever before, need critical tools to read the increasingly bewildering and text-filled world that surrounds them. Those texts can range from the literary to a galaxy of artifacts in the external world. As the students in Martha's class recently pointed out—we met Martha in Chapter 3 as we were studying reader response—texts can include the following: video, TV commercial, billboard, newspaper, magazine, facial expressions.

Adolescents are often, as psychologist William Perry (1970) points out, excessively dualistic in their thinking, which prevents them from being able to imagine, let alone sustain, multiplicity of thought. The dismantling of binaries, which is a requisite part of the deconstructive move, helps adolescents see the limits of binary thinking. According to Terry Eagleton (1983):

> Deconstruction, that is to say, has grasped the point that the binary oppositions with which classical structuralism tends to work represent a way of seeing typical of ideologies. Ideologies like to draw rigid boundaries between what is acceptable and what is not, between self and non-self, truth and falsity, sense and nonsense, reason and madness, central and marginal, surface and depth. Such metaphysical thinking, as I have said, cannot simply be eluded: we cannot catapult ourselves beyond this binary habit of thought into an ultra-metaphysical realm. But by a certain way of operating upon texts—whether "literary" or "philosophical"—we may begin to unravel these oppositions a little, demonstrate how one term of an anti-thesis secretly inheres within the other. Structuralism was generally satisfied if it could carve up a text into binary oppositions and expose the logic of their working. Deconstruction tries to show how such oppositions, in order to hold themselves in place, are sometimes betrayed into inverting or collapsing themselves or the need to banish to the text's margins certain niggling details which can be made to return and plague them. (p. 133)

The unraveling of the binary oppositions also helps unravel the ideology that set those polarities into motion and supported their production. For Jaques Derrida (1989), it is through the dismantling of false binaries that we see the limitations of the ideology they were constructed to support. Deconstruction is often viewed as ultimately antiauthoritarian, a stance needed by those oppressed, as Roland Barthes noted (1981), by the overbearing and oppressive systems around them. Bonnycastle (1996) explains: "Deconstruction is often talked about as though it were primarily a critical method, but it is best understood as a way of resisting the authority of someone or something that has power over you" (p. 112).

This antiauthoritarian aspect of deconstruction has natural appeal for adolescents. But rather than simply stoking their rebellious fires, deconstruction provides adolescents with interpretive tools for critiquing the ideology that surrounds them. It teaches them to examine the very structure of the systems that oppress them, and, in doing so, to intellectually dismantle them, thus making them rebels *with* a cause.

The interpretive openness and flexibility of deconstruction is also appealing to adolescents. In the sense of multiplicity, the appeal is similar in some ways to deconstruction's sloppier cousin, reader response:

> What is especially commendable about deconstruction as an approach for responding to poetry is that readers, especially young readers in classrooms, do not have to be unnerved by self-deprecating fears that their responses to a poem are wrong. Instead of right and wrong answers, deconstruction encourages plural responses. Instead of a hidden meaning that must be revealed, the poetic text is a site where the reader's imagination, experience, understanding, and emotions come into play in unique performances. (Leggo, 1998, pp. 187–188)

Finally, Tyson (2006, p. 240) explains what deconstruction offers readers: "It can improve our ability to think critically and to see more readily the ways in which our experience is determined by ideologies of which we are unaware because they are built into our language."

INTRODUCING DECONSTRUCTION TO ADOLESCENTS

In addition to the music video that begins this chapter, I have found a couple of other ways to introduce deconstruction to secondary students. Sometimes I begin by projecting or passing around a picture of the pop singer Michael Jackson. After the inevitable snickers of discomfort, I ask students to consider why it is that Michael Jackson is so hard to . . . comprehend. He seems to vacillate among several different pairs of constructs: He seems both male and female (I once saw him on TV and thought he was Latoya!); he seems both childlike and adult; and he seems, given a series of plastic surgeries and skin lightening, both Black and White. Michael Jackson is difficult to understand because he straddles the binaries that deconstructionists claim we have created precisely so that we *can* see things. Michael Jackson is a walking example of deconstruction!

I've also used the animated film *Shrek* to introduce deconstruction. As with much postmodern fiction, *Shrek* is a text that does some deconstructive work for us. Besides troubling the archetypal categories of hero/villain, protagonist/antagonist, prince/monster, and princess/heroine, the film deconstructs contemporary notions of beauty and femininity. It also very strategically calls the viewer's story grammar (Applebee, 1978) by beginning the movie with an evocative leather-bound text and ending with a page that calligraphy proclaims "They lived *ugly* ever after." These images act as bookends that present the film as a fairy tale, but one that dissembles our usual assumptions about both character and narrative structure.

Students can also apply several critical lenses to *Shrek*, including deconstruction (see Appendix, Activity 32).

DECONSTRUCTION IN THE LITERATURE CLASSROOM: ONE APPROACH

Once students are introduced to the concept of deconstruction, we are ready to apply it to literature. Many of the definitions offered in the previous section seem understandable to adolescents. I incorporated these definitions into Activity 24 in the Appendix. Many teachers and I have found that when students are allowed to absorb, discuss, and then paraphrase the definitions, they are well on their way to a fairly solid understanding of this difficult concept.

The lesson itself is designed as a kind of heuristic device, first taking students through an explanation of deconstruction, then proceeding to deconstruct some common metaphors and John Donne's poem "Death Be Not Proud," a widely anthologized work that many students may have encountered previously. Finally, either working alone or in small groups, they deconstruct a text of their own. This particular exercise focuses on the aspect of deconstruction that invites us to consider the fact that language is slippery and imperfect, or, as one teacher I know describes it, "Words wiggle."

To underscore the idea of words wiggling, we considered the following commonly used metaphors:

- Love is a rose
- You are the sunshine of my life
- The test was a bear

If, as the deconstructionists argue, language reflects our own imperfection and the fact that words do wiggle, then metaphors may not have the effect the poet intended. Therefore, I asked students to "unpack" the metaphors and describe both the intended and unintended meaning. This exercise also serves as a warm-up for the next section, which asks students to deconstruct John Donne's "Death Be Not Proud."

The value of having students deconstruct a familiar and frequently taught poem is described succinctly by Guth and Rico (1996) in their introduction to a deconstructive reading of Wordsworth's "A Slumber Did My Spirit Seal":

> The following much anthologized poem is accompanied by a deconstructionist reading that clears away much of the apparent surface meaning of the poem. The critic then discovers a new and different dimension of meaning as the language used by the poet dances out its own significance. (p. 863)

As with the deconstructive reading of the Wordsworth classic, the intent of this part of the deconstruction exercise is to help students see how the commonly understood reading of a widely anthologized poem can unravel through the tools of deconstructive analysis. The analysis we used did not employ the deconstruction of the false binaries that Derrida originally offered. Rather, it focuses on Barthes' notions of the "shifting meanings in the weave of the written text" (Moore, 1997, p. 77). Other critics have referred to the shifting and unstable nature of the meaning of a literature text as "undecidability." As Tyson (2006, p. 252) explains, "To reveal a text's undecidability is to show that the 'meaning' of the text is really an indefinite, undecidable, plural, conflicting array of possible meanings, and that the text, therefore, has no meaning, in the traditional sense of the word, at all."

In Activity 24 in the Appendix, I ask students to contrast the author's intended meaning and the tools of traditional literary analysis with the consideration of how the poem might break down and work against the poet's intentions. They are also invited to consider places where the text falls apart, where the threads of meaning begin to unravel. The students attended to inherent contradictions in the poem and noted some of its internal inconsistencies. Here are some of their observations:

> The poem breaks down when he offers that the only way to never have to face death is to die.

> The poem is very contradictory. Donne attempts to dissect death and make it smaller, but the contradictions in the poem thwart the attempt and death ends up staying powerful and frightening.

> He is trying to console himself, not the reader, in this poem. I don't think he successfully manages to console either.

> Although the poet is trying to convey that we must fight off death, that we are stronger than death, we, and he, cannot deny our fate.

> The last line is completely indefensible. The punctuation also seems to add to confusion and may result in some unintended meaning.

The students then worked in pairs and reconsidered a reading on their own, using the heuristic device of the exercise with "Death Be Not Proud." The texts they chose to deconstruct were wide-ranging and included some of those in Figure 8.1.

For each text the students described their understanding of the author's purpose and then gave specific examples of how the text broke apart. Figure 8.2 is an example of how a student read against her own original reading to reveal possible conflicts in interpretation.

Finally, students offered some reflective comments on deconstruction:

Figure 8.1. Texts for Use with the Deconstruction Exercise

Novels and Plays	Poems
1984, George Orwell	"Bright Star, Were I Steadfast as Thou Art," John Keats
A Doll's House, Henrik Ibsen	
A Room of One's Own, Virginia Woolf	"Do Not Go Gentle into That Good Night," Dylan Thomas
Brave New World, Aldous Huxley	"I Saw a Chapel," William Blake
Catcher in the Rye, J. D. Salinger	"I Wandered Lonely as a Cloud," William Wordsworth
Heart of Darkness, Joseph Conrad	
Native Son, Richard Wright	"Kubla Khan," Samuel Taylor Coleridge
Of Mice and Men, John Steinbeck	
Romeo and Juliet, William Shakespeare	"My Papa's Waltz," Theodore Roethke
	"Ode to My Socks," Pablo Naruda
Sister Carrie, Theodore Dreiser	"Shall I Compare Thee to a Summer's Day," William Shakespeare
Snow Falling on Cedars, Dave Guterson	
The Age of Innocence, Edith Wharton	"Sonnet 18," William Shakespeare
	"The Executive's Death," Robert Bly
The Awakening, Kate Chopin	"The Road Not Taken," Robert Frost
The Things They Carried, Tim O'Brien	"The Universe," May Swenson
	"The Unknown Citizen," W. H. Auden
The Trial, Franz Kafka	"Traveling Through the Dark," William Stafford

Deconstruction is cynical.

Deconstruction is very hard to do. When I look at poems they do seem solid, with one main idea and no contradictions. It's extremely interesting, though. I'm going to keep trying, trying to see the contradictions.

Does deconstruction show flaws on the part of the writer or on the part of the reader?

I think that Tim O'Brien has written a story (*The Things They Carried*) that is at war with itself. In some passages he describes war's beauty and seems to love war, yet in other passages he claims to hate it. This is a war of themes. He hasn't decided for himself what he feels, so he puts his feeling on paper, using his emotions as truth and lying for evidence. He admits he can't decide how he feels many times, so I guess my main response is: If he can't decide, how can I, even? Who am I to say whether it is a love or war story?

Figure 8.2. Deconstruction Worksheet

Text: *The Awakening,* by Kate Chopin

When I **deconstruct** this text, here's what happens. I think the main idea the author/poet was trying to construct was:

This society's oppression of women is tragic, preventing their development and fulfillment in life.

But this construct really doesn't work. The idea falls apart. The language and construction of the text isn't able to convey what the author meant to convey. There are places in the text where it just doesn't work. For example:

In the opining island scene with the wives talking, Chopin wants to show how bored the women are (because they have nothing to do), but they end up seeming flighty and dull. Edna's suicide is supposed to be driven by society's oppression only, but her own weakness is very apparent as well.

So, in the end, even though the author meant the work to say

Edna was essentially the victim of an oppressive society.

it really said

Edna ended up killing herself; she had the option of living but just gave up.

(Optional) I'd also like to say that:

Kate Chopin probably had personal doubts that were involved in this book. Perhaps she saw herself in Edna and was attempting to justify her own failures through her.

Deconstruction reveals more than meets the eye. When viewed through the deconstructive literary technique, the main ideas, values, and beliefs of the author are revealed to be neither monstrous nor heroic. This view helps to understand hidden meaning not otherwise apparent.

On the whole, the lens of deconstruction works well with high school students. It seems especially compatible with their adolescent sensibilities, which are often characterized by a burgeoning iconoclasm. The students I worked with, for the most part, took readily to this lens. Yet there is a serious downside to using deconstruction. While all the other lenses we've discussed—reader response, gender, social class—meet with their share of resistance from individual students for particular reasons, the resistance to deconstruction seems especially poignant and potentially harmful. In considering the use of deconstruction, teachers should consider the following incident which occurred when I introduced deconstruction in Martha Hargrove's class. After reading the incident, teachers may want to proceed with caution.

THE DANGER OF DECONSTRUCTION: RACHEL AND HER PLEA

The school year is drawing to a close and the students in Martha's senior English classes have been introduced to a whole variety of critical lenses. It's a dream class—lively, bright, engaged, and a bit feisty. They've taken the class content seriously and have frequently challenged the usefulness and relevance of each theoretical perspective. But today will present a different kind of challenge. It is time to discuss deconstruction, one of the most difficult lenses of all.

The class thinks through the deconstruction handout. We read together the definitions of *deconstruction*. I try to keep the tone light—to keep us all from feeling overwhelmed. We're "playing with deconstruction," I say. We practice with metaphors (Appendix, Activity 24) and discuss intended and unintended meanings. We then consider Donne's' "Death Be Not Proud" and attempt to deconstruct it together. The previous week, these students had completed the AP test. This is probably important; we are not only deconstructing a traditional reading of the poem, we are in effect deconstructing the entire AP test and a particular way of interpreting literature.

The deconstruction exercise works well. Perhaps too well.

After we go through the entire lesson including a deconstruction of a reading of their choice (see the previous section, "Deconstruction in the Literature Classroom"), the students seem both comfortable with their understanding of deconstruction and, at the same time, unsettled by that understanding. They get it and they can apply it—but they hate it. They seem uncomfortable, as if they managed to chew something unpleasant without choking but now the aftertaste is killing them.

Jessica is the first to speak. She has always struck me as a remarkably self-possessed young woman, confident and self-assured. Her high school education will be over in 2 weeks; in the fall she is off to the University of Michigan. Jessica is pragmatic. She takes a no-nonsense approach to many things, including literary interpretation. She seems mostly reality bound—firmly located in the here and now. She is also quite bright and has been able to engage enthusiastically in the varieties of literary discourse we've explored.

Jessica has never been shy about speaking her mind. She's one of the "beautiful people," the kind of girl other girls love to hate; she is part of the "in" crowd. She has gravitas, the weight of popularity surrounding her. She is from a fairly well-to-do family and seemed somewhat resistant to the social class lens when we studied it (see Chapter 4). She appears to be having a relatively successful adolescence and somehow doesn't seem particularly vulnerable to the vagaries of deconstruction.

Today, however, she is positively wailing. "Why did you teach us this? I'm so sorry I know about this. How could you have told us about this? What are you trying to do—destroy us? How am I supposed to live with this knowledge? You've just demonstrated that everything we've learned up to this point has been a sham. Now what? Here I am at the end of my high school education, and now it seems as if everything I was trying to do is worth absolutely nothing. Nothing means anything. Is that what I'm supposed to believe? I feel as if all of my illusions have been torn down. And here we are left with nothing. What am I supposed to replace it with? It's not just what we've studied and how we've studied it—it's everything. Now I feel like everything I've done in school has been a big lie."

Martha and I are absolutely shocked and disturbed by this outburst. The class undertakes a metaphysical debate the likes of which I can't remember ever being a part of before. Sarah says that deconstruction should be taught at home, "We were going to find out all this stuff anyway, right? Better sooner than later."

The class erupts into a debate about whether deconstruction is indeed harmful to kids. No one, oddly enough, is debating whether it is true or not—only whether kids should learn about it. It strikes Martha and me as odd that the very students who generally make a very strong case for their full-fledged adulthood and the rights that go with such status are asking to have something be kept from them. It is not only during the class discussion that students' discomfort with deconstruction is evidenced. Although Jessica and Sarah bravely announced their issues with deconstruction in class, other students waited to confess their confusion in their journals. Kevin echoes Jessica's discontent in this entry from his reading journal:

Earlier this year, I wrote a paper on the literary lens of deconstruction and thought that I had a fairly complete understanding of the concept. I found out today that my understanding was not complete. I love it when I learn something new! I find literary deconstruction to be very thought-provoking but have unresolved conflict within me. I understand the concept of literary deconstruction, but isn't it destructive?

The meaning of any work is questionable, but if some meaning isn't assumed, will we ever get anywhere? I have always believed that assumption is the worst thing any human can do, but educated assumption is necessary for humans to survive. We must assume that the sun will appear every morning and disappear every evening. We must also assume that we won't spontaneously combust.

Assumption is necessary given human emotion. Assumption allows humans to feel comfort which helps them lead a contented life. If we didn't assume that the sun would rise in the morning, many would lead horrible lives. Many would constantly worry and suffer about the future. Yes, assumption is not 100% safe, but nothing in this world is. One can safely assume many things if one takes the time to research things. Those who fear assumption are those who will end up on Prozac and Valium. Mental stability thrives in comfort. Uncertainty does not create comfort.

Are Jessica and Kevin right? Is deconstruction too potentially destructive for adolescents? The challenge doesn't arise as a result of the students' inability to understand such a difficult and complex concept. Oh, they get it all right. The challenge arises because understanding the implications of this particular lens is extremely frightening to them.

Perhaps for Jessica the fragile and artificial constructs on which she's based her entire high school career have come crashing down on her. Perhaps the lens of deconstruction has helped her see that her own adolescence and the constructs she uses to define it may be as artificial and impermanent as the set of the "Torn" video.

Others have addressed this byproduct, as it were, of deconstruction:

> As we have seen, deconstruction asserts that our experience of ourselves and our world is produced by the language we speak, and because all language is an unstable, ambiguous force-field of competing ideologies, we are, ourselves, unstable, ambiguous force-fields of competing ideologies. The self-image of a stable identity that many of us have is really just a comforting self-delusion, which we produce in collusion with our culture, for culture, too, wants to see itself as stable and coherent when in reality it is highly unstable and fragmented. We don't really have an identity because the word identity implies that we consist of one, singular self when in fact we are multiple and fragmented, consisting at any moment of conflicting beliefs, desires, fears, anxieties and intentions. (Tyson, 2006, pp. 250–251)

> In my undergraduate English studies I was trained to look for meaning, like a beagle on the trail of a rabbit. The rabbit might twist and turn and hide, but if I persisted I could outwit the rabbit. Deconstruction reminds me that there is no plump rabbit seeking to avoid my capture and consumption. (Leggo, 1998, p. 187)

The reaction of Jessica and her classmates to deconstruction serves as a caveat to teachers considering using this lens with high school students. While the privileging of "the personal" in reader response and the anti-ideology stances of gender and social class theory seem to be developmentally appropriate for adolescents, deconstruction is intellectually more challenging and psychologically more frightening for students at this age.

In my experience, students have seemed uncomfortable with deconstruction. For the students described in this chapter, at least, deconstruction ultimately proved a somewhat dangerous tool for literary analysis, one that called into question the foundations of their personal identities and core beliefs. As Erik Erikson, James Marcia, Carol Gilligan, and other theorists have noted, adolescents follow a developmental imperative to construct an identity. The fragility and instability of identity construction during adolescence apparently makes the nihilistic nature of deconstruction too painful for adolescents to integrate. The students' ability to understand the theory was not in question. Rather, they just seemed too vulnerable to have their shaky foundations torn from under them. As Bonnycastle (1996) reminds us:

> If you go to deconstruction to find a set of values or a philosophy of life, you enter a world that is anachronistic and solipsistic—a world in which each person is essentially alone and cannot communicate with others, and social groups fall apart because they have no coherence. This, I think, is an almost impossible world to live in, but it is an interesting one to know about. (p. 115)

To be sure, high school students do, as Bonnycastle suggests, find the elements of deconstruction to be "interesting." And, despite its potentially nihilistic side effects, it seems to be worth teaching. Perhaps more than any other literary lens, deconstruction can inspire a particular kind of intellectual suppleness. Like the gender and social class theories, it requires the reader to read ideology. Deconstruction helps students question the certainty of meaning without relying exclusively on the personal lens of reader response. Like reader response, it requires the reader to be an active meaning-maker, but unlike reader response, with its sometimes sloppy overgeneralization and over application, deconstruction requires the rigor of a close reading.

Like the political prisms of social class and gender literary theory, deconstruction teaches students to resist surface meaning and to read ideology—two critical skills students need to become autonomous and powerful adults. It is what they need to make meaning in the world and to evaluate cultural norms and expectations so that they do not merely succumb to them. This is not only important for the interpretation of literary texts, it is essential to the skills of critical interpretation of the media that surround adolescents through print, video, and other new media. Lynn (2007) points out that "a deconstructive stance not only may help us anticipate some of the ways that even simple texts can be misread, it may also help us see what is being excluded or suppressed in a text" (p. 94). Deconstructing an ad for a "Hemingway cap" that plays on constructs of masculinity, Lynn points out that adopting a deconstructive stance encourages an acute alertness to rhetorical strategies and even the assumptions these strategies depend upon (pp. 94–95). This acute alertness contributes to helping young people become vigilant witnesses (hooks, 1994) as they learn to read and resist the ideologies inscribed in the texts that surround them. Students can also use deconstruction to read nonfiction as well (see Appendix, Activity 25).

In *Textual Power*, Robert Scholes (1985, p. 21) creates a metaphor for education. Students, he says, operate in an endless web of growth and change and interaction. As teachers, our task is "to introduce students to the web, to make it real and visible for them" and "to encourage them to cast their own strands of thought and text into this network so that they will feel its power and understand both how to use it and how to protect themselves from its abuses."

By introducing students to the power of deconstruction we may indeed put them at intellectual risk as they call everything into question. Yet with care and guidance, we may finally bestow upon them the "textual power" Scholes calls for by finally removing the artificial barrier between school knowledge and the knowledge that counts in the "real world." As Scholes (1985, p. 24) states: "We must open the way between the literary and verbal text and the social text in which we live."

SUGGESTED NONFICTION SELECTIONS FOR THE DECONSTRUCTION LENS

Tim O'Brien, "Telling Tails" (*The Atlantic*)

Annie Dillard, "Death of a Moth/How I Wrote Death of a Moth" (pdf available online)

Steve Almond, "Once Upon a Time, There Was a Person Who Said, 'Once Upon a Time'" (*New York Times*)

James Baldwin, "If Black English Isn't a Language, Then Tell Me, What Is" (*New York Times*)

Jonathan Swift, "A Modest Proposal" (pdf available online)

Bill Bryson, "How You Became You" (pdf available online)

Amy Tan, "Mother Tongue"* (available online)

Rudolfo Anaya, "Take the Tortillas Out of Your Poetry"* (pdf available online)

G. K. Chesterton, "The Fallacy of Success"* (pdf available online)

*Suggested Common Core Anchor Texts

CHAPTER NINE

Lenses and Learning Styles

Accommodating Student Plurality with Theoretical Plurality

> A man with one theory is lost. He needs several of them, or lots! He should stuff them in his pockets like newspapers.
>
> —Bertolt Brecht

Perhaps one of the biggest misconceptions about the use of literary theory with secondary students is that it is most appropriate for college-bound or AP students. Many teachers choose not to incorporate literary theory into their regular tracked classes because they assume that literary theory is both irrelevant and too difficult for their "average" students. In fact, nothing could be farther from the truth.

Literary theory is not just intellectual cake for adolescent cake eaters—those who are privileged by social status and other factors to have significant educational advantages. Because many of the theories deal with issues of power, students on the margin for particular reasons—ethnicity, class, ability—are often more receptive to the basic ideological premises of these theories than are their more privileged peers, who sometimes respond to theories such as gender and class as using the master's tools to dismantle the master's house.

In fact, kids on the margins seem to be savvier about theory. Many of them have been reading the world and its inequities for a very long time. They naturally challenge hegemonic beliefs as well as the status quo. They've been reading patterns of privilege and inequity their whole lives. As Luis Moll (Gonzalez, Moll, & Amanti, 2005) points out, these students actually have the "funds of knowledge" to apply their perceptions of the world to a literary text.

Lisa Eckert (2006) also believes that literary theory has a particular salience for reluctant learners. In *How Does It Mean*, she writes, "learning how to effectively argue for a particular interpretation is ideally suited for adolescent learners, whose behavior is often oppositional, anyway" (p. 9). Eckert (2006) argues that literary theory requires readers to take an active role in their reading and to become more engaged and involved readers.

> Introducing different theoretical approaches into the literature classroom en-
> courages students to consciously use everything they know to construct mean-
> ing from a text, and gain an understanding of what they are doing when they
> read and respond. They discover how they are constantly interpreting signals
> whenever they read, even though they may not be aware of doing so. (p. 8)

Similarly, Allen Carey-Webb (2001) makes the case that literary theory
makes literature seem more rather than less relevant for our students by
making robust connections between their lives and the literature they read.
He continues:

> It is not so much that our students need to be entertained—though some have
> seen it this way—but that they need to understand the purpose and meaning of
> what we are doing if we are going to succeed in keeping them engaged. (p. 159)

Thus, from both dispositional and motivational perspectives, literary theory
is well suited to a wide variety of adolescent readers.

This is true from a cognitive perspective as well. While there may still be
those who cling to the misperception that literary theory remains the province of the erudite and intellectual elite, or in the case of secondary students,
the definitively college-bound, that is simply not the case. Using multiple
perspectives to read and interpret literature doesn't require that students are
already operating at a certain level of intellectual flexibility; it is an instructional approach that actually helps increase that intellectual flexibility.

To be sure, readers need to be at least "formal operational" from a
Piagetian perspective. In other words, they probably need to be in at least
6th or 7th grade. As Lev Vygotsky (1978) reminds us, learners, regardless of
their ability or their initial predisposition, can learn practically anything if
teachers provide the appropriate scaffolding. This holds true for literary theory as well. With the appropriate guidance and prior knowledge, nearly all
secondary students can read and interpret texts from multiple perspectives.
In fact, most of the activities that accompany this book are constructed as a
kind of scaffolding to allow students of all abilities to participate. Let's look
at one of the activities as an example.

A SAMPLE "MAINSTREAM" LESSON IN MULTIPLE PERSPECTIVES

Activity 30 in the Appendix asks students to read a Gary Soto poem from
three different perspectives. I have worked with teachers who have used both
"Oranges "and "Ode to Family Photographs" for this lesson. First, teach-
ers use some of the introductory activities that are explained in Chapter 2.
Then, teachers offer students the Literary Perspectives Toolkit Handout (see
Appendix, Activity 4), which is specifically written to be accessible to students

with a wide range of abilities. Next, the teacher distributes a brief biographical sketch of Gary Soto. Finally, students read either "Oranges" or "Ode to Family Photographs," poems that are easily readable and comprehensible at the literal level yet are rich enough to yield multiple interpretations.

Ode to Family Photographs

This is the pond, and these are my feet.
This is the rooster, and this is more of my feet.

Mama was never good at pictures.

This is a statue of a famous general who lost an arm,
And this is me with my head cut off.

This is a trash can chained to a gate,
This is my father with his eyes half-closed.

This is a photograph of my sister
And a giraffe looking over her shoulder.

This is our car's front bumper.
This is a bird with a pretzel in its beak.
This is my brother Pedro standing on one leg on a rock,
With a smear of chocolate on his face.

Mama sneezed when she looked
Behind the camera: the snapshots are blurry,
The angles dizzy as a spin on a merry-go-round.

But we had fun when Mama picked up the camera.
How can I tell?
Each of us is laughing hard.
Can you see? I have candy in my mouth.

                          *   *   *

Oranges

The first time I walked
With a girl, I was twelve,
Cold, and weighted down
With two oranges in my jacket.
December. Frost cracking
Beneath my steps, my breath
Before me, then gone,
As I walked toward
Her house, the one whose
Porchlight burned yellow
Night and day, in any weather.
A dog barked at me, until

She came out pulling
At her gloves, face bright
With rouge. I smiled,
Touched her shoulder, and led
Her down the street, across
A used car lot and a line
Of newly planted trees,
Until we were breathing
Before a drug store. We
Entered, the tiny bell
Bringing a saleslady
Down a narrow aisle of goods.
I turned to the candies
Tiered like bleachers
And asked what she wanted-
Light in her eyes, a smile
Starting at the corners
Of her mouth. I fingered
A nickel in my pocket,
And when she lifted a chocolate
That cost a dime,
I didn't say anything.
I took the nickel from
My pocket, then an orange,
And set them quietly on
The counter. When I looked up,
The lady's eyes met mine,
And held them, knowing
Very well what it was all
About.
Outside,
A few cars hissing past.
Fog hanging like old
Coats between the trees.
I took my girl's hand
In mine for two blocks,
Then released it to let
Her unwrap the chocolate.
I peeled my orange
That was so bright against
The gray of December
That, from some distance,
Someone might have thought
I was making a fire in my hands.

The poems, the explanation of the lenses, and the biographical information are all written at a level that is accessible to most students. The skill of reading through multiple perspectives can be taught with students of a wide range of abilities; it is simply the choice of texts that needs to be modified. With students at a higher grade level or with more advanced reading or interpretive skills, one can teach a very similar lesson using a more complex text and more elaborated instructions and explications of the literary lenses. For example, I have used an activity very similar to the one discussed above. Rather than use a fairly accessible, or as some might argue elementary poem, we have used Kate Chopin's "The Story of an Hour" with a set of somewhat more elaborate instructions.

In sum, critical lenses can and should be used with a wide diversity of learners. The following cases, drawn from classrooms across the country with real students in diverse classrooms will help illustrate the range of learners that literary theories can reach.

Marcos

Marcos is a 10th-grader in the English class of Yvonne Sanchez. Yvonne teaches a Puente class in a community a few miles outside of Los Angeles. Puente is a program designed to encourage underrepresented students, especially Latino students, who hope to increase their college readiness. Nearly all of the students in her 10th-grade English class are native Spanish speakers. Yvonne readily admits to skepticism when she first learned about using literary theory with her specific student population at a Puente workshop. But, always adventurous, Yvonne decided to try.

She began by trying the lenses with one of the students' favorite poets, Gary Soto. Modifying the activity described earlier in this chapter, Yvonne had them read the poem "Oranges" from three different theoretical perspectives.

Marcos is a solid if not unusually engaged student; he generally receives Bs and Cs. English, he claims, is not his favorite subject. Marcos is reading exactly at grade level. He tends to read all of the work that is assigned but is not a particularly avid reader and rarely reads on his own for recreation. Marcos is a bit vague about his post-high school aspirations. "I'd like to go to college maybe. I'm just not sure it'll happen."

During Yvonne's lesson on using lenses with the poem "Oranges," Marcos, as with many of his classmates, was easily able to move from the consideration of gender roles and Latino machismo to considerations of class to reader-response associations of first loves. In the activity, Marcos seemed to move comfortably from one theoretical perspective to another. When he read the poem through a gender lens, he pointed out that the "boy was taking charge, showing off to buy his girl something he really couldn't afford. Like he's supposed to be the provider or something. Hey, it's what we're brought up to believe, you know, Latin men take charge. Hey, it's machismo!" Marcos then moved to a consideration of the poem from a social class perspective, the perspective about which Yvonne, like many teachers was the most dubious or wary (especially when it was labeled the "Marxist lens"). Marcos noted in class discussion that the boy in the poem "didn't even have enough money to pay for an orange. . . . He was probably poor or something. Actually I think they both were, because the poem takes place in a grocery store, not a store like Macy's or something. Like who's gonna to go to the corner grocery to buy your girl something in the first place?"

Marcos then moved, somewhat reluctantly, to the reader-response perspective. "Yeah, I mean, I can relate to wanting to give a girl something, though I wouldn't pick a dumb orange. That's for sure. And I guess I want my girl to think I can give her stuff. Um, I liked the ending, too, cause it seems (Marcos blushes) like, when you are with your girl, everything is, um, stronger, more intense, you know, like the sun was in the poem."

Encouraged by this initial success, Yvonne included theory-based activities throughout her year-long class, with canonical works such as *Romeo and Juliet* and more contemporary texts such as *House on Mango Street*. Marcos also used literary lenses as he read adolescent novels such as *The Giver, Monster,* and *Bronx Masquerade*.

In his final exam "reading the world" (see Appendix, Activity 34), Marcos writes:

> Using multiple perspectives broadens my ability to see all sides of the story. It keeps me from feeling personally victimized. It also says a lot about where you grew up economically and socially as well as what type of household you grew up in. It makes you realize where your life is now and why you are there.

In a personal interview, Marcos concludes:

> At first I thought the lenses stuff that Ms. S was teaching us was going to be too hard, but then I tried it and it wasn't that hard. She says this is the way people read poems and stories in college. Hey, I even think about it when I listen to lyrics and stuff. I tell Ms. S she ruined me.

As an experienced teacher of non-native speakers of English, Yvonne believes that lenses are appropriate for her students. "My bilingual kids are actually more adept at switching perspectives than are my English speakers. After all, switching language codes is a survival tactic for them, and we all know that when you switch from one language to the next you also switch perspectives."

Ayanna

Ayanna often thinks of herself as "a stranger in a strange land." She is the only student of color in Greg's AP Literature and Composition class that has 34 majority students. This demographic composition is reflective of the school as a whole, which enrolls fewer than 12% students of color. When Ayanna entered 9th grade, her family moved from their city neighborhood in Minneapolis to this suburb, well known throughout Minnesota for its high-quality school system, so that she could have a better education.

Although she is a successful athlete and generally well-liked by her peers, Ayanna feels as if the social ice she skates on is very thin, and she could "fall through at any moment." At lunch, she is like a social chameleon moving from group to group to try to fit in. Indeed, the climate around her sometimes feels as chilly as a Minnesota winter.

Issues of race come up on an almost daily basis for Ayanna and no more so than in English class, both because of the literature the class reads as well as the general themes that Greg likes to raise. For Ayanna, Greg's diverse curriculum is somewhat of a mixed blessing. Novels such as *Invisible Man*, *Their Eyes Were Watching God*, *Sula*, *Beloved*, *Adventures of Huckleberry Finn*, *Heart of Darkness*, and *Waiting for the Barbarians*, and plays such as *Othello* and *Fences* surely are more adventurous and diverse fare than one finds in most secondary classrooms (Applebee, 1993). At the same time, they also offer the opportunity and necessity, perhaps, for many difficult discussions and uncomfortable moments.

Ayanna used to feel that a giant spotlight would shine on her whenever issues of race were raised in class discussions. And, despite the atmosphere of politeness (referred to as "Minnesota nice") and the lack of overt racial comments, Ayanna often felt uncomfortable. Greg struggled, too. "I want us to be able to go beneath the surface of the texts," he confided, "but every time I see Ayanna's face in this sea of White faces, I can feel myself backing down. I don't want to put her on the spot or make her uncomfortable in any way. For everyone's sake, I wish our classroom were more diverse, but it isn't. And there are things we need to discuss, regardless of who is (and who isn't) in the room."

Somehow, for both Ayanna and Greg, the literary lenses, especially social power and gender, provide a way to discuss the issues more comfortably. The lenses not only move the focus away from her but provide a way to help her classmates see what she has always seen. In a personal interview she explains:

> I guess, as a person of color, I've always had to "read" what's going on in terms of people's attitudes toward race and stuff. I used to think it was just a personal lens, but now [I] see that some of the, like, more political lenses . . . provide a way of thinking about what's going on

in the world, not just what's going on with me. It gives us a way of talking about it that's, um, more, comfortable.

Ayanna remembers when her class read *A Raisin in the Sun* and *Their Eyes Were Watching God*. By using the postcolonial and social class lenses, her classmates were able to see particular issues in ways that were depersonalized and general. It moved the discussion away from Ayanna. The lenses brought issues of power and equity into sharp relief but in a different context:

> The lenses make me feel less isolated. I finally feel as if, being a person of color, I am at an advantage rather than disadvantage. The lenses help my classmates see what I've seen my whole life. This is how I see the world.

Jenny

Jenny is a 10th-grader at Lincoln High School, a comprehensive high school in an inner-ring suburb. At Jenny's school, the graduation rate is less than 70%, and the school has had difficulty meeting the Annual Yearly Progress (AYP) mandated by No Child Left Behind. Less than 60% of the student body attends college or some other form of postsecondary education as compared with the well over 96% who do so at Ayanna's school. Seventy-two percent of the students are White, and 28% are students of color, with the largest percentage of those being African American, followed by Asian, Latino, and Native American.

When Michael, Jenny's 10th-grade American Literature teacher, decided to infuse literary theory into his year-long course, both his colleagues in the English department and his students were mystified. "Isn't this college prep, AP stuff?" one of his colleagues challenged. "Why teach literary theory to students who aren't going to college?" Why, indeed?

Influenced by the work of Bruce Pirie, bell hooks, Robert Scholes and others, Michael believes that his obligation as an English teacher is to help his students become what Scholes (2001) calls "crafty readers." He believes that teaching students to read and teaching students to become able interpreters of literary texts are inextricably intertwined. His approach is what Hephzibah Roskelly has dubbed "an unquiet pedagogy" (Kutz & Roskelly, 1991).

Like Yvonne, Michael teaches all the theoretical perspectives to his students, regardless of what level English course they happen to be enrolled in. He simply modifies the explanatory material using the Literary Perspectives Toolkit (see Appendix, Activity 4) and, of course, considers his students' abilities and interests as he makes his text selections. Michael finds that with students like Jenny, applying the lenses with shorter texts such as short stories or poems seems to be a bit more successful than using it with whole texts, at least initially. Michael also finds that Jenny seems much more interested in applying the lenses to real-world situations than to literary texts.

Jenny is in good company with this preference. Robert Scholes (1985) remarks, "The relationship between the text and the world is not simply a fascinating problem for textual theory. It is, above all others, the problem that makes textual theory necessary" (p. 31). bell hooks (1994) concurs: "Being an 'enlightened witness' means becoming critically vigilant about the world we live in" (p. 60). Bruce Pirie (1997) also invokes the larger textual world that Michael finds students like Jenny can more easily engage:

> It is *not* that we shouldn't care about individual students and texts. We should, and I do. We also recognize, however, that students and texts are embedded in huge, living, sometimes contradictory networks, and if we want students to understand the workings of textuality, then we have to think about those larger systems. (p. 96)

Michael provides his students with several opportunities to apply the multiple perspectives that literary theory affords to everyday events. For both the gender and social class lenses, Michael invites students to consider real-world incidents that can be better understood or explained through a particular theoretical reading. For example, when she was asked to bring in a cultural artifact that needed to be "read" from a particular perspective, Jenny brought in a computer screen shot of a Victoria's Secret advertisement for swimsuits. The assignment asked students to "read" the cultural artifact as a text and to discuss the significance of it using a particular lens. Jenny wrote:

> I found a picture on the Victoria's Secret website while browsing
> through the swimwear. As I was looking at the different swimsuits
> they have to offer, I noticed something about every girl/picture. On
> each picture there would be a girl in her swimsuit with oil on her
> body, looking sort of seductive. Each girl on the entire website was
> extremely skinny. Then I thought about the gender lens, about the
> portrayal of women in society, and here's what I came up with. In
> order to sell their swimwear, they got the skinniest and prettiest
> models. Nowhere on their website, not one place, is there a plus-
> sized or even an average-sized woman. This suggests the idea that
> if they were to have an average- or a plus-sized model their product
> would not sell. Victoria's Secret is not the only place in the world that
> supports the message "skinny sells."

In a final assignment, entitled "From Reading Words to Reading the World: Critical Lenses in Literature and in Life" (see Appendix, Activity 34), Jenny was asked to consider a real-world event or issue and apply lenses to it. She chose to write about fights in the school hallway and described them thus:

> The psychological lens helps me interpret these fights very well. It brings up questions like: Are they scared? Do they enjoy it? Why are they doing it? Do they know what will happen afterwards? This lens increases our understanding by asking why. The gender lens also helps us understand fights. In our society, guys are taught to be "tough" and not take anything from anyone. They often resort to violence and think violence actually solves something, which is absurd. Gender lenses show us that males are more prone to fighting and the sexes are raised in different ways.

The assignment also asked, "How do you think the multiple perspectives can help you understand some things about yourself and your life outside of school?" Jenny responded:

> Being able to use these lenses and perspectives helps me be more open-minded about things. It helps me think about certain situations and events in more than one perspective. It allows me to learn more and think more in depth about issues that I haven't before. It's like taking a look at a picture and noticing something different.

The work of Jenny and her classmates demonstrate that literary theory is not an intellectual parlor game. Through her insights and engagement, she demonstrates that the reading and interpretive skills theory facilitates are just as accessible to, and important for, the large majority of secondary students, students whose worlds may or not include college, students who are ready and eager to read their world and are sometimes even better at it than their college-bound counterparts.

ON THE SUBWAY: CONVERSATIONS ABOUT DIVERSITY

In addition to providing conceptual interpretive tools for a wide variety of students, literary theory can also provide students (and their teachers) with ways to talk more easily and productively about issues of diversity, including race, class, and gender. Molly teaches 11th-grade English in an inner-ring suburban school. Although technically a suburb, like many inner-ring suburbs in the United States, Molly's district is really diverse. Nearly 40% of her students are nonmajority. Twenty-nine percent of all students are on free or reduced lunch.

Molly's classroom reflects the overall diversity of her community. In a building that is both overcrowded and sometimes full of social tension,

Molly wants to create an environment where the students feel safe enough to confront difficult issues in class discussions. She is grateful for the diversity of her classroom, but she also feels, as do many teachers, that it is precisely that diversity that makes such discussions difficult. "I want to teach with honesty and teach edgy stuff that brings up issues of race, class, and gender, but I worry about my ability to lead discussions on touchy issues, or even to ask students to read texts they might find offensive. There is always someone who might be offended," Molly says ruefully.

On the suggestion of a colleague, Molly decides to tackle the poem "On The Subway" by Sharon Olds.

On the Subway

The boy and I face each other.
His feet are huge, in black sneakers
laced with white in a complex pattern like a
a set of intentional scars. We are stuck on
opposite sides of the car, a couple of
molecules stuck in a rod of light
rapidly moving through darkness. He has the
casual cold look of a mugger,
alert under hooded lids. He is wearing
red, like the inside of the body
exposed. I am wearing dark fur, the
whole skin of an animal taken and
used. I look at his raw face,
he looks at my fur coat, and I don't
know if I am in his power—
he could take my coat so easily, my
briefcase, my life—
or if he is in my power, the way I am
living off his life, eating the steak
he does not eat, as if I am taking
the food from his mouth. And he is black
and I am white, and without meaning or
trying to I must profit from his darkness,
the way he absorbs the murderous beams of the
nation's heart, as black cotton
absorbs the heat of the sun and holds it. There is
no way to know how easy this
white skin makes my life, this
life he could take so easily and
break across his knee like a stick the way
his own back is being broken, the

rod of his soul that at birth was dark and
fluid and rich as the heart of a seedling
ready to thrust up into any available light.

—Sharon Olds

Molly is afraid of this poem—afraid to teach it, afraid it might offend and enrage her students, both Black and White. Yet it is this very fear that makes her think she should teach it. Its power and directness make her both shudder and smile as she considers how to approach it. After all, she teaches literature precisely because it is the mirror of human experience, in all its beauty and ugliness, precisely because reading literature offers a way to address important issues with adolescents.

Using the gender, class, reader-response, and formalist lenses, Molly divides the class into four, giving each a separate handout, a separate way into the text (see Appendix, Activities 22–25). The lenses offer a way of triangulating the subject so that students can address the issues without completely personalizing them.

The students meet in their theory groups for about 20 minutes, reading the poem through their assigned lens. Molly then moves them into a "jigsaw" configuration, so that in each group there is a student from each of the previous groups. Thus in each new group, every lens is represented. Molly is pleased as she walks around the room, which fills quickly with voices from each group—high-pitched, engaged, and exuberant. The small groups have allowed even the most reluctant of students to participate, and the lenses seem to offer a way to discuss the undiscussable without fear or embarrassment.

As a closing activity, Molly uses one of her favorite prompts, "What/ So What?" The prompt asks each student to respond to the following questions:

- "What?" (What was the poem literally about?)
- "So What?" (What is the significance or meaning in what you read? Why does it matter?)

Here are three students' responses:

Emma (White female)

What? Sitting across from a Black man on the subway, Sharon Olds discusses the implications of race in society.

So What? In a society where race and racial tensions are regarded as "risky," we must challenge ourselves to challenge our assumptions. Encountering our fear is the only way to overcome it. Literature provides a way for us to step outside our protective bubble into situations that are foreign and scary, and through these encounters embrace and accept our uneasiness as a way to overcome it.

Joe (Latino male)

What? Speaker differentiates himself from the Black man across from him. He leaves no room for gray. . . only black and white. He talks about his fear of him; the Black man's power is in violence. White power is in superior standing. He talks about class difference. He talks about how society promotes this. He talks about the persistence of the minority.

So What? The poem asks or presents the question: Are these thoughts and distinctions of race and gender present or latent in our minds? If so, are they supposed to be there? The "so what" of this poem is the importance of exploring whether or not it is morally wrong to make superficial distinctions. Are these distinctions even superficial? If we are thinking about them, should we keep them to ourselves or discuss them with others? In an age of political correctness, we have a booming responsibility to answer these questions.

Alicia (African American female)

What? A wealthy White woman sits across from a poorer Black boy and contemplates what he could do to her—and what she is doing to him by being White and well off.

So What? It is somewhat of a paradox in race and class relations that the author addresses. The White woman and the Black man are both holding each other hostage in some way—the man through the violence and crime that makes up his life, and the woman by her inherent ability to have money and power. It is a question as to which of these powers is greater—him taking her life by force or her gradually taking away his right to a prosperous life. The author doesn't give us any information that we don't already know about the tensions involved in race, class, and sex. But what this poem does is ask us what the next step is. It helps the reader decide whether it must always be like this (if society is stuck in a rut of prejudices and fear) or if there is room for balance and change. Instead of all new insights the author chooses to pose the questions of societal fate to her readers.

Molly is impressed with these responses. She knows there is a tendency to underestimate "average" students in "regular" classrooms, and she laughs off the skepticism of those who doubt her students' ability to read insightfully and through multiple lenses. Her literary gamble paid off, and she is emboldened to continue to use the lenses to help pave the way for such discussions.

Far from being the singular province of "advanced" students, literary theory, as we have seen from these cases, can serve the needs of diverse learners in diverse classrooms. With the possible exception of deconstruction (see Chapter 8), literary theory is accessible to all different kinds of students at many ability levels.

As we saw in the cases of Marcos, Jenny, and Ayanna, literary theory is not only within the reach of diverse learners, it can actually serve their intellectual and psychological needs. By modifying the difficulty of texts, and using some of the approaches suggested here, all students can enjoy the benefits of viewing both textual and actual worlds through the multiple perspectives that literary theory affords.

CHAPTER TEN

Critical Encounters
Reading the World

> To understand the craft of reading is to understand the world itself as a text and to be able to read it critically.
>
> —Robert Scholes, *The Crafty Reader*

> A better understanding of the world in which we live, it seems to me, automatically comes along for the ride when we study literature, and the study of critical theory makes that enterprise even more productive.
>
> —Lois Tyson, *Critical Theory Today*

> The world is like a huge novel that needs to be interpreted. It has a very broad and confusing plot with a variety of settings and many different cultures and themes.
>
> —Jesse, Grade 11

> Critical lenses are devices of interpretation. Just as they are used to interpret literature they can be used to interpret the world. A critical lens can be used to "read" the world because there is little, if any, difference between what is real and the literature it is customarily used for.
>
> —Carmen, Grade 12

It's a warm May Friday afternoon in St. Paul, Minnesota. The 5th-hour bell has just rung at Groveland High School. The usual formation of rows in Martha's literature classroom has been abandoned in favor of clusters of desks that today are called "learning stations." Over each station is a hand-lettered sign. One station has the name "Gender" over it, another says "Social Power/Class," another says "Reader Response," while another is called "Historical/Biographical." In addition to looking different today, the classroom also sounds different: The blues of Robert Johnson, Miles Davis, Billie Holiday, and Bo Diddley competes with the afternoon announcements for the students' attention—and the blues wins.

In groups of four, the students scurry from one station to the next, one minute considering feminist readings of Bigger Thomas's violence toward women, the next reading biographical data on Richard Wright and considering its relevance to the themes of *Native Son* (see Appendix, Activity

36). As they progress from station to station, the students recall the critical theories they have discussed all year. They adroitly apply and critique each theory. Their minds seem to shift as quickly as their feet as they move from among stations, creating multiple interpretations of an often taught classic of American literature, using contemporary literary theory to guide their way.

Later, in small groups, the students consider how these critical encounters enhanced their understanding of the text. They also evaluate the relative applicability of each lens to *Native Son*. This is no cookie-cutter exercise, no one-theory-fits-all approach. Martha knows that some students will assert that certain theories do not help their reading of this novel. She welcomes the dissonance because she also knows they will be able to explain why certain theories are more useful for particular texts than others. She welcomes the resistance because critical resistance has been something she wanted them to learn. She welcomes the multiple critical encounters her students had with *Native Son*. As she surveys her disorderly room, chairs askew and folders opened at each station, she is reminded of how messy and unpredictable critical encounters can be.

CRITICAL ENCOUNTERS WITH TEXTS

Critical encounters with literature, with the world, and with each other are at the heart of this "theory relay." These critical encounters also form the core of this book. Through the lenses of literary theory, the students and teachers that appear here transformed their study of literature into theoretical odysseys marked by significant critical encounters. Rather than simply covering literature as cultural content or focusing exclusively on the skills of reading and writing, these students and teachers used the lenses of literary theories to construct multiple ways of reading texts. Together they constructed and enacted a different kind of knowing in the literature classroom. As Cochran-Smith and Lytle (1993) remind us:

> We begin with the assumption that through their interactions, teachers and students together construct classroom life and the learning opportunities that are available. Essentially, teacher and students negotiate what counts as knowledge in the classroom, who can have knowledge and how knowledge can be generated, challenged, and evaluated. (p. 45)

Critical encounters with theory help students and teachers reevaluate what counts as knowing in the literature classroom. Contemporary literary theory helps students reshape their knowledge of texts, of themselves, and of the worlds in which both reside. In a special issue of *Theory into Practice* dedicated to the teaching of literary theory in the high school classroom,

Meredith Cherland and Jim Greenlaw (1998) remind teachers of the importance of teaching with theory:

> High school English teachers are under pressure to teach their students to read literature in ways that lead to more flexible formulations of meaning, in ways that are more relevant to their contemporary lives. . . . New forms of literary theory have useful applications in high school English classrooms and they support effective teaching practices in three different ways. First, literary theory has implications for *how people read*. Secondly, literary theory has implications for *what is read*. Thirdly, literary theory simulates the production of ideas and *discourages reductive thinking*. (p. 175)

In her introduction to *Critical Theory Today: A User-Friendly Guide,* Lois Tyson (2006) summarizes the importance of studying theory and how that study transforms what we mean by knowledge:

> For knowledge isn't just something we acquire; it's something we are or hope to become. Knowledge is what constitutes our relationship to ourselves and to our world, for it is the lens through which we view ourselves and our world. Change the lens and you change both the view and the viewer. This principle is what makes knowledge at once so frightening and so liberating, so painful and so utterly, utterly joyful. (p. 10)

Jack Thomson (1993) views contemporary literary theory as a way of helping students control texts, as a way of redistributing the interpretive power in the classroom:

> Too often our students see literary criticism as the practice of subordinating their human, ethical, and political reactions to some ideal of literary value. I think we have a responsibility to help them unravel and evaluate the themes and ideologies of texts they read rather than see them as some divine or secular authority. (p. 136)

Although many of the adolescents in the classes featured in this book were initially skeptical and viewed the lenses as simply another kind of analytical tool for finding the often predetermined, singular "hidden meaning" in literature, they eventually integrated the theories into their own interpretive repertoire and offered appreciative insights about the impact of theory on their literary understanding. The excerpts below are from the reading journals and final exams of several students, representing a range of abilities, educational contexts and backgrounds, who confirm that they found reading with theory created significant and meaningful critical encounters with texts. The students' own words demonstrate how theory became powerfully and positively integrated into their study of literature:

Critical lenses give opportunity to view literature in ways never thought of before and broaden the reader a little more to open up and see things in a different light. The lenses make the reader think.

Critical lenses allow us to look at something in different ways to understand what is taking place around us. If people look at things in different ways, it is possible to see the intent of other people and, in turn, [to] understand them.

It is sometimes difficult to grasp the meaning of a work through one's own eyes. One's experiences in life greatly influence the way one views the world around him; this most likely limits one's understanding of a piece of literature. Literary theories or critical lenses are tools that will open up many windows in one's understanding. They make the reader take on a different personality, with different views of society and [oneself], thus leading to a better, wider, clearer understanding of a work.

THE IMPORTANCE OF MULTIPLE PERSPECTIVES

Critical lenses are about looking into elements of the world in different ways, thinking about things from different perspectives. This will never be a bad thing, no matter what [they are] used to view. . . . Seeing many different sides of stories only benefits everyone.

—Joelle, Grade 11

Multiplicity, or the ability to "see many different sides of stories" as Joelle puts it, is central to the idea of teaching literary theory to adolescents. Students' ability to read texts, the world, and their own lives is enhanced not only by the study of individual theories themselves but also by the notion of multiple perspectives. In his impressive argument for using literary theory to read adolescent novels, John Moore (1997) quotes Henry Louis Gates Jr.'s apt metaphor for theory as prism, one that changes the entire nature of what is viewed when we view it through a different angle of the prism:

Literary theory functioned in my education as a prism, which I could turn to refract different spectral patterns of language use in a text, as one does daylight. Turn the prism this way, and one pattern emerges; turn it that way, and another pattern configures. (p. 187)

By viewing individual texts through the prisms of varied theories, students were able to construct multiple perspectives. Moore (1997) underscores the importance of literary theory in helping students learn to construct and sustain a plurality of perspectives:

We can help our students understand what it means to read literature differently if we value multiple readings (or interpretations) over a single authoritative reading. Literary theory helps us understand that there are many ways to know texts, to read and interpret them, but many secondary school teachers are unfamiliar with the changes that have occurred in literary theory over the last four decades. (p. 4)

This volume not only provides teachers with the tools they need to become more familiar with contemporary literary theory, it also emphasizes the value of multiple perspectives of multiple readings of texts. As I argued in Chapter 2, the ultimate pedagogical goal of teaching with theory is to facilitate students' ability to understand different perspectives. To that end, I encourage teachers to use several different critical theories with individual literary texts. With high school teachers and their students, I have developed variations on the kind of "theory relay" that opened this chapter. (For theory relays on *The Things They Carried,* see Appendix, Activity 31.) This relay helps students consider different critical interpretations side by side. In doing so, they become flexible thinkers, skilled interpreters, and are able to see, as Bonnycastle (1996) reminds us, that the problem of approaches to literature is really "a problem of ideologies" (p. 32).

READING WORLDS

Critical encounters with literary theory also help students to read the world around them. Teachers hope that students will be able to integrate successful strategies for learning in school and to adapt those strategies to life as well. As argued in Chapter 1, students need to learn to read the world around them in order to function as literate participants in an increasingly complex society. Jack Thomson (1993) has written, "All our regular institutional and social practices, including our social rituals and ceremonies, are texts to be read and interpreted" (p. 130).

In *The Crafty Reader,* Robert Scholes (2001) reminds us that, "The human condition . . . is a textual one and has always been so" (p. 78). Learning to read the world as text is an important result of high school literature instruction that includes theory. In a culminating activity called Critical Encounters: Reading the World (see Appendix, Activity 35), I ask students to bring in both artifacts and examples of personal experiences to see if they can use the lenses of literary theory to shed light on these artifacts and experiences. Teachers have used this activity as an assessment tool, a kind of final exam on how well students are able to apply the critical tools they have learned in their literature class to real life situations. Here are some items students brought in for cultural analysis:

- a variety of magazine ads, television commercials, and commercial webpages generally using beautiful, young, thin women to sell everything from toothpaste to milk
- a *People* magazine edition featuring "the 50 most beautiful people in the world"
- body piercing and tattoos (in some cases they offered up themselves)
- credit card ads
- military recruitment posters
- college view books
- music videos

In addition to these artifacts, students also shared particular individual experiences for cultural analysis, including some of the following:

- Quitting a part-time job because of perceived sexual harassment
- A misunderstanding between two friends because one couldn't inhabit the other's perspective
- Overhearing two male friends discussing how women can't be sportscasters because they are not good at it
- Fighting with a sibling over the car
- Listening to gossip and wondering why we do it
- Attending the homecoming dance
- Moving to another school

In groups and as whole classes, the students described how they used particular literary theories to understand these artifacts and incidents. Students offered analyses that were frequently acutely influenced by theories of gender, social power, postcolonialism, and reader response. They noticed, for example, dominant pink and red in print advertisements for sugar substitutes and described how women were visually drawn into the page. They scanned the *New York Times* and noticed the juxtaposition of ads for Cartier watches and luxury cars with articles about the endless cycle of poverty in our cities and around the world. They discussed the power structure of high school, including how power is enacted within their own relationships with peers.

Two teachers, in search of a concrete assessment of literary understanding in this standards-driven world, helped me create another culminating activity called "From Reading Words to Reading the World: Critical Lenses in Literature and in Life" (see Appendix, Activity 34). Here is a compilation of how some of their students, both urban and suburban, "regular" tracked and college-bound, responded to the two final questions, as shown below,

Question: *Now think of something you've heard about or seen outside of class that struck you as worth thinking about. Describe this event or issue and explain why it is important.*

- I think the Virginia Tech shootings were an important event in America history.
- Whether wearing a headscarf indicates oppression and radical Islam or a simple act of being close to one's religion/culture.
- The only time my mom and I have time together is when we are at the grocery store.
- Watching the news this morning, there was a story about underage drinking and how more and more frequently bars are serving alcohol to underage people.
- My parents getting divorced and my dad moving to Cleveland, Ohio. This is important because it changed both my mom's life and mine forever.
- There is a new immigration bill that is an unusual mix between Republican and Democrat views regarding Mexico.
- The new school policy that limits the number of excused and unexcused absences a student can have before being failed or dropped from a class.
- Finding a summer job. This is important because I need to start saving money for college and other stuff.
- The continuing war in Iraq.
- The fights in the hallways at school.
- The response or lack of response to poor people during Hurricane Katrina.

Question: *How do you think the multiple perspectives can help you understand some things about yourself and your life outside of school?*

- Multiple perspectives allow one to attack all aspects of a problem or situation, ultimately leading to an inevitably enhanced level of understanding of the predicament. In terms of myself, I can begin to develop my philosophical rationale, my set of beliefs, as I read literature and am exposed to others' thoughts. I also can apply my learning in this class to my life outside of school so I can understand others' opinions, especially those with opinions that clash with my beliefs.
- I think the multiple perspectives can help me understand how to look at the world through the eyes of a person other than myself. I get sick of just seeing the world through my sheltered eyes; I would like to be able to see every event in many different, opposing ways.
- I think sometimes we only look at things from our perspective because especially as teenagers we don't have a lot of other

experience and our main focus is ourselves. So sometimes we have to make a conscious effort to "put on" other lenses in order to see the different sides of a situation.

- Multiple perspectives allow me to pull away from the event, step back and just examine it before acting upon it. It's like thinking before you act. It can't really do much harm, it can only end up helping me to make better decisions in my life.
- We can use them in the world, and I think that's why we are taught that we've [been using some of] these lenses all along. We actually have a name for it now.

CONCLUSION

The last student comment in the preceding section reminds us that when we teach theory, we are, more than anything else perhaps, naming what it is that we naturally do. We all try to construct a framework or world-view to help us make sense of the seemingly disconnected events that confront us. Our place in the world is a theoried one. As Steven Lynn (2007) writes, "Whether we are aware of them or not, theories of some sort inevitably must guide our perceptions, our thinking, our behavior" (p. xiv). W. Ross Winterowd (1989), in his introduction to Sharon Crowley's book on deconstruction for teachers, makes the case even more strongly:

> Every English teacher acts on the basis of theory. Unless teaching is a random series of lessons, drills, and readings, chosen willy-nilly, the English class is guided by theories of language, literature, and pedagogy. That is, insofar as teachers choose readings and plan instruction, they are *implementing* a theory. The question, of course, is whether or not teachers understand the theory that guides their instruction. If we do not understand the theoretical context in which we function, we are powerless. (p. xiii)

Both teachers and their students have less power over their environment if, as Winterowd said, they do not understand the theoretical context in which they function. We may not be able to name our theories, nor are we always aware of how our ideologies (for that is what they are) become internalized and may in fact prevent us from understanding worlds and perspectives different from our own. We also may not be able to recognize an oppressive ideology when we are confronted with one, whether it's in a textbook, a tracking system in a high school, or in the workplace. The critical encounters encouraged by the approaches in this book will help us name our theories and consider multiple perspectives as we find our place in the texts we read and the lives we lead.

Classroom Activities

Note to teachers: Several of the activities include the original terms *Feminist* and *Marxist*, rather than or in addition to gender and social power/class. Teachers should feel free to adapt the materials for their classrooms.

Free printable PDFs of these Activities are available for download at tcpress.com

ACTIVITY 1

Little
Miss
Muffet

Russell Baker

One of the fascinating aspects of American English is its diversity, and one of the causes of this diversity is the specialized vocabularies of different occupations in America. Russell Baker's report of a conference dealing with Little Miss Muffet, taken from Poor Russell's Almanac, illustrates several varieties of occupational jargon.

Little Miss Muffet, as everyone knows, sat on a tuffet eating her curds and whey when along came a spider who sat down beside her and frightened Miss Muffet away. While everyone knows this, the significance of the event had never been analyzed until a conference of thinkers recently brought their special insights to bear upon it. Following are excerpts from the transcript of their discussion:

Sociologist: We are clearly dealing here with a prototypical illustration of a highly tensile social structure's tendency to dis- or perhaps even de-structure itself under the pressures created when optimum minimums do not obtain among the disadvantaged. Miss Muffet is nutritionally underprivileged, as evidenced by the subliminal diet of curds and whey upon which she is forced to subsist, while the spider's cultural disadvantage is evidenced by such phenomena as legs exceeding standard norms, odd mating habits, and so forth.

In this instance, spider expectations lead the culturally disadvantaged to assert demands to share the tuffet with the nutritionally underprivileged. Due to a communications failure, Miss Muffet assumes without evidence that the spider will not be satisfied to share her tuffet, but will also insist on eating her curds and perhaps even her whey. Thus, the failure to pre-establish selectively optimum norm structures diverts potentially optimal minimums from the expectation levels assumed to. . .

Militarist: Second-strike capability, sir! That's what was lacking. If Miss Muffet had developed a second-strike capability instead of squandering her resources on curds and whey, no spider on earth would have dared launch a first strike capable of carrying him right to the heart of her tuffet. I am confident that Miss Muffet had adequate notice from experts that she could not afford both curds and whey and, at the same time, support an early-spider-warning system. Yet curds alone were not good enough for Miss Muffet. She had to have whey, too. Tuffet security must be the first responsibility of every diner . . .

Book Reviewer: Written on several levels, this searing and sensitive exploration of the arachnid heart illuminates the agony and splendor of Jewish family life with a candor that is at once breathtaking in its simplicity and soul-shattering in its implied ambiguity. Some will doubtless be shocked to see such subjects as tuffets and whey discussed without flinching, but hereafter writers too timid to call a curd a curd will no longer. . .

Editorial Writer: Why has the government not seen fit to tell the public all it knows about the so-called curds-and-whey affair? It is not enough to suggest that this was merely a random incident involving a lonely spider and a young diner. In today's world, poised as it is on the knife edge of . . .

Psychiatrist: Little Miss Muffet is, of course, neither little or a miss. These are obviously the self she has created in her own fantasies to escape the reality that she is a gross divorcee whose superego makes it impossible for her to sustain a normal relationship with any man, symbolized by the spider, who, of course, has no existence outside her fantasies. Little Miss Muffet may, in fact, be a man with deeply repressed Oedipal impulses, who sees in the spider the father he would like to kill, and very well may some day, unless he admits that what he believes to be a tuffet is, in fact, probably the dining room chandelier, and that what he thinks he is eating is, in fact, probably . . .

Student Demonstrator: Little Miss Muffet, tuffets, curds, whey and spiders are what's wrong with education today. They're all irrelevant. Tuffets are irrelevant. Curds are irrelevant. Whey is irrelevant. Meaningful experience! How can you have relevance without meaningful experience? And how can there ever be meaningful experience without understanding? With understanding and meaningfulness and relevance, there can be love and good and deep seriousness and education today will be freed of slavery and Little Miss Muffet, and life will become meaningful and . . .

Child: This is about a little girl who gets scared by a spider. (The child was sent home when the conference broke for lunch. It was agreed that he was too immature to subtract anything from the sum of human understanding.)

ACTIVITY 2

Group Exercise for John Updike's "Separating"

Read John Updike's "Separating" on your own. Then, get into groups of three or four and work together on the following questions.

1. List all the characters that appear in the story.

2. From whose point of view is the story told?

3. Summarize the story from that character's point of view. That is, according to the character you named in Question 2, what happens in this story?

4. Now, pick another character from those you listed in Question 1. Summarize the story from the viewpoint of that character.

5. Reread the last two paragraphs of the story. Speculate together on what will happen next. Is there any reason to believe that Richard and Joan might not separate?

6. Extend the story. Write at least one page *from the point of view of the character you used in Question 4.*

ACTIVITY 3

A Matter of Perspective

Let's explore the notion of perspective. Much contemporary fiction violates traditional narrative expectations by telling the story from the perspective of a variety of characters, rather than from the perspective of a single protagonist.

1. Tell the story of "The Three Little Pigs."

2. Now, look at the children's book *The True Story of the Three Little Pigs, As Told by A. Wolf.* What differences does that switch in perspective make?

3. Think of a family story, preferably one that is retold often, a part of your family mythology. In a paragraph or so, tell that story from your own perspective. Write your version below.

4. Now, think of another family member, and retell the story from his/her perspective. Write that version below.

   Family Member: _____

5. In groups of no more than four, share those stories and discuss the difference perspective makes. How can we know what is the "true" version of the story?

ACTIVITY 4

Literary
Perspectives
Toolkit

Literary perspectives help us explain why people might interpret the same text in a variety of ways. Perspectives help us understand what is important to individual readers, and they show us why those readers end up seeing what they see. One way to imagine a literary perspective is to think of it as a lens through which we can examine a text. No single lens gives us the clearest view, but it is sometimes fun to read a text with a particular perspective in mind because you often end up seeing something intriguing and unexpected. While readers typically apply more than one perspective at a time, the best way to understand these perspectives is to use them one at a time. What follows is a summary of some of the best-known literary perspectives. These descriptions are extremely brief, and none fully explains everything you might want to know about the perspective in question, but there is enough here for you to get an idea about how readers use them.

Reader-Response Perspective: This type of perspective focuses on the activity of reading a work of literature. Reader-response critics turn away from the traditional idea that a literary work is an artifact that has meaning built within it; they turn their attention instead to the responses of individual readers. By this shift of perspective, a literary work is converted into an activity that goes on in a reader's mind. It is through this interaction that meaning is made. The features of the work itself—including narrator, plot, characters, style, and structure—are less important than the interplay between a reader's experience and the text. Advocates of this perspective believe that literature has no inherent or intrinsic meaning waiting to be discovered. Instead, meaning is constructed by readers as they bring their own thoughts, moods, and experiences to whatever text they are reading. In turn, what readers get out of a text depends upon their own expectations and ideas. For example, if you read "Sonny's Blues" by James Baldwin and you have your own troubled younger brother or sister, the story will have meaning for you that it wouldn't have for, say, an only child.

The Archetypal Perspective: In literary criticism, the word *archetype* signifies a recognizable pattern or a model. It can be used to describe story designs, character types, or images that can be found in a wide variety of works of literature. It can also be applied to myths, dreams, and social rituals. The archetypal similarities among texts and behaviors are thought to reflect a set of universal, even primitive ways of seeing the world. When we find them in literary works they evoke strong responses from readers. Archetypal themes include the heroic journey and the search for a father figure. Archetypal images include the opposition of Paradise and Hades, the river as a sign of life and movement, and mountains or other high places as sources of enlightenment. Characters can be archetypal as well, like the rebel-hero, the scapegoat, the villain, and goddess.

The Formalist Perspective: The word *formal* has two related meanings, both of which apply within this perspective. The first relates to its root word *form*, a shape of structure that we can recognize and use to make associations. The second relates to a set of conventions or accepted practices. Formal poetry, for example, has meter, rhyme, stanza, and other predictable features that it shares with poems of the same type. The formalist perspective, then, pays particular attention to these issues of form and convention. Instead of looking at the world in which a poem exists, for example, the formalist perspective says that a poem should be treated as an independent and self-sufficient object. The methods used in this perspective are those of close reading, a detailed and subtle analysis of the formal components that make up the literary work, such as the meanings and interactions of words, figures of speech, and symbols.

The Character Perspective: Some literary critics call this the *psychological* perspective because its purpose is to examine the internal motivations of literary characters. When we hear actors say that they are searching for their character's motivation, they are using something like this perspective. As a form of criticism, this perspective deals with works of literature as expressions of the personality, state of mind, feelings, and desires of the author or of a character within the literary work. As readers, we investigate the psychology of a character or an author to figure out the meaning of a text (although sometimes an examination of the author's psychology is considered biographical criticism, depending upon your point of view).

The Biographical Perspective: Because authors typically write about things they care deeply about and know well, the events and circumstances of their lives are often reflected in the literary works they create. For this reason, some readers use biographical information about an author to gain insight into that author's works. This lens, called biographical criticism, can be both helpful and dangerous. It can provide insight into themes, historical references, social oppositions or movements, and the creation of fictional characters. At the same time, it is not safe to assume that biographical details from the author's life can be transferred to a story or character that the author has created. For example, Ernest Hemingway and John Dos Passos were both ambulance drivers during World War I and both wrote novels about the war. Their experiences gave them first-hand knowledge and created strong personal feelings about the war, but their stories are still works of fiction. Some biographical details, in fact, may be completely irrelevant to the interpretation of that writer's work.

The Historical Perspective: When applying this perspective, you view a literary text within its historical context. Specific historical information will be of key interest: about the time during which an author wrote, about the time in which the text is set, about the ways in which people of the period saw and thought about the world in which they lived. History, in this case, refers to the social, political, economic, cultural, and/or intellectual climate of the time. For example, the literary works of William Faulkner frequently reflect the history of the American South, the Civil War and its aftermath, and the birth and death of a nation known as The Confederate States of America.

New Historicism: New historicism asks us to consider literature in a wider historical context than does traditional historicism. Unlike traditional historicism, new historicism asserts that our understanding of history itself is a result of subjective interpretation, rather than a linear objective set of events. New historicists also believe that it is not simply enough to understand the sociocultural and historical contexts in which a piece of literature was written; we must also consider how our own place and time in history affects our interpretations, since we bring to a text some perceptions, assumptions and beliefs that were not at play when the text was written. For example, the questions that we ask about how women are portrayed in Shakespeare's plays are shaped by contemporary feminist thought and the changes that women's roles in society have undergone in the intervening centuries since Shakespeare's era. New historicism then tells us that literature is influenced by history and that our historical understanding is also influenced by literature. The author, the reader and the critic are all influenced by our own cultural and historical location, and our understanding of, and appreciation for, particular texts will change over time.

The Social-Power Perspective: Some critics believe that human history and institutions, even our ways of thinking, are determined by the ways in which our societies are organized. Two primary factors shape our schemes of organization: economic power and social class membership. First, the class to which we belong determines our degree of economic, political, and social advantage, and thus social classes invariably find themselves in conflict with each other. Second, our membership in a social class has a profound impact on our beliefs, values, perceptions, and our ways of thinking and feeling. For these reasons, the social-power perspective helps us understand how people from different social classes understand the same circumstances in very different ways. When we see members of different social classes thrown together in the same story, we are likely to think in terms of power and advantage as we attempt to explain what happens and why.

The Gender Perspective: Because gender is a way of viewing the world, people of different genders see things differently. For example, a feminist critic might see cultural and economic disparities as the products of a "patriarchal" society, shaped and dominated by men, who tend to decide things by various means of competition. In addition, societies often tend to see the male perspective as the default, that is, the one we choose automatically. As a result, women are identified as the "other," the deviation or the contrasting type. When we use the gender lens, we examine patterns of thought, behavior, value, and power in interactions between the sexes.

Deconstruction: Deconstruction is, at first, a difficult critical method to understand because it asks us to set aside ways of thinking that are quite natural and comfortable. For example, we frequently see the world as a set of opposing categories: male/female, rational/irrational, powerful/powerless. It also looks at the ways in which we assign value to one thing over another, such as life over death, presence over absence, and writing over speech. At its heart, deconstruction is a mode of analysis that asks us to question the very assumptions that we bring to that analysis. Gender, for example, is a *construct*, a set of beliefs and assumptions that we have built, or constructed, over time and experience. But if we *de-construct* gender, looking at it while holding aside our internalized beliefs and expectations, new understandings become possible. To practice this perspective, then, we must constantly ask ourselves why we believe what we do about the make-up of our world and the ways in which we have come to understand the world. Then, we must try to explain that world in the absence of our old beliefs.

Literary Theories: A Sampling of Critical Lenses

Literary theories were developed as a means to understand the various ways people read texts. The proponents of each theory believe their theory is *the* theory, but most of us interpret texts according to the "rules" of several different theories at a time. All literary theories are lenses through which we can see texts. There is nothing to say that one is better than another or that you should read according to any of them, but it is sometimes fun to "decide" to read a text with one in mind because you often end up with a whole new perspective on your reading.

What follows is a summary of some of the most common schools of literary theory. These descriptions are extremely cursory, and none of them fully explains what the theory is all about. But it is enough to get the general idea.

Archetypal Criticism. In criticism *archetype* signifies narrative designs, character types, or images which are said to be identifiable in a wide variety of works of literature, as well as in myths, dreams, and even ritualized modes of social behavior. The archetypal similarities within these diverse phenomena are held to reflect a set of universal, primitive, and elemental patterns, whose effective embodiment in a literary work evokes a profound response from the reader. The death-rebirth theme is often said to be the archetype of archetypes. Other archetypal themes are the journey underground, the heavenly ascent, the search for the father, the Paradise-Hades image, the Promethean rebel-hero, the scapegoat, the earth goddess, and the fatal woman.

Gender/Feminist Criticism. A feminist critic sees cultural and economic disabilities in a patriarchal society that have hindered or prevented women from realizing their creative possibilities and women's cultural identification is as a merely negative object, or "Other" to man as the defining and dominating "Subject." There are several assumptions and concepts held in common by most feminist critics.

- Our civilization is pervasively patriarchal.
- The concepts of gender are largely, if not entirely, cultural constructs, effected by the omnipresent patriarchal biases of our civilization.
- This patriarchal ideology also pervades those writings which have been considered great literature. Such works lack autonomous female role models, are implicitly addressed to male readers, and leave the woman reader an alien outsider or else solicit her

to identify against herself by assuming male values and ways of perceiving. Feeling and acting.

This is somewhat like Marxist criticism, but instead of focusing on the relationships between the classes it focuses on the relationships between the genders. Under this theory you would examine the patterns of thought, behavior, values, enfranchisement, and power in relations between the sexes. For example, "Where Are You Going, Where Have You Been" can be seen as the story of the malicious dominance men have over women both physically and psychologically. Connie is the female victim of the role in society that she perceives herself playing—the coy young lass whose life depends upon her looks.

Social Class/Marxist Criticism. A Marxist critic grounds his theory and practice on the economic and cultural theory of Karl Marx and Friedrich Engels, especially on the following claims:

- The evolving history of humanity, its institutions, and its ways of thinking are determined by the changing mode of its "material production"—that is, of its basic economic organization.
- Historical changes in the fundamental mode of production effect essential changes both in the constitution and power relations of social classes, which carry on a conflict for economic, political, and social advantage.
- Human consciousness in any era is constituted by an ideology—that is a set of concepts, beliefs, values, and ways of thinking and feeling through which human beings perceive, and by which they explain what they take to be reality. A Marxist critic typically undertakes to "explain" the literature in any era by revealing the economic, class, and ideological determinants of the way an author writes, and to examine the relation of the text to the social reality of that time and place.

This school of critical theory focuses on power and money in works of literature. Who has the power/money? Who does not? What happens as a result? For example, it could be said that "The Legend of Sleepy Hollow" is about the upper class attempting to maintain their power and influence over the lower class by chasing Ichabod, a lower-class citizen with aspirations toward the upper class, out of town. This would explain some of the numerous descriptions you get of land, wealth, and hearty living through Ichabod's eyes.

New Criticism is directed against the prevailing concern of critics with the lives and psychology of authors, with social background, and with literary history. There are several points of view and procedures that are held in common by most New Critics.

1. A poem should be treated as primarily poetry and should be regarded as an independent and self-sufficient object.
2. The distinctive procedure of the New Critic is explication, or close reading: The detailed and subtle analysis of the complex interrelations and ambiguities of the components within a work.
3. The principles of New Criticism are basically verbal. That is, literature is conceived to be a special kind of language whose attributes are defined by systematic opposition to the language of science and of practical and logical discourse. The key concepts of this criticism deal with the meanings and interactions of words, figures of speech, and symbols.
4. The distinction between literary genres is not essential.

Psychological and Psychoanalytic Criticism. Psychological criticism deals with a work of literature primarily as an expression, in fictional form, of the personality, state of mind, feelings, and desires of its author. The assumption of psychoanalytic critics is that a work of literature is correlated with its author's mental traits:

1. Reference to the author's personality is used to explain and interpret a literary work.
2. Reference to literary works is made in order to establish, biographically, the personality of the author.
3. The mode of reading a literary work itself is a way of experiencing the distinctive subjectivity or consciousness of its author.

This theory requires that we investigate the psychology of a character or an author to figure out the meaning of a text (although to apply an author's psychology to a text can also be considered biographical criticism, depending upon your point of view). For example, alcohol allows the latent thoughts and desires of the narrator of "The Black Cat" to surface in such a way that he ends up shirking the self-control imposed by social mores and standards and becomes the man his psyche has repressed his whole life.

Reader-Response Criticism. This type of criticism focuses on the activity of reading a work of literature. Reader-response critics turn from the traditional conception of a work as an achieved structure of meanings to the responses of readers as their eyes follow a text. By this shift of perspective a literary work is converted into an activity that goes on in a reader's mind, and what had been features of the work itself—including narrator, plot, characters, style, and structure—is less important than the connection between a reader's experience and the text. It is through this interaction that meaning is made.

Students seem most comfortable with this school of criticism. Proponents believe that literature has no objective meaning or existence. People bring their own thoughts, moods, and experiences to whatever text they are reading and get out of it whatever they happen to, based upon their own expectations and ideas. For example, when I read "Sonny's Blues" I am reminded of my younger sister who loves music. The story really gets to me because sometimes I worry about her and my relationship with her. I want to support her in a way that Sonny's brother does not support Sonny.

New Historicism. New historicism asks us to consider literature in a wider historical context than does traditional historicism. Unlike traditional historicism, new historicism asserts that our understanding of history itself is a result of subjective interpretation, rather than a linear objective set of events. New historicists also believe that it is not simply enough to understand the sociocultural and historical contexts in which a piece of literature was written; we must also consider how our own place and time in history affects our interpretations, since we bring to a text some perceptions, assumptions and beliefs that were not at play when the text was written. For example, the questions that we ask about how women are portrayed in Shakespeare's plays are shaped by contemporary feminist thought and the changes that women's roles in society have undergone in the intervening centuries since Shakespeare's era. New historicism then tells us that literature is influenced by history and that our historical understanding is also influenced by literature. The author, the reader and the critic are all influenced by our own cultural and historical location, and our understanding of, and appreciation for, particular texts will change over time.

Other theories we'll be discussing in class include:

Deconstructionist Criticism. Deconstruction is, by far, the most difficult critical theory for people to understand. It was developed by some very unconventional thinkers who declare that literature means nothing because language means nothing. In other words, we cannot say that we know what the "meaning" of a story is because there is no way of knowing. For example, in some stories (like "Where Are You Going, Where Have You Been") that do not have tidy endings, you cannot assume you know what happened.

Historical Criticism. Using this theory requires that you apply to a text specific historical information about the time during which an author wrote. History, in this case, refers to the social, political, economic, cultural, and/or intellectual climate of the time. For example, William Faulkner wrote many of his novels and stories during and after World War II, which helps to explain the feelings of darkness, defeat, and struggle that pervade much of his work.

ACTIVITY 6

Literary Theory Cards

Choosing Critical Lenses

Remember that the way we read is a *choice;* the interpretation of a text depends on active, conscious decisions on the part of the reader.

Here are some hints to remember when you are sorting through your critical lenses.

1. The lenses are not always mutually exclusive, but you should be aware which are incompatible by understanding the assumptions behind them.

2. No single lens gives the clearest view; all have limitations.

3. Applying different lenses to the same text can reveal new features of that text.

4. It is easier for novices to apply one lens at a time.

5. These descriptions are simplified; many lenses are based on years of scholarly research and debate.

6. Turning these lenses on your experiences—your life—can help you understand and think critically about your own ideologies.

7. Writing about literature and art affords us the ability to discuss real ideas in the realm of imagination; in other words, we can *play.*

Reader-Response Lens

Essential Question: How does this text reflect the experience, beliefs, and understandings of its reader?

Central Concerns: effect, personal reflection, description, subjectivity

Critical Assumptions:

1. The text does not exist without a reader.

2. An author's intentions are unavailable to a reader outside the text.

3. Reading is the active process of evaluating a personal response to a text.

4. A reader's changing perceptions that result from reading are valuable.

What to do:

1. Move through the text carefully and slowly, describing the response of an informed reader at various points; note changes in response.

2. Describe your own responses to the text, using evidence and explanation.

3. React to the text as a whole, expressing the subjective and personal response it engenders.

Archetypal Lens

Essential Question: How does this text show similarities to ancient story designs, character categories, and imagery?

Central Concerns: myth, image, dreams, rituals, pattern, model

Critical Assumptions:

1. Imaginative work is indebted to ancient systems of meaning, including ritual, mythology, and inherited symbolism (the "collective unconscious").

2. There are no new stories.

3. Conflicts, characters, and symbols in fiction and poetry come from the same place as dreams, and can be interpreted the same way dreams are.

What to do:

1. Determine how the text mirrors certain inherited story structures, such as the heroic journey, creation myths, fairy tales, legends, and so forth.

2. Determine how the characters in the text can be said to reflect inherited character types such as the hero, the crone, the wicked stepmother, and so forth.

3. Show patterns in the text that resemble dream logic or seem to be without explicit context.

Biographical Lens

Essential Question: How does this text reflect the experiences, beliefs, and intentions of its maker(s)?

Central Concerns: context, systems of meaning, commentary, society, belief, self-expression

Critical Assumptions:

1. Meaning is contextual.

2. Writing is a product of social, political, and historical forces.

3. Writing reflects the systems of meaning available to the author.

4. Interpretation of writing demands interpretation of its historical or biographical context.

What to do:

I. Research the author's life, and relate that information to the text.

2. Research the author's time—its historical, geographical, political, and intellectual moment—and relate that data to the text.

3. Research the systems of meaning available to the author, and relate those systems to the text.

New Criticism/Formalism Lens

Essential Question: What does analysis of the text's form reveal about the meaning of its content?

Central Concerns: form, unity, ambiguity, resolution, pattern, literacy language

Critical Assumptions:

1. A text will teach you how to read it; the work itself is the only locus of critical interest.

2. The author's intentions are unavailable and irrelevant.

3. A text is valuable if it contains ambiguities, ironies, and complexities that can be resolved through careful analysis of its form.

4. A complex work will reveal a unifying theme.

What to do:

1. Determine oppositions, ambiguities, ironies, and complexities in the text.

2. Read closely; assume there are no "mistakes" in a text, or that any aspect of text is "unintentional." Study the interrelationship of literary elements.

3. Explicate the text by showing how it resolves its ambiguities.

Gender/Feminist Lens

Essential Question: How does this text reinforce, critique, or challenge definitions of masculinity or femininity?

Central Concerns: gender roles, objectivity/objectification, representation, differences

Critical Assumptions:

1. Any text cannot exist outside of a gender frame of reference.
2. Historically, writing (and interpretation) has been dominated by men and masculine perceptions; it is important for women to create a feminine/feminist way of writing and reading.
3. Men and women are essentially different, and differences can be examined in social behavior, ideas, and values; these differences should be recognized.
4. Stereotyping is dangerous and can lead to destructive social norms.

What to do:

1. Consider the gender of the author, the reader, and the characters/voices in the text: how does the text reflect social gender codes?
2. Ask how the text reinforces or undermines gender stereotypes.
3. Imagine yourself as someone of the opposite gender reading this work.

Social Power/Marxist Lens

Essential Question: How does this text comment on or represent class conflict?

Central Concerns: power, economics, class, differences, fairness, society

Critical Assumptions:

1. The way people think and behave is determined by basic economic factors.
2. Class conflict is the same as political conflict.
3. The wealthy class exploits the working class by forcing their own values and beliefs upon them, usually through control of working conditions and money.
4. These ideas can be applied to the study of literature, which is a product of culture and social conflict.

What to do:

1. Explore the way different economic classes are represented in the text.
2. Determine the ideological stance of the text. (Is it radical? Conservative?)
3. Link the text to the social class of its author.
4. Consider how the text itself is a commodity that reproduces certain beliefs and behaviors. What is the effect of the work as means of control?

Psychological Lens

Essential Question: How can we apply psychology and psychoanalytical criticism to gain insights into the behavior and motivations of authors and characters?

Central Concerns: expression, personality, state of mind, designs of author

Critical Assumptions:

1. An author reveals repressed wishes or fears in a literary text.

2. Creative writing, like dreaming, can unlock the subconscious.

3. There are some patterns such as anxiety, repression, fear of death that can be applied both to individual characters and authors as well as generally to human beings.

What to do:

1. Look for an underlying psychological subtext in the work.

2. Discover key biographical moments and relate them to the text.

3. Try to explain the behavior of the characters in psychological terms, such as projection, repression, fear (of abandonment, sexuality, etc.).

Postcolonial Lens

Essential Question: How does this text comment on, represent, or repress the marginalized voices?

Central Concerns: cultural markers, the Other, oppression, justice, society

Critical Assumptions:

1. Colonization—the exploitation of one national or ethnic group by another—is a powerful destructive force that disrupts the identities of both groups.

2. Colonized societies are forced to the margins by their colonizers (called "Othering"), despite having a historical claim to the land they inhabit.

3. Literature written by colonizers distorts the experiences and realities of the colonized; literature written by the colonized often attempts to redefine or preserve a sense of cultural identity.

What to do:

1. Explore how the text represents a colonized or colonized cultural group.

2. Ask how the text creates images of "others." How does it demonstrate a colonial mindset?

3. Ask how conflicts in the text might be viewed as cultural conflicts.

New Historicism Lens

Essential Question: What are the ways in which our understanding of literature and its historical context change over time?

Central Concerns: history as interpretation and cultural construction, literature as dynamic, meaning changes over time

Critical Assumptions:

1. Meaning is contextual.
2. There are divergent viewpoints on the nature of a historical context.
3. History is subjective.
4. Interpretation is a kind of cultural production, marked by a particular context; we cannot look at history objectively, as we too interpret events as a product of our culture and our time.

What to do:

1. Learn about the systems of meaning that were available to the author at the time the work was produced.
2. Consider the ways in which cultural concepts change over time.
3. List the ways in which contemporary events, assumptions and perspectives might shape one's reading of the literary texts.
4. Imagine the ways in which literary works influence reconsiderations of history.

Deconstruction Lens

Essential Question: How does analysis of this text reveal privileged oppositions of meaning and arbitrary nature of language?

Central Concerns: privilege, hierarchies, indeterminacy, sign, signifier

Critical Assumptions:

1. Meaning is not determinate: it is made by binary oppositions (yes/no, positive, negative, etc.), but one item in an opposition is unavoidably favored or privileged over the other.
2. The hierarchy is arbitrary and can be exposed or reversed.
3. Texts contain unavoidable gaps, spaces, absences, contradictions and irresolvable ambiguities that defeat complete interpretation.

What to do:

1. Identify oppositions in the text.
2. Determine which member in a given opposition appears favored, and demonstrate contradiction of that favoring.
3. Expose a text's inability to resolve its ambiguities.

Theory Wars:
Looking at *Star Wars* Through Critical Lenses

In your groups, discuss the following questions. You will be asked to share the fruits of your discussion with the whole class in your symposium.

1. Try to recall the first time you saw this film. In what ways was this viewing different from your first viewing. What were some things you noticed that you didn't notice before? What seemed to be important this time that didn't come through in a previous viewing?

2. Think back to our discussions of archetypes from last year. Describe how characters, plot, conflict or theme in *Star Wars* could be viewed in archetypal terms. For example, is this a classic story of good versus evil, is Princess Leah the typical heroine?

3. Read through the handout on literary theory. Select the two theories that you think might be most helpful in illuminating the film. Write down the theories below.
   1.

   2.

4. Now come up with some statements about the film for each of the theories you named in question 3. For example, if you select feminist criticism you might discuss the lack of female characters and evaluate the role of Princess Leah from a feminist perspective. If you choose reader-response theory you might describe how the film reminded each of you of a personal experience in your struggle with good and evil. (Use loose-leaf paper—journal potential.)

5. After you discuss these interpretations, decide how to present them to the whole class. Your presentation should be no more than about ten minutes of your symposium.

ACTIVITY 8

Literary Theory: Prisms of Possibilities

Please read the Sylvia Plath poem and discuss it in your group using the assigned lens.
We will consider each lens when we reconvene as a large group.

	Reader Response	Biographical	Feminist/Gender	Marxist/Social Class
What aspects of the poem lend themselves to this particular lens?				
Cite specific textual passage(s) that support this reading.				
If you look through this lens, what themes or patterns are brought into sharper relief?				
If you look through this lens, what questions emerge?				
Do you believe in this reading? Why or why not?				

ACTIVITY 9

Upon Seeing an Orange

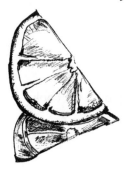

Gender theory asks	Can a woman and a man equally partake of this orange? What possibilities are available to a woman who eats this orange? A man?
Formalism asks	What shape and diameter is the orange? How does the shape of the orange affect its taste?
Social class theory asks	Who does the orange belong to? Who can afford oranges? Who can't?
Postcolonialism asks	Who did the orange used to belong to? Who has it now? Who took the orange away?
Reader-response asks	What are some experiences we have eating oranges? What does the orange taste like? What does the orange remind us of?
Deconstruction asks	In orange juice, what orangeness remains? If there are "oranges" and "non-oranges," which is a tangerine?

Source: Adapted from www.geocities.com/litcrittoolkit/defin.html

Looking Through Lenses: Our First Look

Group Members:

Summer Reading Text:

1. In three or four sentences please summarize the plot of the book.

2. What were some of the most important things you noticed about the text before we read our discussion of lenses?

3. Which two lenses do you think might be most useful to apply to this text?

4. Which lenses do you think might not be particularly useful? Why?

5. Now try applying the two lenses that you selected in #3.

Lens 1

When we viewed this book through the lenses, we looked at:

The lenses help us see the following things that we didn't notice before:

Therefore we see that this might be a book about:

Lens 2

When we viewed this book through the lenses, we looked at:

The lenses help us see the following things that we didn't notice before:

Therefore we see that this might be a book about:

* * * Journal Entry * * * Journal Entry * * * Journal Entry * * *

Reflecting on the above, write an entry in your journal summarizing what you discovered from this activity. What worked, what went "clunk"?

What were the most and least useful elements of this first application of critical lenses?

Reader-Response Chart

Context
(What factors surrounding my reading
of the text are influencing my response?)

Reader (   ) ⟶ **Meaning** ⟵ **Text** (   )
        YOUR NAME

(What personal qualities or events   (What textual features might
relevant to this particular book   influence my response?)
might influence my response?)

Context

Reader Response and *Native Son*

Context
(What factors surrounding my reading
of the text are influencing my response?)

Reader (_____ **)** ➝ **Meaning** ⬅ **Text (*Native Son*)**

      YOUR NAME

(What personal qualities or events
relevant to this particular book
might influence my response?)

(What textual features might
influence my response?)

Context

ACTIVITY 13

Key Ideas of Marx

Stages of History

Marx believed that history moved in stages: from feudalism to capitalism, socialism, and ultimately communism.

Materialism

Each stage was mainly shaped by the economic system. The key to understanding the systems was to focus on the "mode of production." (For example, most production under feudalism was agricultural, while most production under capitalism was industrial.) It also was necessary to focus on who owned the "means of production." (Under capitalism a small class—the bourgeoisie—owned the factories. Under socialism, the factories would be owned by the workers.)

Class Struggle

"The history of all hitherto existing society is the history of class struggles." Each system, up to and including capitalism, was characterized by the exploitation of one class by another.

The Dialectic

Marx believed that great historical changes followed a three-step pattern called thesis-antithesis-synthesis. Any idea or condition (thesis) brought into being its opposite (antithesis). For example, the existence of the ruling bourgeoisie under capitalism made necessary the existence of its opposite, the proletariat. The two opposites would conflict until they produced a new, higher stage (synthesis).

Internal Contradictions

Each class system therefore contained the seeds of its own destruction, which Marx sometimes called "internal contradictions." Capitalism, he believed, was plagued by such contradictions, which would get worse and worse until they destroyed it.

Capitalism

Marx saw capitalism as the cruelest, most efficient system yet evolved for the exploitation of the working majority by a small class of owners. It was the nature of capitalism, Marx believed, for wealth and ownership to be concentrated into an ever-shrinking class of megarich. This was one of many internal contradictions of capitalism that would inevitably destroy it.

Working-Class Misery

It was the nature of capitalist production methods to become more and more technologically efficient, requiring fewer and fewer workers to produce more and more goods. Therefore, capitalism would be plagued by bouts of high unemployment. As machines made a worker's skill less important, wages would be pushed ever downward. As each worker became simply an appendage of a machine, his job would be less satisfying and he would become more alienated.

Class Consciousness

Such total exploitation of so many by so few could not last forever. The workers would inevitably develop "class consciousness," or an awareness of their predicament. When that occurred, it would be fairly simple to take over the factories and the state.

End of History

Since class conflict was the engine that drove history, and since under communism there would be no class distinctions, history would come to its final resting place in a system free of exploitation.

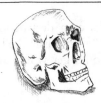

Reading *Hamlet* Through the Marxist/Social Class Lens

Act 1—Warm-up Discussion

First things first. This stuff can be pretty cool but takes a bit of practice. It can be hard, but I've heard you're pretty smart readers. So here goes. Have you considered Marxist/social class literary theory in your reading before? With what texts? How did that consideration affect your reading of the text as a whole?

The article you read, "Marxist Criticism" by Stephen Bonnycastle, states that in order to understand *Hamlet* from a Marxist perspective, you need to know something about Shakespeare's times and the class struggle present then. What *do* you know about that?

An *ideology* is a view of the world, a prevailing set of beliefs. What are some examples of ideologies you have come across?

What is the prevailing ideology that is represented in *Hamlet?* Are there other differing views of the world that fight with one another within the text? Explain.

Act 2—In Trios and Then as a Class

"Marxist/social class criticism pays a lot of attention to the social structures that allocate power to different groups in society." List some of the social groups that are represented in *Hamlet*.

We've all heard the term *social ladder*. Try plotting some of the *Hamlet* characters on the social ladder graph below.

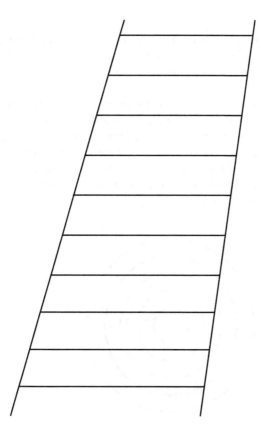

Name some of the primary power struggles that the play portrays. Who has the power and who doesn't?

Conflict Between:

Has Power	Has No Power

Put a * next to the power struggles that could be considered class conflicts.

Act 3—On Your Own

The following questions should be done on your own. You don't have to share your responses to the first one, but we may discuss your responses to the second and third questions in class tomorrow.

Marxist literary theory asserts the importance of paying attention to class conflicts, power struggles and how we place ourselves within the particular social structure in which we find ourselves. Draw a picture or diagram, if you can, of the existing power or class structure in which you live. You can do it like the social ladder we used above, or you can draw concentric circles, or you can map or web, anything is fine. Where are you, relative to where power and money is located?

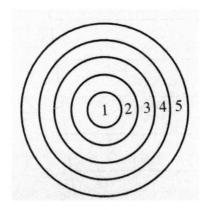

To what degree do you think this location may have affected your reading of *Hamlet?* What characters in *Hamlet* do you feel most closely represent where you are socially.

Marxist literary theory encourages us to look at the big political questions that surround our more personal concerns. List below some of the big questions that emerge for you as a result of reading *Hamlet* through a Marxist lens.

Now think of one or two smaller, more personal and perhaps more important questions that emerge for you as you think about issues of class conflict, ideologies or beliefs, and struggle. List them below.

ACTIVITY 15

Blue Collar Brilliance: Using Literary Lenses to Read Nonfiction

As we have seen, we can use literary lenses to read nonfiction as well as fiction. As with fiction, different lenses bring different aspects of the text into sharper relief. Let's look at the essay "Blue Collar Brilliance"* by Mike Rose through the reader-response lens and the class lens. You may find it helpful to read through your theory cards as you consider each lens.

The Reader-Response Lens

Mike Rose begins this piece by telling us about his mother who was a waitress. How does this personal example affect your response to this essay? To the writer?

What experiences have you had with the body-mind connection that Rose explores?

Do you buy Rose's argument that we undervalue certain kinds of manual labor?

Are you proud of your parent(s)' occupation? Explain.

How do you think your own identification with a particular social class affects your response to Rose's argument?

The Class Lens

What is surprising or significant about the title of the essay?

In what ways does this essay trouble our assumptions about intelligence?

In what ways does this essay trouble our assumptions about social class? How are our assumptions about intelligence and social class connected?

Rose's mother was a waitress and his uncle worked at General Motors. How do the examples of his family members bring social class into the essay?

Putting It All Together

Why does Rose use the personal examples of his mother, a waitress, and his uncle, a factory worker, to make his argument about the intelligence of blue-color workers?

How do the lenses of reader response and class interact to help construct your overall reading of the piece?

Do you find Rose's discussion about intelligence to be persuasive? Explain.

*Note to teachers: this essay can be easily found online.

ACTIVITY 16

Dumpster Diving:
Using Literary Lenses
to Read Nonfiction

We can use literary lenses to read nonfiction as well as fiction. Let's look at this frequently read essay "On Dumpster Diving"* through three lenses. You may find it helpful to read through your theory cards as you consider each lens.

Approach One: The Reader-Response Lens— A Personal Transaction with a Nonfiction Piece

What is your initial response to the essay?

Did you find any sections of the essay disagreeable or repugnant?

Do you have any sympathy for the writer? Why or why not?

Have you ever known someone who is or has been homeless? How does that experience or lack of it affect your response to the essay?

Approach Two: The Formalist Lens—A Close Reading of a Nonfiction Piece

Who do you think the writer imagines his audience to be? Are you part of that intended audience?

Comment on the overall structure of the essay.

What effect does the use of the present tense have on the overall effect of the story?

Give several examples of the writer's use of figurative language.

Find some examples of the use of the following rhetorical strategies in this essay:

    Comparison-contrast/cause/effect, definition, description, process

    Analysis, classification

How would you describe the *tone* of the essay?

How does the style of the writing intersect in surprising ways with the content of the essay?

Approach Three: The Class Lens—
Reading Nonfiction Through a Political Lens

In what ways is this piece a commentary on the situation of the homeless in the United States?

What larger point about America's class system is the writer trying to make in this essay?

What do the dumpster's contents indicate about those who throw the food away?

How is the writer not a typical homeless person? How might that affect your response to his situation?

In what ways is government implicated in the plight of the homeless?

Is the writer's situation of his own making or are there societal implications that could be considered?

Putting It All Together

Which lens seemed to be most useful in your reading of this essay? What does each contribute to your overall understanding of the essay? Based on the essay itself, which lenses do you think the writer considered as he wrote this essay?

*Note to teachers: this essay can be easily found online.

ACTIVITY 17

Looking at
The Great Gatsby
Through Critical Lenses

Literary theories were developed as a means for understanding the various ways in which people read texts. The proponents of each theory believe their theory is *the* theory, but most of us interpret texts according to the "rules" of several different theories at a time. All literary theories are lenses through which we can see texts. There is nothing to say that one is better than another or that you should read according to any of them, but it is sometimes fun to read a text with one in mind because you often end up with a whole new perspective on your reading. We are going to apply two lenses to *The Great Gatsby*, the Marxist/social class lens and the gender lens.

Definitions:

Social Class Criticism. Social class criticism grounds its theory and practice on the economic and cultural theory of Karl Marx and Friedrich Engels, especially on the following claims:

1. The evolving history of humanity, its institutions and its ways of thinking are determined by the changing mode of its "material production"—that is, of its basic economic organization.
2. Historical changes in the fundamental mode of production effect essential changes both in the constitution and power relations among social classes, which carry on a conflict for economic, political, and social advantage.
3. Human consciousness in any era is constituted by an ideology—a set of concepts, beliefs, values, and ways of thinking and feeling through which human beings perceive and by which they explain what they take to be reality. A social class critic typically undertakes to "explain" the literature in any era by revealing the economic, class, and ideological determinants that inform the way an author writes, as well as to examine the relationship of the text to the social reality of the time and place in which it is set.

This school of critical theory focuses on power and money in works of literature. Who has the power/money? Who does not? What happens as a result?

Strategies for Applying the Social Class Lens:

1. Explore the ways in which different groups of people are represented in texts. Evaluate the level of social realism in the text—How is society portrayed?
2. Determine the ideological stance of the text—What worldview does the text represent?
3. Consider how the text itself is a commodity that reproduces certain social beliefs and practices. Analyze the social effect of the literary work.

Gender Criticism. This is somewhat like social class criticism, but instead of focusing on the relationships among social classes it focuses on the relationships between the genders. In using this theory, you would examine the patterns of thought, behavior, values, enfranchisement, and power in relations between the sexes. There are many different kinds of gendered literary theory. Some theorists examine the language and symbols that are used to see how language and use of symbols is gendered. Others remind us that men and women write differently and analyze how the gender of the author affects how literature is written. Many gender theory critics look at how the characters, especially the female characters, are portrayed and ask us to consider how the portrayal of female characters "reinforces or undermines" sexual stereotypes. Gender literary theory also suggests that the gender of the reader affects his or her response to a text. For example, gender critics may claim that certain male writers address their readers as if they were all men and exclude the female reader.

Much gender theory reminds us that the relationship between men and women in society is often unequal and reflects a particular patriarchal ideology. Those unequal relationships may appear in a variety of ways in the production of literature and within literary texts. Gender theory invites us to pay particular attention to the patterns of thought, behavior, values, and power in those relationships.

Gender critics remind us that literary values, conventions, and even the production of literature, have themselves been historically shaped by men. They invite us to consider writings by women, both new and forgotten, and also ask us to consider viewing familiar literature through a gendered perspective.

Strategies for applying the gender lens:

1. Consider the gender of the author, the characters. What role does gender or sexuality play in this work?
2. Specifically, observe how sexual stereotypes might be reinforced or undermined. Try to see how the work reflects or distorts the place of women (and men) in society.

3. Think about how gender affects and informs relationships between the characters.
4. Consider the comments the author seems to be making about society as a whole.

You can now use both of these lenses to interpret characters, passages, and themes in *The Great Gatsby*.

The Question of Power:

Name some of the primary power struggles that the novel portrays. Who has the power and who doesn't?

From the Perspective of Gender

Has Power	Has No Power

From the Perspective of Class

Has Power	Has No Power

Passages:

Using the social class lens, what is the significance of this passage:

Every Friday five crates of oranges and lemons arrived from a fruiterer in New York—every Monday these same oranges and lemons left his back door in a pyramid of pulpless halves. There was a machine in the kitchen which could extract the juice of two hundred oranges in half an hour if a little button was pressed two hundred times by a butler's thumb.

Using the gender lens, what is the significance of this passage:

Well, she was less than an hour old and Tom was God knows where. I woke up out of the ether with an utterly abandoned feeling, and asked the nurse right away if it was a boy or a girl. She told me it was a girl, and so I turned my head away and wept. "All right," I said, "I'm glad it's a girl, and I hope she'll be a fool—that's the best thing a girl can be in this world, a beautiful little fool."

Themes:

Finish these sentences:

From the social class perspective, *The Great Gatsby* is a novel about . . .

From a gender perspective, *The Great Gatsby* is a novel about . . .

Further Questions:

Social class and gender literary theories encourage us to look at the big political questions that surround our more personal concerns. List below some of the big questions that emerge for you as a result of reading *The Great Gatsby* through social class and gender lenses.

Social Class Questions:

Gender Questions:

Now think of one or two smaller and more personal questions that emerge for you as you think about issues of class conflict, ideologies or beliefs, gender, and power. List them below.

ACTIVITY 18

 What Color Are Your Walls? The Feminist/Gender Lens

1. What is the feminist/gender lens?

Feminist/gender literary criticism helps us look at literature in a different light. It applies the philosophies and perspectives of feminism to the literature we read. There are many different kinds of feminist/gender theory. Some theorists examine the language and symbols that are used and how that language and use of symbols is "gendered." Others remind us that men and women write differently and analyze how the gender of the author affects how literature is written. Many feminist critics look at how the characters, especially the female characters, are portrayed and ask us to consider how the portrayal of female characters reinforces or undermines sexual stereotypes. Feminist literary theory also suggests that the gender of the reader often affects our response to a text. For example, feminist critics may claim that certain male writers address their readers as if they were all men and exclude the female reader.

Like feminism itself, feminist literary theory asks us to consider the relationships between men and women and their relative roles in society. Much feminist literary theory reminds us that the relationship between men and women in society is often unequal and reflects a particular patriarchal ideology. Those unequal relationships may appear in a variety of ways in the production of literature and within literary texts. Feminist theorists invite us to pay particular attention to the patterns of thought, behavior, values, and power in those relationships.

Feminist literary critics remind us that literary values, conventions, and even the production of literature have themselves been historically shaped by men. They invite us to consider writings by women, both new and forgotten, and also ask us to consider viewing familiar literature through a feminist perspective.

2. Consider Gertrude and Ophelia from *Hamlet*

For each character, write two descriptive statements—one from a "traditional" masculine perspective and the second from a feminist perspective.

Gertrude:

Traditional statement:

Feminist statement:

Ophelia:

Traditional statement:

Feminist statement:

3. How do we apply the feminist lens?

We apply it by closely examining the portrayal of the characters, both fe-male and male, the language of the text, the attitude of the author, and the relationship between the characters. We also consider the comments the author seems to be making about society as a whole. Let's try to interpret the following concrete poem in two ways, from a traditional perspective and from a feminist perspective:

—Pedro Xisto

4. Now, think about "The Yellow Wallpaper"

Using the feminist lens, write a brief analysis of the narrator, her situation, and perhaps Perkins' intent in writing the piece. Consider Perkins' audience as well. Finally, what meaning(s) did you derive from the text as you applied the feminist lens? (Note: this is very similar to the kind of analysis you may be asked to do in a college English class.)

A Lens of One's Own:
Using Feminist/Gender Literary Theory

1. What is the feminist lens?

Feminist/gender literary criticism helps us look at literature in a different light. It applies the philosophies and perspectives of feminism to the literature we read. There are many different kinds of feminist/gender literary theory. Some theorists examine the language and symbols that are used and how that language and use of symbols is "gendered." Others remind us that men and women write differently and analyze how the gender of the author affects how literature is written. Many feminist critics look at how the characters, especially the female characters, are portrayed and ask us to consider how the portrayal of female characters reinforces or undermines sexual stereotypes. Feminist/gender theory also suggests that the gender of the reader often affects our response to a text. For example, feminist critics may claim that certain male writers address their readers as if they were all men and exclude the female reader.

Like feminism itself, feminist literary theory asks us to consider the relationships between men and women and their relative roles in society. Much feminist literary theory reminds us that the relationship between men and women in society is often unequal and reflects a particular patriarchal ideology. Those unequal relationships may appear in a variety of ways in the production of literature and within literary texts. Feminist theorists invite us to pay particular attention to the patterns of thought, behavior, values, and power in those relationships.

Feminist literary critics remind us that literary values, conventions, and even the production of literature, have themselves been historically shaped by men. They invite us to consider writings by women, both new and forgotten, and also ask us to consider viewing familiar literature through a feminist perspective.

2. How do we apply the feminist lens?

We apply it by closely examining the portrayal of the characters, both female and male, the language of the text, the attitude of the author, and the relationship between the characters. We also consider the comments the author seems to be making about society as a whole.

3. Is Virginia Woolf a feminist?

In groups of two or three, state whether the feminist literary lens would meet with Virginia Woolf's approval. Does she agree that our readings are "gendered"? Does she believe that women characters and writers are marginalized? Be prepared to defend your statement with at least two quotations from *A Room of One's Own*.

Our position is:

Quotation 1:

Quotation 2:

4. Application: Looking through the feminist lens

Select two female characters from novels with which you are very familiar. They could be from our summer reading, from works we have read together, or from texts you have read in previous English classes. For example, you might choose Daisy from *The Great Gatsby*, Hester Prynne from *The Scarlet Letter*, Sonya from *Crime and Punishment*, or other female characters from the texts we've read.

For each character, write two descriptive statements—one from a traditional masculine perspective and the second from a feminist perspective.

Character 1:

Traditional statement:

Feminist statement:

Character 2:

Traditional statement:

Feminist statement:

ACTIVITY 20

Death of a Salesman and the Social Construction of Gender

1. Consider the following words:

    fashion, football, breadwinner, pilot, strength, flower, ambitious, perseverance, compassionate, bossy, helpless, thoughtful, soft, brassy, dangerous, perpetrator, victim, attractive, opinionated, hostile, emotional

Using your first instinct and without over-thinking, write each in the column that seems most appropriate:

Male	Female	Both	Neither

2. Our ability to assign gender to words or constructs has to do with what some people call the social construction of gender. Using the feminist lens is one way to examine gender construction, but the notion of the social construction of gender broadens the lens to more fully consider how both men and women are affected by this social construction.

Read through the following explanations of the social construction of gender:

The Construction of Gender

This theory acknowledges that men and women are actively involved in constructing their own gendered identities. We adopt different masculinity and femininity practices depending on our situations and beliefs. Our understandings of gender are dynamic, changing over time with maturity, experience, and reflection. Thus, we are active in constructing our own gender identities. The options available to us are not unlimited, however. We are influenced by the collective practices of institutions such as school, church, media, and family, which construct and reinforce particular forms of masculinity and femininity.

These widely accepted, dominant notions of gender often construct masculinity and femininity as opposites, ignoring a vast array of shared human characteristics, and traditionally valuing masculinity as more powerful. Such ideas may be accepted, challenged, modified, or rejected as individuals develop and shape their gender identities:

> In their lives in family and community, and before they come to school, children learn socially approved ways of interacting as female or male. As a consequence, many girls and boys develop narrow and limited concepts of masculinity and femininity, concepts which impoverish their existence.
>
> (National Action Plan for the Education of Girls, 1993–1997, p. 7)

The construction of different ways of being feminine or masculine is a dynamic process in which we all play a part. Students need the critical skills to understand and assess narrow messages about the way they can live their lives.

—Adapted from http://education.qld.gov.au/students/
advocacy/equity/gender-sch/issues/gender-under.html

The Social Construction of Gender

Underlying the different assumptions of the treatment of women and men is a whole series of complex ideologies that seek to explain (and create) the differences between men and women, observed as well as constructed. **Sex differences,** or the biological differences between males and females, are often cited as the basis for unequal treatment. Although we understand **gender differences** between men and women to represent socially constructed norms regarding the division of labor, the distribution of power, and differing responsibilities and rights between men and women, the basis for differentiation continues to be traced back to biological difference. However, it is obvious that the biological differences between men and women are minimal and insignificant when compared with the similarities. Biological difference becomes magnified or exaggerated to represent an **ideology of sex difference,** which we refer to as the ideology of gender. It is used to justify unequal treatment of women and men. The power of the ideology of gender lies in the way it encompasses fundamental cultural and social values relating to the relations between men and women, as well as the force of history underlying its evolution.

The ideology of gender determines:

- What is expected of us
- What is allowed of us
- What is valued in us

The ideology of gender also determines the nature and extent of:

- Disadvantage
- Disparity
- Discrimination

The manifestation of gender difference can be found in the construction of:

- *Roles:* What women and men do
- *Relations:* How women and men relate to each other
- *Identity:* How women and men perceive themselves

The ideology of gender thus contains norms and rules regarding appropriate behavior and determines attributes; it also reproduces a range of beliefs and customs to support these norms and social rules.

—Adapted from www.hku.hk/ccpl/events/training/2003/27032003/4.doc

Briefly jot down your response to these explanations and any questions they raise for you:

3. Consider this list of characters and the descriptions, adapted from a well-known reader's guide to the play. As you read, circle the words that are "gendered":

Willy Loman: An insecure, self-deluded traveling salesman. Willy believes wholeheartedly in the American Dream of easy success and wealth, but he never achieves it. Nor do his sons fulfill his hope that they will succeed where he has failed. When Willy's illusions begin to fail under the pressing realities of his life, his mental health begins to unravel. The overwhelming tensions caused by this disparity, as well as those caused by the societal imperatives that drive Willy, form the essential conflict of *Death of a Salesman*.

Biff Loman: Willy's 34-year-old elder son. Biff led a charmed life in high school as a football star with scholarship prospects, good male friends, and fawning female admirers. He failed math, however, and did not have enough credits to graduate. Since then, his kleptomania has gotten him fired from every job that he has held. Biff represents Willy's vulnerable, poetic, tragic side. Biff cannot ignore his instincts, which tell him to abandon Willy's paralyzing dreams and move out West to work with his hands. He ultimately fails to reconcile his life with Willy's expectations of him.

Linda Loman: Willy's loyal, loving wife. Linda suffers through Willy's grandiose dreams and self-delusions. Occasionally, she seems to be taken in by Willy's self-deluded hopes for future glory and success, but at other times, she seems far more realistic and less fragile than her husband. She has nurtured the family through all of Willy's misguided attempts at success, and her emotional strength and perseverance support Willy until his collapse.

Happy Loman: Willy's 32-year-old younger son. Happy has lived in Biff's shadow all of his life, but he compensates by nurturing his relentless sex drive and professional ambition. Happy represents Willy's sense of self-importance, ambition, and blind servitude to societal expectations. Although he works as an assistant to an assistant buyer in a department store, Happy presents himself as supremely important. Additionally, he practices bad business ethics and sleeps with the girlfriends of his superiors.

Charley: Willy's next-door neighbor. Charley owns a successful business and his son, Bernard, is a wealthy, important lawyer. Willy is jealous of Charley's success. Charley gives Willy money to pay his bills, and Willy reveals at one point, choking back tears, that Charley is his only friend.

Bernard: Bernard is Charley's son and an important, successful lawyer. Although Willy used to mock Bernard for studying hard, Bernard always loved Willy's sons dearly and regarded Biff as a hero. Bernard's success is difficult for Willy to accept because his own sons' lives do not measure up.

Ben: Willy's wealthy older brother. Ben has recently died and appears only in Willy's "daydreams." Willy regards Ben as a symbol of the success that he so desperately craves for himself and his sons.

The Woman: Willy's mistress when Happy and Biff were in high school. The Woman's attention and admiration boost Willy's fragile ego. When Biff catches Willy in his hotel room with The Woman, he loses faith in his father, and his dream of passing math and going to college dies.

Howard Wagner: Willy's boss. Howard inherited the company from his father, whom Willy regarded as "a masterful man" and "a prince." Though much younger than Willy, Howard treats Willy with condescension and eventually fires him, despite Willy's wounded assertions that he named Howard at his birth.

Stanley: A waiter at Frank's Chop House. Stanley and Happy seem to be friends, or at least acquaintances, and they banter about and ogle Miss Forsythe together before Biff and Willy arrive at the restaurant.

Miss Forsythe and Letta: Two young women whom Happy and Biff meet at Frank's Chop House. It seems likely that Miss Forsythe and Letta are prostitutes, judging from Happy's repeated comments about their moral character and the fact that they are "on call."

—Adapted from www.sparknotes.com/lit/salesman/

3a. In what ways do these descriptions contribute to the gendered stereotypes of the characters?

3b. Select one of the four members of the Loman family. Describe the ways in which this character may be held hostage to social expectations of gender and say how those expectations affect the character's actions within the play. Now, as you think about the film version of the play, how did the social construction of gender affect the actor's portrayal of the character?

ACTIVITY 21

Getting to the Heart of the "Other": The Postcolonial Lens and *Heart of Darkness*

THE WHAT

Let's first review the basic tenants of postcolonial theory.

Postcolonial Literary Theory

Assumptions

1. Colonialism is a powerful, usually destructive historical force that shapes not only the political futures of the countries involved but also the identities of colonized and colonizing people.
2. Successful colonialism depends on a process of "othering" the people colonized. That is, the colonized people are seen as dramatically different from and lesser than the colonizers.
3. Because of this, literature written in colonizing cultures often distorts the experiences and realities of colonized people. Literature written by colonized people often includes attempts to articulate more empowered identities and reclaim cultures in the face of colonization.

Strategies

1. Search the text for references to colonization or current and formerly colonized people. In these references, how are the colonized people portrayed? How is the process of colonization portrayed?
2. Consider what images of "others" or processes of "othering" are present in the text. How are these "others" portrayed?

Analyze how the text deals with cultural conflicts between the colonizing culture and colonized or traditional culture.

Here's another definition of postcolonial theory:

Postcolonial literary theory attempts to isolate perspectives in literature that grow out of colonial rule and the mindset it creates. On one hand, it can examine the ways in which a colonizing society imposes its world-view on the peoples it subjugates, making them "objects" of observation and denying them the power to define themselves. The colonizers are the "subjects," those who take action and create realities out of the beliefs they hold to be important. On another hand, it can focus on the experiences of colonized peoples and the disconnection they feel from their own identities. Postcolonialism also focuses on attempts of formerly colonized societies to reassert the identities they wish to claim for themselves, including national identities and cultural identities. When this lens is used to examine the products of colonization, it focuses on reclamation of self-identity.

One thing that postcolonial theory shares with deconstruction is the attempt to isolate "false binaries," categories that function by including dominant perspectives and excluding the rest, relegating outsiders to the status of "other." Colonized people are always seen as existing outside the prevailing system of beliefs or values. As the dominant ideology asserts itself, it creates a sense of normalcy among the ideas of the colonizers and a sense of the exotic, the inexplicable, and the strange among the customs and ideas of "the other."

In your own words, what is postcolonial literary theory?

THE WHY

Here's how one teacher explains why she teaches the postcolonial lens:

"In other words, I am fully convinced that students can come to a clear understanding of the poststructuralist and gendered notions of socially-constructed subjectivity, and of postcolonial perspectives that reveal the presence of 'the self' in 'the other' (the master in the slave; the slave in the master), if they can find personal and cultural connections to those peoples they would otherwise perceive as antithetical to them. (Few of my mainstream American students can imagine there is any commonality, any common humanity, between themselves and 'Communists' or 'Arabs' or 'lesbians' or 'gays' or any of those groups demonized so often in our national consciousness. The task that I face in my classrooms most often is to allow students to see a hint of that common humanity, to deconstruct their preconceptions as a way to see that others, no matter how putatively different, might in other circumstances and ideological convictions than those we presently inhabit and uphold, be our colleagues, our comrades, our friends.)"

—Lindsay Aegerter

Respond to this quotation in a short paragraph:

THE HOW

1. Rephrase from a postcolonial perspective the following sentence: *Christopher Columbus discovered America.*

2. Read the poem "Sure You Can Ask Me a Personal Question." In groups of three or four, construct a postcolonial reading and explain it below.

THE TEXT

Using the table below, list all the characters you have met in the novel in terms of their stance as the colonized and the colonizers.

The Colonizers	The Colonized

If it is true that the master is in the slave and the slave is in the master, select one character from each column and explain how they embody both categories. Work with one other person on this question.

The Questions

Using the postcolonial lens, what kind of questions emerge from your reading of this text? Write at least four questions below.

Reading Nonfiction and Art:
A New Historical Approach

The Emancipation Proclamation

Spend some time studying the painting located at http://upload.wikimedia.
org/wikipedia/commons/1/11/Stephens-reading-proclamation-1863.jpeg
Then write a brief paragraph that describes your response to it.

Now read the historical document located at http://www.nps.gov/ncro/anti/
emancipation.html

Return to the painting. What do you notice that you didn't notice before?

This painting was completed in 1863. How do you think your reaction
to the painting might differ significantly from the response of the artist's
contemporaries?

"How It Feels to Be Colored Me"

Consider the essay "How It Feels to Be Colored Me" by Zora Neale Hurston, located at http://destee.com/index.php?threads/how-it-feels-to-be-colored-me-by-zora-neale-hurston.71938/

This essay was written in 1928, 65 years after the Emancipation Proclamation. Does Hurston's essay reflect an "emancipated" reality for African Americans?

In what ways is the historical context of the essay important to your understanding of it?

Does her essay revise your viewing of the painting?

What elements of Hurston's essay seem relevant today? Which seem outdated?

Metaquestion: How does history shape and reshape our reading of artistic and literary works?

The Interplay of Nonfiction and Poetry

Please read the poem "In Response to Executive Order 9066: All Americans of Japanese Descent Must Report to Relocation Centers" by Dwight Okita, available at dwightland.homestead.com/ABOUTPOEMS.html

Using the **reader-response lens**, write your own personal reaction to the poem:

Now look at the historical document on which the poem is based, located at www.archives.gov/historical-docs/todays-doc/?dod-date=219

How does this historical document enhance your understanding of the context of the poem? Contrast the way that language is used in the poem and in the historical document.

Now read what the poet Dwight Okita says about the poem, available at dwightland.homestead.com/ABOUTPOEMS.html
How does this additional information change your reading of the poem?

Do you think this background is necessary to gain a full understanding of the poem?

Metaquestion: How does the poem and your reading of it change your understanding of the historical event represented in "Executive Order 9066"?

Deconstruction

Deconstruction is, by far, the most difficult critical lens for people to understand. It is an intellectually sophisticated theory that confuses many very smart people, but we think so much of you, that we know you can understand it. It is a postmodern theory, and like most postmodernism, it questions many of the basic assumptions that have guided us in the past. In the traditional study of literature, those basic assumptions include:

- language is stable and has meaning we can all agree on
- the author is in control of the text s/he writes
- works of literature have an internal consistency
- works of literature have an external relevance
- you can take the author's or poet's word for what s/he writes
- there is a set of interpretive tools that you can reliably use to interpret a literary text

Deconstruction calls all of these assumptions into question. It asks you to read resistantly, to not take a work of literature at its face value and to question the assumptions, both literary and philosophical, that the work or the author asks you to make. It is this kind of resistance that you folks are so good at. And it is that resistance, that ability to look beyond what seems to be intended, that will be a useful skill in the "real world." It helps us to become careful and skeptical consumers of culture, not passive recipients of "great works."

Deconstructionist critics ask us to probe beyond the surface or recognizable constructs of a finished story or text. By "construct," we mean something that has been constructed by mental synthesis. That is, constructs are created when we combine things we know through our senses or from our experiences. They do not exist naturally; they are products of our intervention into the order of the universe. When we reexamine and challenge the constructs employed by the literary writer, we "deconstruct." The term does *not* simply mean to take it apart. It means we need to look thoughtfully beyond the surface of the text—"to peel away like an onion the layers of constructed meanings." It doesn't mean the same thing as analyzing. In the traditional sense, when we *analyze* a piece, we put it back the way it was and appreciate it more. When we *deconstruct* a piece of literature, we realize that there is something wrong or incomplete or dishonest or unintended with how it was put together in the first place.

Here is one good explanation of deconstruction:

Having been written by a human being with unresolved conflicts and contradictory emotions, a story may disguise rather than reveal the underlying
anxieties or perplexities of the author. Below the surface, unresolved tensions
or contradictions may account for the true dynamics of the story. The story
may have one message for the ordinary unsophisticated reader and another
for the reader who responds to its subtext, its subsurface ironies. Readers
who deconstruct a text will be "resistant" readers. They will not be taken in
by what a story says on the surface but will try to penetrate the disguises of
the text. . . They may engage in radical rereading of familiar classics. (Guth
& Rico, 1996, p. 366)

Here is another useful definition:

Deconstruction is a strategy for revealing the underlayers of meaning in a text
that were suppressed or assumed in order for it to take its actual form. . . . . Texts
are never simply unitary but include resources that run counter to their assertions and/or their authors' intentions. (Appignanesi & Garratt, 1995, p. 80)

We're going to play with deconstruction today in three steps: first with some
common metaphors, then with a traditional poem, and then with some texts
you've read for this class.

1. Unpacking metaphors:

Let's take some metaphors and see if there is anything false or unintended
about their meaning. Under each, please write the obvious surface meaning,
and an unintended meaning that may lie beneath the surface.

Love is a rose.
Intended:

Unintended:

You are the sunshine of my life.
Intended:

Unintended:

The test was a bear.
Intended:

Unintended:

2. Deconstructing a text:

Let's read the following poem, one that's often subject to traditional analysis:

Death Be Not Proud

Death be not proud, though some have called thee
Mighty and dreadful, for though art not so;
For those whom thou think'st thou dost overthrow
Die not, poor death, nor canst thou kill me.
From rest and sleep which but thy pictures be
Much pleasure—then from thee much more should flow;
And soonest our best men with thee do go,
Rest of their bones and souls delivery.
Thou art slave to fate, chance, kings and desperate men,
And dost with poison, war, and sickness dwell;
And poppy and charms can make us sleep as well,
And better than thy stroke. Why swell'st thou then?
One short sleep passed, we wake eternally,
And death shall be no more; death, thou shalt die.

—John Donne

What is the poem supposed to say? How would you approach it for, say, the AP exam? What traditional tools of analysis might you employ to unpack the meaning of the text?

Where does the poem break down? How might it work against the author's intentions? Write down some specific places where the text falls apart.

3. Reconsidering a reading:

Now, think of a poem, short story or novel you've read that cannot be taken at face value, that may reveal, because of internal inconsistencies or unintended conflict and the failure of language to really communicate what we mean (even in the hands of gifted writers), a mixed message or an unintended meaning. On your own or with a partner, please complete the following sentences about the text. We will ask you to detach this page from the handout and turn it in.

Name(s):

Text:

When I **deconstruct** this text, here's what happens. I think the main idea the author/ poet was trying to construct was:

But this construct really doesn't work. The idea falls apart. The language and construction of the text isn't able to convey what the author meant to convey. There are places in the text where it just doesn't work. For example:

So, in the end, even though the author meant the work to say:

it really said:

(Optional) I'd also like to say that:

ACTIVITY 25

A Modest Proposal: Deconstruction and Nonfiction

Deconstruction reminds us of the instability of meaning. This is because people use language to name categories into which our experiences don't neatly fit. Similarly, satire requires us to construct a particular meaning based on an understanding of such categories—one that uses and then reverses their meanings. Let's see how deconstruction works with this very famous nonfiction essay, "A Modest Proposal"* by Jonathan Swift

1. Summarize the literal meaning of the piece. What exactly does Swift say he is proposing?

2. Give some examples of words or phrases that fit into the following categories that Swift presents in his essay. For example, what happens when he describes "a child just dropped from its dam"?

People	Animals	Food	Other

3. How do these categories contribute to the literal meaning of the essay?

4. In what ways do these categories become unstable or imprecise and betray themselves to reveal a different meaning?

5. Find three or four sentences that lead you to believe Swift intends a different meaning than the one that is directly stated.

6. Rewrite your response to #1, restating what you think is the *intended* meaning of the essay.

7. How does Swift use language to convey one thing and mean another?

8. How might the **social class lens** provide a useful reading to this piece? If you read this piece through that lens, what might be brought into sharper relief?

*Note to teachers: this essay can be easily found online.

"On the Subway," by Sharon Olds:
The Gender Lens

1. Read the poem aloud in your group.

2. Using the theory cards, glossaries and any other information that you have, please summarize what you think it means to apply a gender lens to a text.

3. As a group, underline lines that are particularly relevant to a gendered reading.

4. As a group, complete this sentence (more than one meaning statement might result).

Using the gender lens, we think the poem means

because

5. What larger questions about society does this reading raise for you?

6. Pick a reporter to summarize your group's findings.

"On the Subway," by Sharon Olds:
The Formalist or New Critical Lens

1. Read the poem aloud in your group.

2. Using the theory cards, glossaries, and any other information that you have, please summarize what you think it means to apply a formalist lens to a text.

3. As a group, list some of the important poetic devices that Olds employs to convey her meaning.

4. Underline lines that contain those poetic devices.

5. As a group, complete this sentence (more than one meaning statement might result).

Based on a formalist analysis we think the poem means

because

6. Does this reading raise larger questions about society for you?

7. Pick a reporter to summarize your group's findings.

"On the Subway," by Sharon Olds: The Social Class Lens

1. Read the poem aloud in your group.

2. Using the theory cards, glossaries, and any other information that you have, please summarize what you think it means to apply a social class lens to a text.

3. As a group, underline lines that are particularly relevant to a social class reading.

4. As a group, complete this sentence (more than one meaning statement might result).

Based on a social class reading, we think the poem means

because

5. What larger questions about society does this reading raise for you?

6. Pick a reporter to summarize your group's findings.

"On the Subway," by Sharon Olds:
The Reader-Response Lens

1. Read the poem aloud in your group.

2. Using the theory cards, glossaries, and any other information that you have, please summarize what you think it means to apply a reader-response lens to a text.

3. Have each person list the personal qualities and/or personal experiences that are relevant to the poem.

4. Have each person underline lines that are particularly relevant to those personal experiences.

5. Have each person in the group complete the following sentence:

Based on my own reading, I think the poem means

because

6. Pick a reporter to summarize your group's findings.

"Ode to Family Photographs": Three Perspectives

The Reader-Response Perspective

Reread the poem with these questions in mind and then discuss them with three other classmates:

- What family photos of your own come to mind as you read the poem?
- Who is your usual family photographer? Why?
- What might people be able to tell about your family from the photographs?

The Formalist Perspective

Reread the poem with these questions in mind and then discuss them with three other classmates:

- List some of the images that are conjured as you read the poem.
- In what ways is this different from most poems you've read?
- How would you describe the tone of the poem? Support your response with specific lines or phrases from the poem.

The Biographical Perspective

Read the brief biography of Gary Soto that we provided and then reread the poem with these questions in mind. Discuss them with three other classmates:

- What images or specific references do the two pieces share?
- What else do the pieces seem to have in common?
- In what ways does the information in the bio affect your reading of the poem?

ACTIVITY 31

Literary Theory:
Among the Things We Carry

Please consider the stories from Tim O'Brien's *The Things They Carried* from the perspective of the four theories listed below. Each group will consider a particular lens and then we will discuss this together as a whole class. Note, too, that your paper assignment is also related to this exercise. Here is a list of the stories: "The Things They Carried," "Love," "Spin," "On the Rainy River," "Enemies," "Friends," "How to Tell a True War Story," "The Dentist," "Sweetheart of the Song Tra Bong," "Stockings," "Church," "The Man I Killed," "Ambush," "Style," "Speaking of Courage," "Notes," "In the Field," "Good Form," "Field Trip," "The Ghost Soldiers," "Night Life," "The Lives of the Dead."

	Reader Response	Historical	Feminist/Gender	Marxist/Social Class
Which stories lend themselves to this particular lens?				
Cite specific textual passage(s) that support this kind of reading:				

Interpret at least one character through this lens.			
If you look through this lens, what questions emerge?			
If these stories are to be considered as a coherent whole, what is the nature of the "glue" that holds them together?			
Do you believe in this reading? Why or why not?			

Contemporary Literary Theory and *Shrek*

First, consider the opening and the closing minutes of the film. In what ways are we invited to read this film like a story? What are some of the assumptions about stories that you have internalized? (Some theorists call this a story grammar.) How do you know that the film will resist the traditional story line?

Next, let's review the basic assumptions of the five lenses on the other side. Fill in each square in the accompanying table as we discuss the lenses.

View the film. Write down particular moments that strike you on a separate piece of paper. Then fit those moments under the appropriate lens if it works.

Now, with a partner, think about the messages that *Shrek* may be trying to convey. Together, discover the significance of *Shrek* from the perspective of each lens.

	Gender	Social Class	Deconstruction	Archetypal	Reader-Response
LENS					
What are the basic assumptions of this lens?					
List at least two episodes, moments, or incidents that seem to exemplify this perspective.					
Given this perspective, what is the film trying to say?					

The Interplay of Fiction and Nonfiction

"Everyday Use": A SAMPLER OF APPROACHES

Nonfiction can help us read and appreciate fictional works. Let's see how a nonfiction essay can illuminate our understanding of a short story, even after we view it through two other lenses.

Approach One: The Reader-Response Lens—A Pre-Reading Activity "Object Lesson" or Everyday Uses

- Bring an object from home that has some sentimental value to you. Briefly describe the history of this object and how it came to be in your possession.

- Why did you choose this particular object? Summarize what it means to you. Does this object represent anything besides itself (e.g., ring symbolizes love)?

- Does anyone else in your family have any use for or feelings about this object? Explain. (This question is particularly relevant to our reading of "Everyday Use.")

- Now, get into groups with three other people. Share your objects and responses to questions 1–3 with each other. Spend about 10 to 15 minutes doing this.

- Respond individually to what you've just done as a group. Write a brief (four- to five-sentence) reaction to something someone in your group said about his/her object.

Approach Two: The Formalist Lens—A Close-Reading Activity

Now let's read "Everyday Use" by Alice Walker. Review our formalist theory card and use the formalist lens to do a close reading. As you read, consider the following questions:

- Who is the *speaker* of the story?
- How would you describe the *tone* of the story?
- Find some of the most striking examples of *figurative language*. How does this use of language help establish the *mood* of the story as well as the characters?
- What might the quilt *symbolize*?
- What is the *significance* of the title?
- What is the *purpose* or *overall theme* of the story?

Approach Three: The Biographical Lens Using Nonfiction

Read Alice Walker's essay, "In Search of Our Mother's Gardens."

- After you read the essay, skim through the story again. What do you notice that you didn't notice before?

- What are the advantages and disadvantages of having your students read this essay before they read the story?

- Quilts appear both in the essay and the story. How does the mention of the quilt in the essay affect your reading of the story?

- How does reading this essay inform your response to/interpretation of the story? Does it change what you think the purpose of the story might be?

From Reading Words to Reading the World: Critical Lenses in Literature and in Life

We've spent a lot of time this year focusing on critical lenses. For a culminating activity, we would like you to reflect on the ways in which you personally have made sense of the lenses as a tool for reading texts and the world.

1. Reflect on our reading and discussion over this past year. Which lenses did you find particularly useful, interesting, or thought provoking? Which lenses seemed to offer the most explanatory power for your reading of literary texts? Rate the following lenses from 1 through 8, where 1 is the *lowest* rating and 8 is the *highest*:

_____ reader-response theory

_____ formalist theory (New Criticism)

_____ archetypal theory

_____ postcolonial theory

_____ historical theory

_____ psychological theory

_____ gender theory

_____ social class theory

In one to two paragraphs, explain why you have ranked the lenses as you did.

2. Now, think of something you've heard about or seen outside of class that struck you as worth thinking about.

It could be related to school:

- an interaction between two people
- a school policy
- a social group
- academics
- athletics
- something about the building itself
- how the school day is structured

OR

Something outside of school:

- a state, national, or world event or circumstance
- a political situation or event
- a family situation
- a personal event

Describe this event or issue and explain why it is important.

Consider this event from at least two of the lenses we've been working with. What do you notice or what questions emerge for you as you apply these critical perspectives to that event? How do these lenses affect or increase your understanding of the event/issue?

3. How do you think the multiple perspectives can help you understand some things about yourself and your life outside of school?

Critical Encounters: Reading the World

Literary theory raises those issues which are often left submerged beneath the mass of information contained in the course, and it also asks questions about how the institution of great literature works. What makes a "great work" great? Who makes the decisions about what will be taught? Why are authors grouped into certain historical periods? The answers to fundamental questions like these are often unarticulated assumptions on the part of both the professor (teacher) and the students.

Socrates said that the unexamined life is not worth living. . . . Literary theory is at its best when it helps us realize what we are really doing when we study literature.

—S. Bonnycastle

1. Based on our reading as well as class discussions, briefly describe in your own words, the following literary theories. (Spend no more than a few minutes on this part of the exercise.)

Psychological criticism:

Feminist/gender literary theory:

Marxist/social class theory:

Reader-response theory:

Other? (Choose one as a group):

2. In groups of three or four, select a literary work with which you are all familiar. It could be a poem, a short story, a play, or a novel. Or, focus on the novel you are currently using for your reader's choice. Then, think of two theories that would be fruitful to use to explore that text. In the spaces below, briefly describe how each of those two theories might be used to illuminate the text.

Theory 1:

Theory 2:

3. Now, think of something you've read, heard, or seen outside of class that particularly struck you as worth thinking about. It could be an interaction between two people, a MTV video, a song, a film or a scene from a film, a magazine article or ad. Briefly explain it below.

4. What lens might you use to help you understand this event or artifact? How would that lens affect or increase your understanding?

5. Can we use critical lenses to "read" the world? Explain.

6. What, if anything, do you find difficult about reading literature with critical lenses?

Theory Relay: *Native Son*

For the next hour in groups of three or four, please consider *Native Son* from a variety of theoretical perspectives: reader response, historical/biographical, feminist/gender, and Marxist/social class. We'll be doing this as a kind of relay. There are four theory stations around the room. Spend approximately 10 minutes at each station. Each person should turn in one of these sheets to your teacher on Monday. Make certain you've completed the journal entry at the end of the sheet.

Name:

Group Members:

Reader-Response Station

Reread the explanation of reader response and study your reader-response diagram. In the space below, write at least three meaning statements that are the result of your personal interaction with the text.

1.

2.

3.

Historical/Biographical Station

Skim together "How Bigger Was Born" (in your copy of *Native Son*) and skim the biographical articles that you find at this station. How does what you've learned, as well as any additional experience of reading you've had with other works of Richard Wright, affect and inform your understanding of *Native Son*?

Feminist/Gender Station

Consider the quotation you find at the feminist/gender station. As a group, construct an interpretation of the quotation that is informed by your collective understanding of feminist literary theory. When you consider *Native Son* from a feminist perspective, what characters, incidents, or themes are brought into greater relief? Write your response below.

Marxist/Social Class Station

Consider the quotation you find at the Marxist/social class station. As a group, construct an interpretation of the quotation that is informed by your understanding of Marxist literary theory. When you consider *Native Son* from a Marxist perspective, what characters, incidents or themes are brought into greater relief? Write your response below.

   ***Journal Entry:

Reflect on your group's efforts this hour to read *Native Son* through a variety of critical lenses. Which lens seemed to be most consistent with the intention of the novel. Which lens was the most difficult to apply? Which was the most informative? (This entry should be at least two full paragraphs. Write it on a separate piece of paper that you attach to this sheet.)

Through
Rose-Colored Glasses:
The Feminist/Gender Lens

1. What is the feminist/gender lens?

Feminist literary criticism helps us look at literature in a different light. It applies the philosophies and perspectives of feminism to the literature we read. There are many different kinds of feminist literary theory. Some theorists examine the language and symbols that are used and how that language and use of symbols is "gendered." Others remind us that men and women write differently and analyze at how the gender of the author affects how literature is written. Many feminist critics look at how the characters, especially the female characters, are portrayed and ask us to consider how the portrayal of female characters "reinforces or undermines" sexual stereotypes (Lynn, 2010). Feminist literary theory also suggests that the gender of the reader often affects our response to a text. For example, feminist critics may claim that certain male writers address their readers as if they were all men and exclude the female reader.

Like feminism itself, feminist literary theory asks us to consider the relationships between men and women and their relative roles in society. Much feminist literary theory reminds us that the relationship between men and women in society is often unequal and reflects a particular patriarchal ideology. Those unequal relationships may appear in a variety of ways in the production of literature and within literary texts. Feminist theorists invite us to pay particular attention to the patterns of thought, behavior, values, and power in those relationships.

Feminist literary critics remind us that literary values, conventions, and even the production of literature have themselves been historically shaped by men. They invite us to consider writings by women, both new and forgotten, and also ask us to consider viewing familiar literature through a feminist perspective.

2. How do we apply the feminist/gender lens?

We apply it by closely examining the portrayal of the characters, both female and male, the language of the text, the attitude of the author, and the relationship between the characters. We also consider the comments the author seems to be making about society as a whole.

3. Application: Looking through the feminist/gender lens

Select two female characters from novels with which you are very familiar. They could be from works we have read together or from texts you have read in previous English classes. For example, you might choose Daisy from *The Great Gatsby*, Hester Prynne from *The Scarlet Letter*, or Sonya from *Crime and Punishment*.

Name each character and write two descriptive statements for each— one from a traditional masculine perspective and the second from a feminist perspective.

Character 1:

Traditional statement:

Feminist/gender statement:

Character 2:

Traditional statement:

Feminist/gender statement:

4. Try to interpret this concrete poem in two ways, from a traditional perspective and from a feminist/gender perspective:

—Pedro Xisto

5. Can the feminist lens be useful in everyday life? Please write a sentence about the following objects or situations using a traditional perspective and then applying the feminist lens:

- Mount Rushmore

- The Miss America pageant

- Hillary Clinton's bid for the Democratic nomination for President

- The popularity and ups and downs of Britney Spears/Paris Hilton/ Lindsay Lohan

- The hooplah surrounding Sarah Palin as Vice-Presidential candidate

- "Ugly Betty"

6. Can you think of anything that has happened to you or to a friend of yours in the past two weeks that could be better explained or understood through a feminist/gender lens? Pick a partner and share stories.

Selected Literary Texts

NOVELS, SHORT STORIES, AND PLAYS

Achebe, C. (1994). *Things fall apart*. New York, NY: Knopf Publishing Group.

Chopin, K. (1899). *The awakening*. New York, NY: Simon and Schuster.

Chopin, K. (2005). The story of an hour. In *The awakening and selected short fiction*. New York, NY: Barnes & Noble.

Cisneros, S. (1991). *The house on Mango Street*. New York, NY: Vintage Books.

Coetzee, J. M. (1982). *Waiting for the barbarians*. New York, NY: Penguin Group.

Conrad, J. (1995). *Heart of darkness*. Peterborough, Ontario: Broadview Press.

Conrad, J. (2008). The secret sharer. In *Heart of darkness & The secret sharer*. New York, NY: Penguin Group.

Crane, S. (1983). *The red badge of courage*. New York, NY: Penguin Group.

Crews, F. (2003). *Pooh perplex*. Chicago, IL: University of Chicago Press.

Ellison, R. (1995). *Invisible man*. New York, NY: Knopf Publishing Group.

Enger, L. (2001). *Peace like a river*. New York, NY: Atlantic Monthly Press.

Erdrich, L. (1988). *Tracks*. New York, NY: Henry Holt.

Faulkner, W. (1991). *As I lay dying*. New York, NY: Knopf Publishing Group.

Fitzgerald, F. S. *The great Gatsby*. New York, NY: Scribner, 1953.

Frank, A. (1993). *The diary of a young girl*. New York, NY: Bantam Books.

Gilman, C. P. (1989). The yellow wallpaper. In *The yellow wallpaper and other writings*. New York, NY: Bantam Books.

Glaspell, S. (1920). *A jury of her peers*. Boston, MA: Small, Maynard, & Company.

Guest, J. (1976). *Ordinary people*. New York, NY: Viking Press.

Guterson, D. (1994). *Snow falling on cedars*. New York, NY: Vintage Books.

Hansbery, L. (1995). *A raisin in the sun*. New York, NY: Random House Publishing.

Hawthorne, N. (1962). *The scarlet letter*. New York, NY: The Modern Library.

Hegi, U. (1997). *Stones from the river*. New York, NY: Simon & Schuster.

Hurston, Z. N. (1991). *Their eyes were watching God*. Urbana, IL: University of Illinois Press.

Ibsen, H. (1972). *A doll's house*. New York, NY: S. French.

Katz, J. (1992). *Running fiercely toward a high thin sound: A novel*. Ithaca, NY: Firebrand Books.

Kleber, F. (Ed.). (1936). *Beowulf* (3rd ed.). Boston, MA: Houghton Mifflin.

Knowles, J. (1996). *A separate peace*. New York, NY: Simon & Schuster Adult Publishing Group.

Lee, H. (2006). *To kill a mockingbird*. New York, NY: HarperCollins.

Lionni, L. (1974). *Fish is fish*. New York, NY: Random House Children's Books.

Loewen, J. (1995). *Lies my teacher told me: Everything your American history textbook got wrong*. New York, NY: Norton.

Mann, C. (2005). *1491: New revelations about the Americas before Columbus*. New York, NY: Knopf.

Miller, A. (1976). *Death of a salesman*. New York, NY: Penguin Group.

Milne, A. A. (1988). *Winnie the pooh*. New York, NY: Penguin Young Readers Group.

Morrison, T. (1987). *Beloved*. New York, NY: New American Library.

Morrison, T. (1993). *Sula*. New York, NY: Random House.

O'Brien, T. (1990). *The things they carried: A work of fiction*. Boston, MA: Houghton Mifflin.

Remarque, E. M. (1929). *All quiet on the western front*. London, England: Little, Brown and Company.

Said, E. (1979). *Orientalism*. New York, NY: Vintage.

Said, E. (1999). *Out of place: A memoir*. New York, NY: Knopf.

Salinger, J. D. (1951). *The catcher in the rye*. London, England: Little, Brown and Company.

Scieszka, J. (1996). *The true story of the 3 little pigs by A. Wolf*. New York, NY: Penguin Group.

Shakespeare, W. (1985). *Hamlet, prince of Denmark*. Cambridge, U.K. and New York, NY: Cambridge University Press.

Shakespeare, W. (1994). *Macbeth*. In *The complete works of William Shakespeare*. New York, NY: Barnes & Noble.

Shakespeare, W. (1994). *Much ado about nothing*. In *The complete works of William Shakespeare*. New York, NY: Barnes & Noble.

Shakespeare, W. (1994). *Othello*. In *The complete works of William Shakespeare*. New York, NY: Barnes & Noble.

Shakespeare, W. (1994). *The merchants of Venice*. In *The complete works of William Shakespeare*. New York, NY: Barnes & Noble.

Shelley, M. (1984). *Frankenstein, or, the modern Prometheus*. Berkeley, CA: University of California Press.

Silko, L. M. (1986). *Ceremony*. New York, NY: Penguin Group.

Sophocles. (2006). *Oedipus rex*. In *The Theban plays: Oedipus rex, Oedipus at Colonus, and Antigone*. Mineola, NY: Dover Publications.

Steinbeck, J. (1965). *Of mice and men*. New York, NY: Viking Press.

Steinbeck, J. (2002). *The grapes of wrath*. New York, NY: Penguin Group.

Swift, J. (2004). *Gulliver's travels*. New York, NY: Barnes & Noble.

Thiong'o, N. W. (1990). *The river between*. New York, NY: Longman.

Tolkien, J. R. R. (1999). *The hobbit, or there and back again*. Boston, MA: Houghton Mifflin.

Twain, M. (2008). *Adventures of Huckleberry Finn*. New York, NY: Barnes & Noble.

Updike, J. (1929). Separating. In *Problems and other stories*. New York, NY: Knopf.

Wilson, A. (1986). *Fences*. New York, NY: Penguin.

Woolf, V. (1929). *A room of one's own*. New York, NY: Harcourt, Brace.

Wright, R. (1945). *Black boy: A record of childhood and youth*. New York, NY: Harper & Row.

Wright, R. (1940). *Native son*. New York, NY and London, England: Harper & Brothers.

POETRY

Arnold, M., "Dover beach"

Burns, D., "Sure you can ask me a personal question"

Donne, J., "Death be not proud"

Frost, R., "The road not taken"

Olds, S., "On the subway"

Plath, S., "Mushrooms"

Roethke, T., "My papa's waltz"

Soto, G., "Ode to family photographs"

Soto, G., "Oranges"

Stevens, W., "Thirteen ways of looking at a blackbird"

MOTION PICTURES

Adamson, A., & Jenson, V. (Directors). *Shrek* [Animated motion picture]. United States: Dreamworks Animated Studio, 2001.

Coppola, F. F. (Director). *Apocalypse Now* [Motion picture]. United States: Paramount Pictures, 1979.

Costner, K. (Director). *Dances with Wolves* [Motion picture]. United States: Majestic Films, 1990.

Ford, J. (Director). *The Searchers* [Motion Picture]. United States: Warner Bros., 1956.

Jeffs, C. (Director). *Sylvia* [Motion picture]. United States: Universal Studios, 2003.

Lucas, G. (Writer/Director). *Star Wars* [Motion picture]. United States: 20th Century Fox, 1977.

References

Appignanesi, R., & Garratt, C. (1995). *Introducing postmodernism*. New York, NY: Totem Books.

Applebee, A. (1978). *The child's concept of story: Ages two to seventeen*. Chicago, IL: University of Chicago Press.

Applebee, A. (1993). *Literature in the secondary school: Studies of curriculum and instruction in the United States*. Urbana, IL: National Council of Teachers of English.

Appleman, D. (1992). I understood the grief: Reader-response and *Ordinary People*. In N. Karolides (Ed.), *Generating reader's responses to literature* (pp. 92–101). New York, NY: Longman.

Appleman, D. (1993). Looking through critical lenses: Teaching literary theory to secondary students. In S. Straw & D. Bogdan (Eds.), *Constructive reading: Teaching beyond communication* (pp. 155–171). Portsmouth, NH: Boynton/Cook.

Appleman, D. (2000). *Critical encounters in high school English: Teaching literary theory to adolescents* (2nd ed.). New York, NY: Teachers College Press.

Appleman, D., Caligiuri, Z., & Vang, J. (2014). At the end of the pipeline: Can the liberal arts liberate the incarcerated? In A. Nocella II, P. Parmar, & D. Stovall (Eds.), *From education to incarceration, Dismantling the school-to-prison pipeline* (pp. 192–209). New York, NY: Peter Lang.

Appleman, D., Smith, M. W., & Wilhelm, J. D. (2014). *Uncommon core*. Thousand Oaks, CA: Corwin.

Baldwin, J. (1985). *The price of the ticket*. New York, NY: St. Martins.

Barnet, S. (1996). *A short guide to writing about literature* (7th ed.). New York, NY: HarperCollins.

Barry, P. (2002). *Beginning theory*. Manchester, England: Manchester University Press.

Barthes, R. (1981). Theory of the text (I. McLeod, Trans.). In R. Young (Ed.), *Untying the text: A post-structuralist reader* (pp. 31–47). London, England: Routledge.

Beach, R. (1993). *A teacher's introduction to reader-response theories*. Urbana, IL: National Council of Teachers of English.

Beach, R., Appleman, D., Hynds, S., & Wilhelm, J. (2006). *Teaching literature to adolescents*. Mahwah, NJ: Erlbaum.

Bonnycastle, S. (1996). *In search of authority: An introductory guide to literary theory* (2nd ed.). Peterborough, Ontario, Canada: Broadview Press.

Boomer, G. (1988). *Metaphors and meaning: Essays on English teaching* (B. Green, Ed.). Norwood: Australian Association for the Teaching of English.

Brannigan, J. (1998). *New historicism and cultural materialism.* New York, NY: St. Martins.

Carey-Webb, A. (2001). *Literature and lives: A response based, cultural studies approach to teaching English.* Urbana, IL: National Council of Teachers of English.

Carnegie Corporation of New York. (2013). Opportunity by design: New high school models for student success. Available at carnegie.org/fileadmin/Media/Programs/Opportunity_by_design/Opportunity_By_Design_FINAL.pdf

Cherland, M., & Greenlaw, J. (Eds.). (1998). Literary theory in the high school English classroom. *Theory into practice, 37*(3), 175.

Cochran-Smith, M., & Lytle, S. L. (Eds.). (1993). *Inside/outside: Teacher research and knowledge.* New York, NY: Teachers College Press.

Coleman, D., & Pimentel, S., (2013). Revised publishers' criteria for the Common Core State Standards in English language arts and literacy. Grades 3–12. Available at www.corestandards.org/assets/Publishers_Criteria_for_3-12.pdf

Common Core Standards in English Language Arts, Reading: Informational Text; Grade 11–12 (2014). *Common Core State Standards Initiative.* Available at www.corestandards.org/ELA-Literacy/RI/11-12/

Cooper, J. D. (2014). Literacy, literature and learning for life. Available at www.eduplace.com/rdg/res/literacy.html

Crews, F. C. (1965). *The Pooh perplex.* New York, NY: Dutton & Co.

Crowley, S. (1989). *A teacher's introduction to deconstruction.* Urbana, IL: National Council of Teachers of English.

Derrida, J. (1989). Structure, sign, and play in the discourse of the human sciences. In P. Rice & P. Waugh (Eds.), *Modern literary theory: A reader* (pp. 149–165). London, England: Edward Arnold.

Desai, L. (1997). Reflections on cultural diversity in literature and in the classroom. In T. Rogers & A. Soter (Eds.), *Reading across cultures: Teaching literature in a diverse society* (pp. 161–177). New York, NY: Teachers College Press.

Dimitriadis, G., & McCarthy, C. (2001). *Reading and teaching the postcolonial: From Baldwin to Basquait and beyond.* New York, NY: Teachers College Press.

Eagleton, T. (1983). *Literary theory: An introduction.* Minneapolis, MN: University of Minnesota Press.

Eckert, L. S. (2006). *How does it mean: Engaging reluctant readers through literary theory.* Portsmouth, NH: Heinemann.

Elkind, D. (1986). *All grown up and no place to go: Teenagers in crises.* Reading, MA: Addison-Wesley.

Emig, J. (1990). Our missing theory. In C. Moran & E. F. Penfield (Eds.), *Conversations: Contemporary critical theory and the teaching of literature* (pp. 87–96). Urbana, IL: National Council of Teachers of English.

Fairclouth, N. (1989). *Language and power.* New York, NY: Longman.

Fetterley, J. (1978). *The resisting reader: A feminist approach to American fiction.* Bloomington, IN: Indiana University Press.

Fitzgerald, F. S. (1964). *The crack-up.* New York, NY: New Directions.

Foucault, M. (1982). *The archeology of knowledge.* New York, NY: Vintage.

Forrester, V. (1980). What women's eyes see (I. de Courtivron, Trans.). In E. Marks & I. de Courtivron (Eds.), *New French feminisms* (pp. 181–182). Amherst, MA: University of Massachusetts Press.

Freire, P., & Macedo, D. P. (1987). *Literacy: Reading the word and the world.* Westport, CT: Praeger/Greenwood.

Furman, N. (1988). The politics of language—Beyond the gender principle? In G. Green & C. Kahn (Eds.), *Making a difference—Feminist literary criticism.* New York, NY: Routledge.

Galda, L. (1983). Research in response to literature. *Journal of Research and Development in Education, 16*(3), 1–6.

Gallagher, C., & Greenblatt, S. (2000). *Practicing new historicism.* Chicago, IL: University of Chicago Press.

Gates, H., Jr. (1992). *Loose canons: Notes on the culture wars.* New York, NY: Oxford University Press.

Gonzalez, N. E., Moll, L. C., & Amanti, C. (2005). *Funds of knowledge.* Mahwah, NJ: Lawrence Erlbaum.

Goodwin, B., & Miller, K. (2012). Research says/nonfiction reading promotes student success. *Educational Leadership, 70*(4), 80–82. Available at www.ascd.org/publications/educational-leadership/dec12/vol70/num04/Nonfiction-Reading-Promotes-Student-Success.aspx

Graff, G. (1987). *Professing literature: An institutional history.* Chicago, IL: University of Chicago Press.

Graff, G. (1989). Co-optation. *The new historicism.* New York, NY: Routledge.

Graff, G. (1992). *Beyond the culture wars: How teaching the conflicts can revitalize American education.* New York, NY: Norton.

Graff, G. (1995). Organizing the conflicts in the curriculum. In J. F. Slevin & A. Young (Eds.), *Critical theory and the teaching of literature: Politics, curriculum, pedagogy.* Urbana, IL: National Council of Teachers of English.

Greenblatt, S. (1989). *Towards a poetics of culture. The new historicism.* New York, NY: Routledge.

Greene, M. (1988). *The dialectic of freedom.* New York, NY: Teachers College Press.

Greene, M. (1993). The passions of pluralism: Multiculturalism and the expanding community. In T. Perry & J. Fraser (Eds.), *Freedom's plow* (pp. 185–196). New York, NY: Routledge.

Griffith, P. (1987). *Literary theory and English teaching.* Philadelphia, PA: Open University Press.

Guerin, W. L., Labor, E. G., Morgan, L., & Willingham, J. R. (1992). *A handbook of critical approaches to literature* (2nd ed.). New York, NY: Oxford University Press.

Guth, H., & Rico, G. (1996). *Discovering literature.* Upper Saddle River, NJ: Prentice Hall.

Hillis Miller, J. (1989). Deconstruction and *Heart of darkness.* In R. C. Murfin (Ed.), *Heart of darkness: A case study in contemporary criticism.* New York, NY: Bedford-St. Martins.

Hines, M. B. (1997). Multiplicity and difference in literary inquiry. In T. Rogers & A. Soter (Eds.), *Reading across cultures: Teaching literature in a diverse society* (pp. 116–134). New York, NY: Teachers College Press.

hooks, b. (1994). *Teaching to transgress: Education as the practice of freedom.* London, England: Routledge.

hooks, b. (1997). *Cultural criticism & transformation* [movie transcript]. Northampton, MA.

Hopkins, E. (2014). Nonfiction quote. Available at http://www.examiner.com/article/ellen-hopkins-an-interview-and-a-poem-written-just-for-chicagoans

Hynds, S., & Appleman, D. (1997). Walking our talk: Between response and responsibility in the literature classroom. *English Education, 29*(4), 272–294.

Johnson, B. (1981). Translator's introduction. In J. Derrida, *Dissemination* (pp. xv–xvii). Chicago, IL: University of Chicago Press.

Johnson, A., & Ciancio, S. (2008). Shades of power: Deconstructing relationships in Lester's Othello. In A. O. Soter, M. Faust, & T. Rogers (Eds.), *Interpretive play: Using critical perspectives to teach young adult literature* (pp. 145–160). Norwood, MA: Christopher Gordon.

Kaplan, S. J. (2000). On reaching the year 2000. *Signs, 25*(4), 1167–1170.

Kolondy, A. (1989). Dancing through the minefield: Some observations on the theory, practice, and politics of a feminist literary criticism. In E. Showalter (Ed.), *The new feminist criticism: Essays on women, literature, and theory* (pp. 144–167). New York, NY: Pantheon.

Kutz, E., & Roskelly, H. (1991). *An unquiet pedagogy: Transforming practice in the English classroom.* Portsmouth, NH: Boyton-Cook.

Leggo, C. (1998). Open(ing) texts: Deconstruction and responding to poetry. *Theory into practice, 37*(3), 186–192.

Lionni, L. (1974). *Fish is fish.* New York, NY: Random House Children's Books.

Loewen, J. (1995). *Lies my teacher told me: Everything your American history textbook got wrong.* New York, NY: Norton.

Lucas, G. (Writer/Director). (1977). *Star Wars* [Motion picture]. United States: 20th Century Fox.

Lynn, S. (1990). A passage into critical theory. *College English, 52*(3), 258–271.

Lynn, S. (2010). *Texts and contexts: Writing about literature with critical theory* (6th ed.). New York, NY: Pearson Longman.

Lynn, S. (1990). A passage into critical theory. In C. Moran & E. F. Penfield (Eds.), *Conversations: Contemporary critical theory and the teaching of literature* (pp. 99–113). Urbana, IL: National Council of Teachers of English.

Mann, C. (2005). *1491: New revelations about the Americas before Columbus.* New York, NY: Knopf.

Marshall, J. (1991). Writing and reasoning about literature. In R. Beach & S. Hynds (Eds.), *Developing discourse practices in adolescence and adulthood* (pp. 161–180). Norwood, NJ: Ablex.

McCormick, K. (1995). Reading lessons and then some: Toward developing dialogues between critical theory and reading theory. In J. Slevin & A. Young (Eds.), *Critical theory and the teaching of literature: Politics, curriculum, pedagogy* (pp. 292–315). Urbana, IL: National Council of Teachers of English.

Moore, J. N. (1997). *Interpreting young adult literature: Literary theory in the secondary classroom*. Portsmouth, NH: Boynton/Cook.

Moore, J. N. (1998). Street signs: Semiotics, Romeo and Juliet, and young adult literature. *Theory into practice: Literary theory in the high school English classroom, 37*(3), 211–219.

Mosle, S. (2012, November 22). What should children read. *The New York Times*. Available at www.opinionator.blogs.nytimes.com/2012/11/22/what-should-children-read

Murfin, R. C. (Ed.). (1989). *Heart of darkness: A case study in contemporary criticism*. New York, NY: Bedford-St. Martins.

Nelms, B. (Ed.). (1988). *Literature in the classroom: Readers, texts and contexts*. Urbana, IL: National Council of Teachers of English.

Perkins Gilman, C. P. (1973). *The yellow wallpaper*. Old Westbury, NY: Feminist Press. (Original work published 1892)

Perry, W. G. (1970). *Forms of intellectual and ethical development in the college years: A scheme*. New York, NY: Holt, Rinehart, & Winston.

Pirie, B. (1997). *Reshaping high school English*. Urbana, IL: National Council of Teachers of English.

Probst, R. (1988). *Response and analysis: Teaching literature in junior and senior high school*. Portsmouth, NH: Boynton/Cook.

Purves, A., Rogers, T., & Soter, A. O. (1990). *How porcupines make love: Notes on a response-centered curriculum* (2nd ed.). New York, NY: Longman.

Rabinowitz, P. (1987). *Before reading: Narrative conventions and the politics of interpretation*. Ithaca, NY: Cornell University Press.

Rabinowitz, P. J., & Smith, M. W. (1998). *Authorizing readers: Resistance and respect: The teaching of literature*. New York, NY: Teachers College Press.

Reis, S. M., Eckert, R. D., McCoach, D. B., Jacobs, J. K., & Coyne, M. (2008). Using enrichment reading practices to increase reading, fluency, comprehension, and attitudes. *Journal of Educational Research, 101*, 299–315.

Rogers, T., & Soter, A. O. (Eds.). (1997). *Reading across cultures: Teaching literature in a diverse society*. New York, NY: Teachers College Press.

Rose, M. (1999). *Possible lives: The promise of public education in America*. New York, NY: Penguin.

Rosenblatt, L. (1976). *Literature as exploration* (2nd ed.). New York, NY: Noble & Noble.

Ryan, M. (1998). *Literary theory: An introduction*. Oxford, England: Blackwell Press.

Said, E. (1979). *Orientalism*. New York, NY: Vintage.

Said, E. (1999). *Out of place: A memoir*. New York, NY: Knopf.

Scholes, R. (1985). *Textual power: Literary theory and the teaching of English*. New Haven, CT: Yale University Press.

Scholes, R. (2001). *The crafty reader*. New Haven, CT: Yale University Press.

Scieszka, J. (1989). *The true story of the 3 little pigs by A. Wolf*. New York, NY: Penguin Books.

Selden, R. (1989). *A reader's guide to contemporary literary theory*. Lexington, KY: University Press of Kentucky.

Showalter, E. (Ed.). (1985). *The new feminist criticism: Essays on women, literature, and theory* (pp. 125–143). New York, NY: Pantheon.

Slevin, J. F., & Young, A. (Eds.). (1995). *Critical theory and the teaching of literature: Politics, curriculum, pedagogy.* Urbana, IL: National Council of Teachers of English.

Smith, M. W., & Wilhelm, J. (2002). *Reading don't fix no chevys: Literacy in the lives of young men.* Portsmouth, NH: Heinemann.

Sontag, S. (1969). *Against interpretation, and other essay.* New York, NY: Dell.

Spivak, G. C. (1988). *Other worlds: Essays in cultural politics.* London, England: Methuen.

Staton, S. F. (1987). *Literary theories in praxis.* Philadelphia, PA: University of Pennsylvania Press.

Strauss, V. (2012, December 5). List: What Common Core authors suggest high schoolers should read. *The Washington Post.* Available at www.washingtonpost.com/blogs/answer-sheet/wp/2012/12/05/list-what-common-core-authors-suggest-high-schoolers-should-read/

Thomson, J. (1993). Helping students control texts: Contemporary literary theory into classroom practice. In S. Straw & D. Bogdan (Eds.), *Constructive reading: Teaching beyond communication* (pp. 130–154). Portsmouth, NH: Boynton/Cook.

Tyson, L. (2006). *Critical theory today: A user-friendly guide.* New York, NY: Routledge.

Veeser, H. A. (1989). *The new historicism.* New York, NY: Routledge.

Vygotsky, L. (1978). *Mind in society: The development of higher psychological processes.* Cambridge, MA: Harvard University Press.

Willis, A. (1997). Exploring multicultural literature as cultural production. In T. Rogers & A. Soter (Eds.), *Reading across cultures: Teaching literature in a diverse society* (pp. 116–132). New York, NY: Teachers College Press.

Winterowd, W. R. (1989). Introduction. In S. Crowley (Ed.), *A teacher's introduction to deconstruction.* Urbana, IL: National Council of Teachers of English.

Wolf, D. P. (1988). *Reading reconsidered: Literature and literacy in high school.* New York, NY: College Entrance Examination Board.

Index

About the Author

Deborah Appleman is the Hollis L. Caswell Professor of educational studies and director of The Summer Writing Program at Carleton College in Northfield, Minnesota. She has been a visiting professor at Syracuse University and at the University of California-Berkeley. Prior to earning her doctorate at the University of Minnesota in 1986, she was a high school English teacher for 9 years, working in both urban and suburban schools. She continues to work regularly in high school English classrooms with students and teachers across the country.

Professor Appleman's primary research interests include adolescent response to literature, multicultural literature, adolescent response to poetry, and the teaching of literary theory at the secondary level. She is the author of many articles and book chapters and, with an editorial board of classroom teachers, helped create the multicultural anthology *Braided Lives*. In addition to the Third Edition of *Critical Encounters in Secondary English: Teaching Literary Theory to Adolescents*, her books include *Adolescent Literacy and the Teaching of Reading*, *Reading for Themselves: How to Transform Adolescents into Lifelong Readers Through Out-of-Class Book Clubs*, *Teaching Literature to Adolescents* with Richard Beach, Susan Hynds, and Jeffrey Wilhelm, *Reading Better, Reading Smarter* with Michael Graves, and her most recent book with Michael Smith and Jeffrey Wilhelm, *Uncommon Core: Where the Authors of the Standards Go Wrong About Instruction and How You Can Get It Right*.

Professor Appleman's recent work has focused on education and the incarcerated. She teaches literature and creative writing classes regularly at a high security men's prison in Minnesota. The work of her incarcerated students can be found in the creative writing anthology, *From the Inside Out: Letters to Young Men and Other Writing*.